PRAISE FOR *OZARK FOLK MAGIC*

"Weston's piece is reference book, recipe book, and working book all in one. Insightful and personal, his insider perspective and lived experience as an Ozark person combined with his astute academic mind make for a useful and pleasurable guide to the folk magical ways of the Ozark region … This work not only provides the reader with the ability to see how people made do with what they had in the past, it provides the valuable service of preserving this cultural knowledge in such a way that it is still useful, practical, and, most importantly, connective for the people interested in this region today."

—Rebecca Beyer, founder of Blood and Spicebush

"Those of us who practice these old and peculiar traditions always welcome new and experienced voices writing about folkways that are little known but cherished still. Brandon Weston's book is one of those—a gem of discovery for historians, folklorists, and humble healing folks. This is a solid addition to any library."

—H. Byron Ballard, teacher and author of *Staubs and Ditchwater*

"This is an honest, clear look at American witchcraft and folk magic, veering far away from the fantasy realm magic."

—Marcus McCoy, blacksmith at Troll Cunning Forge
and editor of the Verdant Gnosis book series

"Brandon takes you on a remarkable journey into the Ozarks, giving a well-documented and unique vision into the mysteries of Ozark medicine, myth, and magic. Brandon, a healer from this bio region, is able to interpret the stories he's collected, giving cultural context … The information gleaned from this process is invaluable and a real treasure to ensuring these traditions will not be forgotten and are understood. He provides a strong foundation and thorough overview of the magical considerations that formulate this system and how the modern practitioner can incorporate it into their praxis today."

—Catamara Rosarium, convener of the
Viridis Genii Symposium and
proprietor of Rosarium Blends

ABOUT THE AUTHOR

Brandon Weston is a witch, writer, and folklorist living in the Arkansas Ozarks. He is the owner and operator of Ozark Healing Traditions, a collective of articles, lectures, and workshops focusing on traditions of medicine, magic, culture, and folklore all from the Ozark Mountain region. He comes from a long line of Ozark hillfolk and works hard to keep the traditions that he's collected alive and true for generations to come.

OZARK ★ FOLK ★ MAGIC

PLANTS, PRAYERS & HEALING

BRANDON WESTON

Llewellyn Publications
Woodbury, Minnesota

FIRST EDITION
Third Printing, 2022

Book design by Donna Burch-Brown
Cover design by Kevin R. Brown
Zodiac Man © Mary Ann Zapalac, other interior art by the Llewellyn Art Department

Llewellyn is a registered trademark of Llewellyn Worldwide Ltd.

Library of Congress Cataloging-in-Publication Data
Names: Weston, Brandon
Title: Ozark folk magic : plants, prayers & healing / Brandon Weston.
Description: First edition. | Woodbury, Minnesota : Llewellyn Publications,
    [2021] | Includes bibliographical references. | Summary: "Experience
    traditional hillfolk magic through the eyes of an authentic
    practitioner. This book provides lore, herbs, magical alignments, verbal
    charms, and more"-- Provided by publisher.
Identifiers: LCCN 2020042619 (print) | LCCN 2020042620 (ebook) | ISBN
    9780738767253 (paperback) | ISBN 9780738767437 (ebook)
Subjects: LCSH: Witchcraft--Ozark Mountains Region. | Magic--Ozark
    Mountains Region. | Ozark Mountains Region--Folklore.
Classification: LCC BF1577.O93 W47 2020 (print) | LCC BF1577.O93 (ebook)
    | DDC 133.4/3097671--dc23
LC record available at https://lccn.loc.gov/2020042619
LC ebook record available at https://lccn.loc.gov/2020042620

Llewellyn Worldwide Ltd. does not participate in, endorse, or have any authority or responsibility concerning private business transactions between our authors and the public.

All mail addressed to the author is forwarded, but the publisher cannot, unless specifically instructed by the author, give out an address or phone number.

Any internet references contained in this work are current at publication time, but the publisher cannot guarantee that a specific location will continue to be maintained. Please refer to the publisher's website for links to authors' websites and other sources.

Llewellyn Publications
A Division of Llewellyn Worldwide Ltd.
2143 Wooddale Drive
Woodbury, MN 55125-2989
www.llewellyn.com

Printed in the United States of America

Dedicated to my family,
who first told me tales of the Ozarks.

DISCLAIMER

The old-fashioned remedies in this book are historical references used for teaching purposes only. The recipes are not for commercial use or profit. The contents are not meant to diagnose, treat, prescribe, or substitute consultation with a licensed healthcare professional. New herbal recipes should be taken in small amounts to allow the body to adjust.

Please note that the information in this book is not meant to diagnose, treat, prescribe, or substitute consultation with a licensed healthcare professional. This book is not intended to provide medical advice or to take the place of medical advice and treatment from your personal physician. Readers are advised to consult their doctors or other qualified healthcare professionals regarding the treatment of their medical problems. Neither the publisher nor the author take any responsibility for any possible consequences from any treatment, action, or application of medicine, supplement, herb, or preparation to any person reading or following the information in this book.

CONTENTS

All names have been
changed for the privacy
and protection of
individual informants.

Foreword

IF YOU TAKE AWAY ONE message from this book, it should be Brandon Weston's assertation that Ozark folklore is not static. Folklore is a term that carries a lot of baggage, including the assumption that our nation's folklore is outdated, untrue, and backward. This is especially true for the Ozarks and its regional cousin, Appalachia. However, folklore, at its most basic, is defined as traditions shared and learned within a community. It is those practices we learn from our neighbors, friends, and fellows—not in the classroom, but from observation and imitation. It is our food, stories, art, holidays, rituals, music, and so on. It is our traditional belief systems. It is traditional, yes, but traditions are created and changed every day.

Through *Ozark Folk Magic*, Weston is following in the footsteps of a long history of folklore collecting in the United States and in the Ozarks in particular. Collectors have ranged from amateur collectors and community scholars to professional folklorists working in a discipline over a hundred years old. The American Folklore Society, as an example, is one of the nation's oldest academic societies and was founded in 1888 by scholars situated at the confluence of anthropological and literary studies. It is important to note that Weston falls into the former category of community scholar, which often includes tradition-bearers with an interest in their own communities. Weston's terminology and methods might differ from a professional folklorist today, but the role of community scholar and/or amateur folklorist is no less important. Our nation's archives owe a great to deal to community scholars collecting personal histories and traditions from the communities to which they belong. As Weston beautifully demonstrates, often it is only the community members themselves who can access a community's deepest layers of tradition.

As a professional folklorist myself, and an outsider to native Ozark culture, I find *Ozark Folk Magic* to be a deeply fascinating and personal work. Part personal memoir and part folklore collection, this volume contributes to an important and timely conversation about cultural pride and cultural appropriation in an increasingly globalized nation and world. *Ozark Folk Magic* is a book that needed to come from an insider like Brandon Weston. As a member of the Ozarks community himself, Weston is not only privy to knowledge that might not have been accessible to outsiders, but he also has access to the language and vocabulary used by the communities within which he works. As a folklorist born outside the Ozarks community, I can attest to the strength, smarts, and resiliency of Ozarks cultures, but I would not feel comfortable using the term hillbilly. As an outsider, I would fear this term would imply my derision and condescension. Weston, however, is an insider to this culture and has access and entitlements that I do not have.

Weston straddles an interesting divide between older methods of research and a more postmodern approach to his role as researcher. His collecting methods harken back to older forms of folklore collecting, where large swaths of folklore content were distilled into compilation books that did not necessarily highlight the biographies of the informants. Diverging from contemporary professional folklore practice, Weston does not give overt details about the identities and situations in which he collected his content, likely with the intent to protect the identities of practitioners operating within stigmatized traditions. Professional folklorists today would be more likely to include a great deal of context for each instance of folklore collected—the who, what, where, when. Folklorists stress context to reinforce the role individuals have in shaping their community's folklore—traditions are tweaked depending on teller, audience, time, and place. What you see written down in *Ozark Folk Magic* is the culmination of Weston's conversations with many folks, and his methods are important where traditions have been historically shunned and feared. However, I caution you to remember that it does not make it the final and official account of Ozark folk belief. Taking *Ozark Folk Magic* as the definitive and final account risks cementing, and stagnating, what Weston stresses is a live, growing, and changing tradition. Folklore is alive and well in the Ozarks, and *Ozark Folk Magic* is a snapshot of a moment in time.

Again, it is important to remember that despite situating himself within the lineage of folklore collecting in the Ozarks, Weston is collecting as a member of the community himself. When Weston refers to the cold, scientific approach of folklorists toward informants, he is referring to a style of research more characteristic of the early- to mid-twentieth century when folklorists often followed the anthropological trend of documenting the "other," while also attempting to justify the "objective," scientific nature of their work. Folklorists today do not operate as they did decades ago. Over the last several decades, professional folklorists have become increasingly focused on their obligations to their collaborators in the field, as well as in understanding the ways in which their presence may affect what and how folklore is collected. By acknowledging his own responsibilities to his informants, Weston intuitively works much more like a contemporary professional folklorist. This is important because it means that Weston's research is reciprocal. In an era where cultural appropriation endlessly takes from and consumes the communities that are supposedly "admired," Weston actively works to ensure sensitivity and respect for the cultures whose healing traditions have coalesced in the Ozarks.

Finally, do not let the theme of simplicity in *Ozark Folk Magic* cause you to think the people of the Ozarks are not savvy—despite the stereotypes imposed on this region, Weston demonstrates that you may not encounter a more clever and creative people.

—Virginia Siegel, MA
Folk Arts Coordinator
Arkansas Folk and Traditional Arts
University of Arkansas

Introduction

> *"We always lie to strangers."*
> —TRADITIONAL OZARK SAYING

DOC GREEN WAS A WITCH *and everyone around knew it. Not a soul dared ever call him that word, though. Folks around Nelson's Holler had heard too many tales about Doc Green's temper. Ol' Buddy Pickett had a cousin who let his lips flap during church one Sunday about how Doc Green had two-colored eyes, one that stared into this world, and the other—well that one was reserved for seeing haints and the Little People. A crow called outside the meetinghouse just as Tanner Pickett finished his story. His heart raced at the sound, knowing damn well that crows were the devil's messenger, and Doc Green was about as close to the devil as you could get in Nelson's Holler.*

Tanner sat in a cold sweat through the rest of the sermon. It was a long one this Sunday. Tanner swore under his breath, then winced at the sin and swore again. He'd be all right if he could get home and take the cuss off the situation. He'd already crossed all his fingers and turned out his pants pockets, but he wasn't sure it would be enough to counter Doc Green's magic.

As soon as the last "amen" sounded from the congregation, Tanner rushed toward the meetinghouse exit, nearly knocking poor Miss Jenkins to the ground on his way out. The old woman stumbled, but Deacon Evers caught her arm before she hit the ground. She thanked the man, then thought of Tanner Pickett and mumbled Psalm 35:23 under her breath: "Stir up thyself, and awake to my judgment, even unto my cause, my God and my Lord." She smiled, slung her purse back over her arm, and followed Deacon Evers to the fellowship hall for coffee.

Tanner ran all the way home. He ran until his heart nearly stopped, then ran some more. Every now and then he'd see a crow out of the corner of his vision. He mumbled the Lord's Prayer to himself as a defense. When he reached the cabin, he tore through the front door, slamming it shut behind him and locking it. His folks were still back at the church gossiping with the others. The cabin was quiet apart from Tanner's heaving breath. He threw himself into a chair nearby to rest.

A loud "Caw!" sounded above the cabin. The boy jerked up from his chair. He grabbed some salt from the dining table and threw it onto the glowing coals in the fireplace. Sparks popped from the bed of coals, twisting little trails of light up the chimney. Tanner listened closely, his hand over his mouth to steady his breathing.

"Caw! Caw!" the crow called again, this time from just outside the front door. Tanner fell backward to the floor. He slid himself in a panic toward his parents' bed. He tore off his shirt, turned it inside out, and then put it back on. He'd learned this method of countering the dark arts from some older boys at school.

"Caw! Caw!" the demon cried again, clawing and scraping at the wood of the door with its claws and beak. Tanner bit his cheek trying to pull himself out of his frozen panic. The taste of blood woke him up. He ran across the cabin and grabbed his dad's muzzleloader rifle, a bag of powder, and some bullets. He searched through the lead shot, looking for one his dad always kept around. His fingers found the object. He pulled out a shiny ball of silver, smiled to himself, and packed the gun the way his dad had taught him.

With the gun secured, Tanner ran out the back door of the cabin. "Sounds like the devil's still over in the dog run," Tanner whispered to himself, cupping his hand behind his ear to hear better. Just then a crow flew overhead, traveling like mad toward the woods. Tanner brought the sights to his eyes but couldn't get a shot.

Tanner ran across the yard toward the woods, keeping the bird always in his eyes. He jumped over rocks and logs. He ran through puddles leftover from yesterday's rainstorms. He slipped some spicebush leaves into his mouth to better his luck and stuck an owl feather from his pocket into the brim of his hat to improve his vision. The crow growled and cawed as it flew, never once stopping to perch. "The damn thing's leading me somewhere," Tanner said.

A couple of times the boy swore he could get in a shot, but then the bird would turn at the last second, almost as though it knew his thoughts. The two creatures, a boy and a demon, played chase for a mile more. Tanner never stopped running, even though his legs were dead tired. He was bound and determined to end this curse if it was the last thing he did. The bird picked up speed as though some evil hellfire fueled its flight. Tanner swore under his breath and ran faster. He ran and ran through the cedar break, the flat ground letting him catch up. He ran and ran through the hickory trees and *oaks, through sharp blackberry canes and twisting briar vines. In the distance the land turned jagged with big rocks. He ran toward the incline. There was no going around. He ran and ran until...*

Tanner had never experienced flight before, but he imagined what he was feeling now went right along with it. He was falling. The gun went first, down through the darkness of the cave crevice, and he followed after. He stared up toward the bright summer sky. He stared until the crack looked like just a little sliver of light. Then all the lights went out. Silence reigned, apart from the single cawing of a crow.

———

The story above, and others you'll find throughout this work, are retellings from examples I've collected from my family and other storytellers across the Ozark region. The introduction to my own culture came at a young age in the form of family stories like these. I'm a multigenerational Ozarker on both sides. Through my own genealogical work, I've traced the twisting branches of my family tree back to the time of the first settlement of the area. These were outsiders who rushed to claim new land in the early 1800s, after the forced removal of the Osage to Oklahoma by the Indian Removal Act, signed by President Andrew Jackson in 1830. Before that, like most other Ozark families, my people came from various places across the Appalachian Mountains. It's often said that the wandering mountain families and clans decided to settle in the Ozarks because it reminded them so much of their Appalachian home. If you've ever visited both areas, you'll likely agree with them that the landscapes are remarkably similar, as are the flora and fauna. We Ozarkers have always had a hard time defining ourselves. We're not quite Southern, not quite Midwestern, not quite Appalachian. In many ways, we're a mixture of all three areas, with a whole lot more added in. It's because of this unique mixture that many of our cultural traditions and folkways stand out to people on the outside looking in. For me, they were always just a part of day-to-day life.

The most memorable stories from my childhood were always about healers and monsters—hardly ever placed alongside each other in tales, though. The monsters always lurked in the darkness of the woods or hid out in deep, cavernous tunnels underground; critters like the "hoop snake," who can bite his own tail and roll at fast speeds like a tire across the ground. It's said that if one ever catches you, it'll wrap around your neck and spit poison in your eyes. Its cousin is the "blue racer," another deadly fast serpent used by Ozark parents to scare their children out of venturing too far from home.

The healers of old mountain tales were likewise always given equal amounts of respect and distrust, like my great-uncle Bill, who could buy warts off of you for a penny or dime (more about wart charmers in chapter 3). Everyone in the family knew he had the "gift," but they hardly ever talked about that fact. There was a secret belief that talking about such power would somehow tempt the Fates, who would take it away forever. Even when talking to Bill himself, he'd always just say he was "born with a gift, and that's that."

I was always fascinated by the mystery surrounding these mountain magicians, and I still am. There's an important part of the folk-healing process involved in the idea of mystery; a quality that's heightened by almost-epic tales of miraculous powers that often accompany well-known healers who work for the public. No matter the age, for just a moment while listening to the words pour from a storyteller's mouth, listeners truly believe that anything is possible. I can say today that stories like these have continued to be the lifeblood of my work. Everything I know, everything that is important to me, has come in the form of folklore. Blame it on a culture born from mostly illiterate hillfolk if you'd like, but we Ozarkers are a people who thrive on tall tales.

OZARK FOLKLORE

Stories can fuel our bodies and spirits like food. But all too often we don't pay much attention to the ingredients, or sometimes even to the process of eating at all. The act can become a meaningless part of our day-to-day life. That's how stories became for me after childhood, when the fantastic was transformed by the weight of the world into the mundane. I never questioned the tales my family told. I never wondered why my friends at school weren't as terrified of the hoop snake as I was, or why they didn't like playing outside in the woods. Growing up I had little awareness of my culture, or the Ozarks at all, really. The stories and people in my life who might have been considered fantastical by others were so commonplace for me that I didn't even give them a second thought. It was only when I picked up a copy of Vance Randolph's *Ozark Magic and Folklore* my freshman year of college that everything changed.

Vance Randolph is, without a doubt, the most famous Ozark folklorist in publication. His works span what historians call the "old Ozarks," from settlement in the 1830s to around the turn of the twentieth century. As I read his work, I was dumbstruck that my hillbilly upbringing was actually a point of anthropological study. The more I read from Randolph, the more I realized that the stories my family told actually fit into the tapestry of folk beliefs from this amazingly unique place called the Ozarks. It was the first time in my life that I started to question what it was that I believed. "You mean the hoop snake doesn't really exist?" I found myself asking. I now cursed the constant fear I had growing up about getting attacked while wandering the woods during the summertime. This illumination would forever change my hiking trips, as well as my interactions with gullible friends.

I started writing what would become this book almost immediately after finishing Randolph's *Ozark Magic and Folklore*. What struck me the most about his research was his constant use of the word *superstition*. It's still a constant annoyance for me to this day. Randolph was a folklorist and a collector, but above all else, he was an academic. Superstition denotes removal and distance from the culture you're talking about. Few people would willingly call themselves superstitious. No, we call the beliefs of other people superstitions, not our own. There's something primal in this notion. Something that goes way back to our ancestors desperately trying to convince their kids not to marry the bumpkins on the other side of the holler. "Them folks is dead superstitious o'er thar!" you might hear an old-timer say. "Not like us, though!" No, not like the bumpkins on *this* side of the holler.

There are other famous Ozark folklorists besides Vance Randolph, although few outside our small community would likely not have heard of them. There's Mary Celestia Parler, Randolph's wife, whose collection rivals that of her husband even though she has received very little credit over the years. Then there's Otto Ernest Rayburn, whose *Ozark Encyclopedia* is a massive rat's nest of ancient newspaper clippings, dried plant samples, and personal sketches. All three came from mostly academic settings. Parler's collection was used mainly for her own research into Ozark folklore and music. Randolph and Rayburn also published for entertainment. It's really no wonder to me now why they all chose to use the word superstition so frequently in their works. In fact, Randolph's *Ozark Magic and Folklore* was called *Ozark Superstitions* in its original printing. At least Parler kept her commentary to a minimum, opting instead to act only as organizer and encourager for the students she sent out to collect their own family folklore. Her most famous work is the massive *Folk Beliefs from Arkansas*, a multi-volume collection of thousands of anecdotes, all submitted by her folklore students over the course of her long career as professor at the University of Arkansas.

As I continued my studies, a thought always remained in the back of my mind like the constant ticking of a clock. It's a saying made famous by Randolph, and he even named a book of Ozark folktales after the adage: "We always lie to strangers." I couldn't help but wonder whether Randolph's informants were really all that honest with him. To this day, many Ozarkers, especially in the rural areas, are extremely distrustful of strangers. At one time, isolation meant survival for many families out in the hills. You've got to stick with the people you know.

As the more populated areas of the Ozarks grew up around bust flatland communities and farms, people started looking to the hills for entertainment. Going out to see the bare-foot hillbilly was once big business for city folk, not only from the Ozarks but from across the country. One could argue that it still is in places, like Branson, Missouri, where people from all over flock into town to catch a glimpse of the old Ozarks. The clash of cultures that occurred early on made folks in the hills isolate themselves in their traditions even more as their distrust for outsiders grew and grew.

These are the people I come from. The kind of people who never use the word superstitious, not in any meaningful way. They might use it to hide their most secret beliefs though, like the praying granny I met in Marble, Arkansas, who used certain verses from the Bible to heal and drive away evil but would "never pay any mind to them old superstitions." Ozarkers always do, though. We still plant by the moon and read omens out of crow calls, owl hoots, and cicada hums. These aren't really superstitions, mind you. Even tales of witches, boogers, and other mountain monsters, usually told around campfires for entertainment, have an edge of reality to them. They all still have a tinge of something sinister and very real.

I figured out early on in my studies that I needed to get to the source of the river to find the clearest water. The folklorists did their best, bless their hearts. But I came to understand that just reading the folklore wasn't enough; I needed something deeper than just anecdotes. I needed to know, for instance, why people around the Ozarks are always carrying nuts from the buckeye tree (*Aesculus glabra*) for good luck. Or why the sassafras (*Sassafras albidum*) and pawpaw (*Asimina triloba*) are called "witch trees" and looked at with great suspicion by mountain folk. Or why you never pick up a penny off the ground, despite what city folk might claim about its luckiness. My curiosity didn't stop with just the existence of a belief. I needed not only to figure out *why* people believed what they did, but also to make connections with other cultural traditions I knew about. For example, tracing the long lineage of a verbal charm for healing back through the Appalachian Mountains, then across the Atlantic to Britain, then to Medieval Latin sources in Rome. Just knowing that someone once spoke the charm, somewhere, sometime ago, was far from enough of the story for me.

I soon read through everything I could find from the published folklorists. Anyone researching the Ozarks will find out pretty quickly that there's not a lot out there published on even the history of the region, let alone what people have considered superstitions. I decided the best use of my time and energy would be to go out and collect my own information. What could be clearer than that? And this would give me an opportunity to look at how these folkways might have changed since Randolph published *Ozark Magic and Folklore* in 1947. I was certain that a lot had changed since then, considering many of his informants would have likely died over the years. Would their children or grandchildren still know the old stories? I also wondered about the influx of other cultures laying down roots in the area and what these new traditions were adding to Ozark culture.

I decided to start with my own family first, then branched out as I got more used to the process of collecting folklore. I recorded everything I could get my hands on, from anyone willing to talk to me. I was shocked at the amount of valuable information I was able to collect, not only from my family, but from complete strangers. Sometimes in one session alone, stories of childhood quickly turned into anecdotes about foodways, then those led into home remedies, and eventually I found myself recording what I always called the "good stuff," stories about healers and magic.

Now, I figured out early on that I couldn't just start talking about magic right out of the gate. Because the Ozark people have historically been both religiously and socially conservative, there are still a lot of hang-ups about magic and the ever-dreaded witchcraft. This is happily changing today, though, as more and more people are now identifying as witches and pagans in the area. Some you might not expect, like the fourth-generation healer and herbalist I once met outside of a very conservative Arkansas town, who was happy to identify herself as an animist and witch despite the strange looks she got from her neighbors. But, when you look at the material collected by Randolph and others in the first part of the twentieth century, and when you're talking to older generations who would have also been exposed to the culture of the old Ozarks, you have to take a few things into consideration.

MOUNTAIN RELIGION

The hillfolk settlers who made their way from the Appalachian Mountains west into the Ozarks were mostly of Scots-Irish and German stock. Many of these clans also had family from among the indigenous peoples of the Southeast, namely the Cherokee, Yuchi, Muscogee, and Koasati. Others were of African ancestry, and still more were a melting pot of many different nations and cultures. The majority of these families were Protestant Christians, belonging to any number of different churches including Baptists, Presbyterians, Brethren, Unitarians, Methodists, and many others. There were also those from independent churches without any denominational leanings. This of course is not to say there weren't any other churches represented, because we know many Roman Catholic families settled in the region early on, not to mention the wealth of different religious and cultural backgrounds that came to the area later on. When we look at the traditions we see represented in the works of Ozark folklorists like Randolph, we have to take into consideration the religious beliefs and overarching cosmology of the time. The religion would have most commonly been Protestant Christianity, based on the fundamental ideas of simplicity in worship, emphasis on a personal relationship with the Divine, and free access to the Bible in English. These three have influenced Ozark cosmology in more ways than I'm able to record, but I'll mention a few.

One stream of thought that kept popping up for me as I collected folklore and healing knowledge from across the Ozarks was the idea of simplicity in the work of the healer. Many writers and practitioners alike tend to make a firm separation between what they might call "folk magic" and what is labeled as "ceremonial" or "high magic." Ceremonial magic has long been considered the domain of the astute academic with their stacks of tomes and grimoires, staying up until the wee hours of the morning studying arcane lore. Folk magic has a long history of being considered just that other stuff, the bits and pieces the poor and illiterate managed to pick up while snooping on their local wizard's strange rites. This divide still exists in many communities today. Folk magic is somehow seen as being *lesser* than work that involves complicated celestial timings and ancient recitations.

In the Ozarks, where the vast majority of rural people were illiterate well into the twentieth century, the magic of the people was born in a simple yet powerful way. This simplicity is reflected in both the religious beliefs of the Ozark people and their healing practices. In religion, this simplicity manifests in an interesting connection between the people, nature, and the Divine. God is seen as always present in every living (and sometimes even nonliving) aspects of nature. God is in the ripening corn, the river where baptisms are always held, in the spring rain, and even in the wood used to build the church house. Even today, this connection with nature as a part of the Divine can still be seen in the more rural areas of the Ozarks, where people are still fiercely protective of their solitude, the quiet, and the natural world around them.

Another powerful way this idea of simplicity has manifested in the Ozarks is in the repurposing of household objects for magical works. Items like lamps, scissors, knives, axes, brooms, candles, string, and even the cabin itself are all given second lives as tools for wondrous healing. Healing in the Ozarks is simple because at one time, it was required to be simple. People in the hills were scraping out as best of a life as they could, with little to no extra money to spend on specialized healing equipment. Healers in the Ozarks have always used what was at hand, what words they could remember or summon in the moment, what could be grown, and what could be gathered in the wild. While I live a very different life today, my ancestors who were a part of this early system of magical healing would have needed quick work for a busy life. Healing had to fit into a packed schedule of hard, manual labor from sunrise to sunset, usually every day of the week apart from Sunday. Healing couldn't take longer than it needed to, and it had to be free.

The Ozark people have often been described as being incredibly stubborn and at times violently protective of their own personal rights and freedoms. This goes back to the very beginning of settlement in the area. The first outsiders to the mountains were small families and clan groups heading west, seeking new land and new opportunities—but not to farm, make businesses, and grow wealth. They wanted to be left alone. These hillfolk clans found a perfect home in the isolated hills and hollers of the Ozarks. Some of them formed small communities; others embraced the extreme solitude of the wilderness. A natural distrust of strangers grew among these groups. To this day in many places around the Ozarks, people are more likely to shoot first and ask questions later.

This intense desire for personal freedom has influenced the religious foundation of the Ozarks greatly. Religious belief is still seen as something intensely personal and therefore rarely talked about outside of church. As many in the old Ozarks were illiterate, their knowledge of the Bible came from what they could pick up from a church service or traveling preacher. Many of the verbal charms and healing prayers we have today would have likely been first picked up from someone hearing the verse, not reading it from their own Bible. This gave rise to many charms that are said to be from the Bible but aren't really there. One healer I met said she was passed an old "Bible charm," as she called it. She recited the verse to me and curious as I was, I did a quick internet search and couldn't for the life of me find it anywhere in the Bible. I decided not to confront the woman about this discovery.

Healing work is often seen as something just as personal as someone's religion. Folks might go to a magical healer to help them out but wouldn't dare tell anyone. That's not so much out of fear but the idea that it's no one else's business what a person does in their free time. Healers often say they were "born with the gift," or "discovered" their healing abilities through some encounter with nature or a vision of the Divine. The power to heal is considered a calling, just like preaching and teaching, as one healer told me. These callings are always intensely personal. A healer might learn some verbal charms or remedies from another skilled mountain doctor, but what I've found on my own journeys is that for most healers today, it's completely up to them to discover their own power. Someone might be born with the gift for healing, but that doesn't mean they'll be a healer, no more than baptism means someone is always a member of the church. A healer begins their lifelong journey the day they accept this power, and as with many aspects of Ozark life, it's a journey one makes alone.

The last idea to have influenced both religious beliefs and healing traditions in the Ozarks was the availability of the Bible in English. While there were few in the Ozarks who could actually read, a family Bible was still a feature of nearly every home. Though no one in the family could read it, the Bible itself was often seen as a talisman against illness, harm, and evil. As schools were built in small communities and more people began to read, passages from the Bible began to be widely used as prayers for healing and other magical works. The Bible became a powerful grimoire for those with eyes to see the true purpose of the book. These sorts were often said to be gifted themselves. Healers and lay people alike memorized certain magical verses like the famous "blood charm," Ezekiel 16:6, "I passed by you, and saw you flailing about in your blood. As you lay in your blood, I said to you, 'Live!'"[1] This verse is still used by mountain healers today to stop a wound from bleeding. As with other household objects, healers quickly found a whole host of good uses in the verses of the Bible, not just for healing, but for love, drawing in money and luck, protection, banishing evil spirits, and even cursing.

The spiritual landscape of the Ozarks has changed greatly over the years, even since I was a kid. Northwest Arkansas, where I live, is now a region rich in diverse cultures, religions, and traditions. I can even remember when we got our first Buddhist temple in the area.

I'm always getting asked in my workshops and lectures, "What is Ozark magic?" And unfortunately, that's not an easy question to answer. For many, it's a rigid form of traditionalism based specifically in Protestant Christianity, with an emphasis on the healing power of prayer and the use of certain medicinal plants in various preparations. Some would say that Ozark folk healing and magic is *always* this or *never* that. For example, "Ozark folk healing is *always* Christian." "Healers *never* work with anything but the Bible and Jesus." "Witchcraft is *always* evil." Those are just a few I've heard over the years from some very zealous traditionalists who have obviously never met many other Ozarkers. These notions

---

1.   Ezekiel 16:6 (New Revised Standard Version).

might very well have been true at one time or another, when the area was much less populated and folks were isolated from each other, still holding on to the conservative folk
beliefs from their European ancestry. But I tend to question even this idea that the Ozarks
have always been one way or another. I've met plenty of healers who also considered themselves pagans, witches, or just something very apart from Christianity in general. These
people weren't transplants from California, either. They were multigenerational Ozarkers,
about as Ozark as they come. So, who's to say that what they practice isn't traditional or
Ozark? That's one of the purposes in writing this book, to help dispel some of the myths
surrounding this tradition and to help bring it peacefully into an ever-evolving world.

MAGIC, HEALERS, AND WITCHES

Ozark culture has historically carried with it many traditions from across Europe, specifically Ireland, Britain, and Germany. Because of this, there's an ingrained belief in many of
the older generations that magic and witchcraft are always associated with the forces of
evil. In the old Ozarks, magic always referred to malign, supernatural work as performed
by witches. So, what then is a witch? Ozark cosmology situates the individual in a constant
battle between the forces of good and evil. On a daily basis, each soul is seen as being under
attack from an entire world of invisible and malign forces. These hosts include not only
the traditional Christian concept of a demon or devil but also unidentifiable "haints," or
ghosts, who wander the land terrorizing the living. On the opposite end of the spectrum
from these evil hosts, you have forces of good including God, Jesus, and sometimes the
saints, angels, and departed loved ones who are seen as always watching over their family.
In between these two primal forces, you have certain intermediary entities that most often
represent the neutrality of nature itself. This group includes land or nature spirits and the
"Little People." The Little People represent an interesting blending of folk beliefs about
fairies, or the "good folk," from across Europe, and beliefs about the *yvwitsunsdi*, or "Little
People," a Cherokee tradition, that would have entered into the proto-Ozark folklore while it
was still developing in the Appalachian Mountains.[2] In the Ozarks, the Little People are
seen as both tricksters and helping spirits, depending solely upon how they're approached
by a mortal. For the selfish, they can bring terrible sickness and ruin, but for those of pure
heart they often impart magical or healing knowledge. This gift often comes at a price,

---

2. Mooney, *Sacred Formulas of the Cherokees*, 330–35.

though, as with one healer who told me the Little People gave him the power of *dowsing*, or to magically locate underground water sources, but took the vision in his left eye.

In each position on the spectrum, there are certain individuals who are able to harness these cosmic forces and use them in the physical world. It can be said that magic is the spectrum itself. Magic is formless, genderless, neither traditionally good nor evil, but can encompass either aspect. Where one sits on the spectrum is defined by how they use this neutral magic. Traditionally, on the side of good is the healer, or "doctor" as they're often called in the old Ozarks. The healer uses this neutral magic solely for doctoring, helping, cleansing, protecting, and purifying, all words traditionally used in the Ozarks. The healer can be born with this gift, learn it from an elder, or learn it through certain visionary experiences of the Divine, as in the case of the woman I met who gained the power of healing after her baptism. Being born with the gift is seen as the most socially acceptable option, as it denotes an inborn calling sent from God above. The healer, often against their better judgment, accepts their gift and is then able to work wonders in their community. Often those born with the gift will be identified at a young age by an elder healer in the community who will slowly pass them their magical knowledge, piece by piece, until their student is ready to go off on their own. Many times, though, I've seen the belief pop up that if you're born with the gift it will naturally manifest, whether you learn any verbal charms, rituals, remedies, or not. The power inside the healer itself shows them how to heal; they need only accept it and let it guide them. This seems to be a more common belief today where there are far fewer experienced elder healers around with this knowledge than there used to be. Others might learn certain healing techniques from the spirits of their ancestors, or nature, or even the Little People. This form of learning is more popular today, where it bears less of a stigma than it once did in a more conservative era. One healer I interviewed told me she learned her healing prayers as a child by listening to the song sung by the river near her family's cabin.

Conservative communities have historically seen the power of healing as having its source in God and God alone, and they have therefore looked at this form of magical learning with great suspicion. Many of the healers I know who gained their power in this way have told me they always heal and avoid telling anyone where their gift came from, lest they risk being ostracized by their community. Healers oftentimes don't just limit their work to healing, but might also include work for settling disputes, saving marriages, or for helping someone become lucky or prosperous. As long as the work is seen as doing good and not harming anyone, it's generally accepted by the community. In more conservative areas, though, even these healers are seen with suspicion. One informant told me a story about his grandpa, who remembered a time in his childhood when a man was run out of town for selling love potions to some of the good church folk. The idea behind this suspicion is that in areas of love and luck, God rules all, and changing that is like trying to force the hand of the Divine, said to be the work of witches.

On the opposite end of the spectrum is the character of the witch, sometimes also called by other traditional European terms like warlock, magician, conjurer, and sometimes sorcerer. I say *character* because today in the Ozarks, the witch is left to stories and folklore. There are few who still believe in the witch as a real force for evil in their lives. The witch is said to use the neutral magic of the universe for evil or selfish purposes like hurting, harming, cursing, hexing, stealing, maiming, disfiguring, etc. What separates the witch from the healer, besides how they use this magical power, is how the power is obtained. Some people in the Ozarks believe the witch can be born with their power just like a healer can, but also like the healer, it's ultimately up to the individual to choose how to use their gift. Vance Randolph has an anecdote in his *Ozark Magic and Folklore* about certain "carriers" of the power, left to them by an elder witch in their family line.[3] The individual doesn't become a witch until choosing to use this inborn power in an evil way. Like the healer, the witch might also gain their power through apprenticing with an elder in the community or through encounters with the neutral spirits of the land and Little People. There are just about as many stories about people learning healing words from the Little People as there are about learning how to curse or throw a hex.

We know now that thousands of innocent lives have been lost to witch accusations throughout history, if not more. The murders of innocent people accused of being witches aren't just a tragic moment in our past—they continue throughout the world even today. Ozark folklore is filled with stories about witches, how to tell if a person is a witch, and how to kill them once they're found. These depictions of the character of the witch follow the stereotypical European formulas of an older woman, usually a widow, who lives on the edge of town or out in the woods and who is overly fond of nature and eating small children.

The earliest creations of witches were aimed at removing anyone who might be different from the community, whether they had any purported magical powers or not. Those who most often suffered were already the most disenfranchised of the society: widows,

---

3.   Randolph, *Ozark Magic and Folklore*, 266.

people with physical or mental disabilities, and those who would now be a part of the LGBTQIA+ community were all fair game for ostracizing, and it generally only took a handful of accusations from prominent churchgoers to send the community into a frenzy. I'm happy to say that the view of witches in the Ozarks has changed greatly since these older times. This is in part due to so many younger generations now happily reclaiming the word for themselves to define their beliefs and practices in a way no other word really could.

I've even seen the character of the witch change in more conservative communities. Even amongst older healers who still hold to some of the more conservative traditions, the witch they might be fighting against is no longer an actual person but has been transformed into the evil "other" itself. Prayers and formulas no longer target specific people (for the most part) but instead are aimed at the "witch over the mountain" or the "witch deep in the woods." In this way, the client is still able to feel like there is someone to blame for their misfortune and the healer is still able to cast evil away to some other place, far from the one they're healing. The witch is no longer a physical person, but the manifestation of sickness and evil itself.

The separation between "black" and "white" magic, healers and witches, still exists in some communities throughout the Ozarks. This separation needs to be talked about, mostly because all of our recorded folklore is full of this more conservative way of thinking. But, in my own travels and personal experience as a healer and folk magic practitioner, I've been able to observe the growth of gray or "neutral" magic as a phenomenon amongst younger generations of Ozark healers. Like the Little People and spirits of the land itself, this gray magic exists in between conservative notions of good and evil, black and white, light and darkness. When Mother Nature sends a storm that floods a town, was it evil? When hail dents your car up, is that the working of a maleficent force? Those who work in this gray area often consider their practice to always be beneficial, no matter if it's healing or cursing. Their work becomes the work of nature itself.

I've only spoken to a few old-timers who would admit to any kind of retribution work. One told me he always sent curses, or "goomering" as it's called in the Ozarks, back to its source, whether it harmed the sender or not. This sort of benevolent cursing is fairly common to see amongst younger generation practitioners who feel like this kind of "sending back" is just a natural part of healing work. Others dip their toes a little deeper into what might be labeled by more conservative individuals as witchcraft. These practitioners might consider preemptively cursing an unfaithful spouse or a backstabbing business partner, for instance, as equally important as cleansing and healing work. This "graying" of magic is hardly new, even in the Ozarks. The problem is that because we looked at many of these practices with so much disdain and fear, we have little recorded material about healers who actually might have worked in similar ways. Today, gray magic is becoming the norm with so many practitioners. I myself consider the magical work I do to exist within this neutral realm of magical power. I see it as being an extension of nature itself, and in the Ozarks we are often so close to nature that it only makes sense for me to work in this way. I'm happy that others now feel comfortable enough to reclaim their own connection to the Divine, within themselves and the natural world.

DIVERSE PRACTICES

Traditional Ozark healing and magic itself has evolved over the years to include many diverse practices and systems of medicine. Take, for instance, the mountain man I know who has in his mental repertoire around a hundred different medicinal plants native to the Ozarks, but who was also at one time trained in acupuncture and traditional Chinese medicine. I asked him if he thought what he was doing was still considered "Ozark," and he just smiled, laughed a little, and replied, "Ozark people have always used what worked, no matter where it came from." This idea sums up a great deal about how Ozark folk practices developed in the first place. I often use terms like "Ozark traditional healing" or "Ozark folk magic" to encompass a corpus of beliefs, remedies, rituals, and practices with a wide range of histories in both this country and around the world. We can dig deep, and many folklorists have, to trace certain practices back to original sources across the Western and Eastern worlds. Many of the folk traditions we have recorded from the old Ozarks are unique to this area, centered mostly on certain native plant varieties only found here in the New World. For instance, beliefs surrounding the pawpaw tree.

The pawpaw is a native fruit here in the Ozarks. It's been a food for the people here for hundreds of years and fed the indigenous people of the region for even longer. Its texture and flavor are in between a banana and a pineapple. Apart from being an excellent food, there is a great deal of folklore surrounding this tree. Some people still refer to the pawpaw as a witch tree and believe the tree itself is known to attract spirits of the dead and other supernatural entities. This is because pawpaw trees, along with the sassafras, both attract certain species of the swallowtail butterfly. At certain times of the year you can find hundreds of these butterflies fluttering around in the branches of these trees. In Ozark cosmology, spirits of the dead often appear to humans in the form of the butterfly, so seeing a tree filled with so many of one kind is taken as a very auspicious "token," or omen.

There are many more folk beliefs unique to the Ozarks, some of which will be discussed in this work, but we also have to remember that much of what makes up this tradition can be traced to influencing factors from outside the region. Ozark folk traditions bear the fingerprints of many other cultures and practices. The vast majority of our plant knowledge alone, for example, comes from interactions with the indigenous people of the Southeast, specifically those groups in the Appalachian Mountain region like the Cherokee and Muscogee Creek. Without this valuable knowledge, the European settlers would have been left to only the few varieties of plants they brought with them from their homeland. While a great deal of this relationship was defined by violence on the part of European colonizers, there was also a peaceful exchange of knowledge between these groups. Many indigenous peoples added medicinal plants native to Europe, like mullein (*Verbascum thapsus*) and plantain (*Plantago major*), to their own healing repertoire while simultaneously teaching about the plants of this land.

Like many people from the Appalachian cultural region, my own ancestry is a complicated blend of Europe and the New World. In my travels across the Ozarks I've collected stories from a wide variety of people, all of whom have considered themselves a part of Ozark culture. Some still consider themselves a part of the Old Settler Cherokee groups who were given a large amount of land in northwest Arkansas around 1817, prior to their forced removal along with the Osage to what is now Oklahoma. I've also met descendants of slaves, children and grandchildren of the few Black communities to have survived a period of widespread lynching throughout the Ozarks between about 1894 and 1909.[4] These cultures had a great deal of influence upon the culture of the southern Ozarks. In many of the practices I've studied I see pieces taken from Hoodoo, also called Rootwork or Conjure, a practice exemplified in Arkansas by the famous Newport resident root doctor and spiritualist Aunt Caroline Dye. Many whites in the Ozarks have scoffed at my mentioning of these interactions, choosing to wrongfully believe that all of our Ozark traditions have come from Europe alone. This is far from the truth of the matter, and as we enter into an era where vast amounts of new information can be accessed in the blink of an eye, we're learning more and more about how diverse our practices really are. But I've known

---

4. Harper, *White Man's Heaven*.

this for a long time. It's amazing how much truth you can discover by actually going out and talking to people.

I knew when I started collecting stories that I would find more than I could ever deal with all at once. The few tidbits I had from my family were nothing compared to what I found when I started traveling out to rural parts of the Ozarks. It seemed like every new informant had at least three buddies I was also encouraged to talk to, and each of them had even more. The traditions of the Ozarks, especially those surrounding more personal beliefs like religion, magic, and folk healing, are as diverse as the people still practicing these traditions. When I'm giving talks or workshops, I preface everything with, "Well, this is how *I* was taught to do it." That's because for every remedy, for every healing ritual, there are a hundred other varieties out there equally as effective.

One example I like to give is of the horseshoe as a talisman of good luck. Now, many of us will recognize this symbol, and I'm willing to bet many of you reading this have one hanging up on your wall right now, but let me ask you a question: do you hang a horseshoe with the prongs up or down? Some of you will have a gut reaction to this question, but what I found collecting folklore around the Ozarks is that there's about a fifty-fifty split between people who believe the horseshoe prongs should face upward, creating a bowl to hold good luck, and those who reverse that and have the prongs face down, so as to pour luck over whoever walks underneath it. So, which side is correct? Maybe we have to accept that they both are, at least in their own way.

This diversity of practices is what has made me most excited about studying the Ozarks. As a practitioner and healer myself, I found I was able to rely less upon strict teaching from an erudite elder and instead let my path follow my visions, dreams, and a more winding road, like the twisting of hills and hollers. The beliefs and practices contained in this book are ones that I've commonly found throughout the Ozark region. These are the traditions that almost everyone I met seemed to know about. But just like I mentioned earlier, while many of these remedies and rituals might have had a long career of use in the old Ozarks, they might not be appropriate for a modern world. This is why it's so important that we are able to look at our folkways and practices as ever-evolving and changing. We should always be able to integrate new and better information into our practices whenever it comes along.

At the heart of the many diverse practices and beliefs of the Ozarks is a core connection to the earth, plants, animals, and landscape itself, and the fervent belief that the world of spirits, or the "otherworld," is constantly at hand but separated by a thin veil. This is the heart of the Ozarks, and this is what we can bring with us into the modern world as a new generation of Ozark magical practitioners.

THE MODERN OZARKS

The influx of newer traditions mixing with the old, the common use of the word witch as a positive term, and the budding of gray magic amongst younger practitioners has led many traditionalists to say there are no longer Ozark practices. We again have to ask the question, "What does *Ozark* mean exactly?" As a practitioner of this magical tradition myself, it's fascinating for me to see how our folkways have evolved over the years and yet stayed true to the heart of Ozark folk belief, as mentioned in the previous section. Take again, for instance, the lowly pawpaw. Many of my own family remember eating this fruit as a part of their seasonal diet. They're high in protein and other nutrients, and they were often a welcome sight at the table. Love of the pawpaw skipped my parents' generation though, like so many other folkways. But with my generation, there's been a resurgence of interest in some of the old traditions, especially surrounding food. People my age are now growing pawpaw trees again and using them in ways the old-timers might not have thought about, like in my favorite: ice cream. Along with this, they are spreading the good news about our native Ozark flora and encouraging people to grow the trees themselves.

This push for sharing and updating many of the old traditions is becoming more and more commonplace these days, and I say bring it on! When we look back on the stacks and stacks of material Vance Randolph and Mary Parler alone collected, a lot of what we see encompasses traditional, not modern, folkways. There are certain traditions that are very Ozark, but that shouldn't be brought into the modern world: inhumane practices, like cutting off the end of a cat's tail and swiping the blood across your eye to heal a painful sty, or even ingesting certain poisonous chemical substances like turpentine or kerosene as remedies for illnesses like sore throat and cough. These folkways might have been commonplace at one time, but they have no place in practice anymore, especially with so many modern advances in medicine. You have to remember that many of these old remedies were born out of desperation, at a time when you couldn't just go pick up a cream or pill from the pharmacy.

We also have to consider if these beliefs might target a certain group of people for ostracization. Unfortunately, there are many of these when we read back through published folklore. I've already mentioned witch accusations, but there's another tradition mentioned by Randolph of certain taboos established for pregnant women, lest their child be born with a so-called "deformity." For example, it's said that if a pregnant woman steps on a rock and hurts her foot, her child will be lame in that leg. Or, if a bull scares a pregnant woman, her child will be born with a cow-shaped birthmark. These beliefs are interesting in the context of folklore, but they have no place in actual practice in the modern world. I once spoke with an old man who believed the large, bloodred birthmark across his face was put on him because his mother helped with butchering a hog while pregnant, which was apparently taboo. As a child, everyone in his small community knew the story and made him suffer because of it for most of his life. It was only when he moved away to a larger town a few hours away that he felt he was truly free from the laughter and gazes.

This, and others like it, are unfortunately common stories across much of the Ozarks, where physical and mental impairment might still be looked at as cursed conditions or punishment for some family sin. We're living in a world with so much potential for growth and bringing people together; we need to remember our priorities and examine all of our beliefs, not just in our folklore, to see if they bear the seeds of violence or hatred.

MY OWN PATH

My life forever changed the minute I walked out my door and went to meet my first informant. Being new to the work, I stumbled over my words and failed to remember the advice that had been given to me about avoiding the subject of magic until the person got to know me better. But regardless, I considered the information I collected, however small, to be a treasure still. The more people I found, the easier the work became.

The trust I developed with people came from the fact that I was an Ozarker, just like them, and I was young, which always impressed the old-timers who all bemoaned the fact that their kids and grandkids no longer cared about their stories. I also approached my work in a different way from other folklorists, even other amateur ones. I recorded stories, yes, but I've never had any intention of releasing those recordings, and I made sure the people I talked to knew that. It was because of this trust that I was able to approach certain subjects like childhood, which for the majority of old-timers across the Ozarks wasn't a happy one. For most, it was filled with hard labor, even at a young age, sickness, little food, and often abuse that went unnoticed by the outside world. For many of my informants, I was the only one they'd ever shared such intimate stories of their lives with. For some, even their kids were shocked by what they chose to reveal to me. This put me in a position I hadn't accounted for. I couldn't be as cold and academic as other folklorists who chose to ignore the emotional responses of their informants in order to collect material. I was unable to separate myself from the lives and stories I was listening to.

Growing up I was always more sensitive to the world around me and I still am, if I'm honest. It's my Cancerian nature, I reckon. I always preferred the quiet of the woods to being around a lot of people. I even remember at a young age wondering why all of my friends were so weird and didn't want to play outside. I soon learned that in the eyes of most people around me, I was the weird one. As I grew up, I learned to funnel my deep, spiritual connection with the world into what I was told were useful activities like writing stories, performing in school plays, music, and being active in church. "He's just got an overactive imagination," people would say. "Don't worry, he'll grow out of it." I'm glad they were wrong. Despite having hidden a lot about myself—including, but not limited to, my hillbilly heritage, my own sexual and gender identity, my sensitivity to the spirit world, and an overactive imagination—I learned through collecting stories that the tale of my own life was just as important as the ones I was gathering. I often wondered, *What would people say about me when I left this world?*

While out on the road, I had a revelation. It was a cool morning. A breeze blew across my face from the open window beside me. Sunlight poured across the valley and I saw three peach trees full of pink blossoms, just opened in the warmth of spring. I realized that this place was *my* home too. I was collecting stories like I was trying to discover something hidden inside my own life. I was no longer a folklorist, but a part of this living story, and the continuation of the lives of my ancestors.

This feeling stayed with me for a long while. I stopped recording my informants and instead just sat and listened to what they had to say. I came to realize that their lives and histories could have easily been the same as my great-grandparents, or even farther back, to those ancestors whose stories I never got to hear. My long-dead family began appearing in spirit around me as I visited with new storytellers. It was as though they were drawn in by what was being told as well.

One summer evening I met a particularly rambunctious healer who, instead of just telling me what I wanted to hear, was sensitive enough to the spiritual lives of other people to tell me something very important, something I had been secretly dreading since day one: "You've got the gift too, you know?"

I felt like screaming, or laughing, or both. "No, not me," I answered with a chuckle.

The old woman across from me smiled and pinched my blushing cheek. "Yes, you do." She was kind yet firm in her response, cutting through the barrier I had put up like a hot knife through butter.

Up until this point I had avoided thinking about the possibility of my own gift. I'd ignored the fairies I visited in the woods when I was a kid. I'd ignored the dreams I had about talking with long-dead relatives and the spirits I saw smiling and laughing at family reunions. I'd hidden a lot about myself deep inside, behind layers upon layers of guilt, study, seriousness, and a reality that so many unreliable people wanted me to buy into. I just needed someone to call me out, and that's what I got.

From that point on, some door inside of me opened up. I started dreaming more, and my connection to the land and my ancestors was renewed, refreshed by some spring that had been plugged up for too long. I started going back through the stories I collected, and this time I listened and read with a new perspective. I realized that I wasn't just collecting interesting anecdotes anymore, but a living, breathing knowledge that I could incorporate into my own life as a budding gifted individual.

While I know a whole lot more than I used to when I started down my path as a healer almost twelve years ago, I'm still learning. My lessons still come from old-timers out in the hills and hollers, and from those not-so-traditional Ozarkers using whatever means necessary to heal. I'm still learning from spirits of my ancestors, the healers who have gone before me, and spirits of the land alike. I still leave out food every Christmas Eve for the Little People, throw cornmeal into waterfalls as an offering, and pray in twisting lines of tobacco smoke. My journey is nowhere near finished, and I hope it never will be. As I've learned from others, this path is never-ending. It's like the hoop snake from my childhood—the Ozark *ouroboros*, some might say—an ancient alchemical symbol of eternity, round as the full moon and constantly consuming its own tail. A cycle of death and rebirth.

PART
ONE

MOUNTAIN HERITAGE

I FACE AN INTERESTING CHALLENGE in the work I do in attempting to understand *where* certain traditions I've collected come from. I still have a compulsion to find the source of the waters, not just play in the stream.

The Ozark people are rarely of one ethnic or cultural heritage, but the problem is that you can't always trust family legends. Many times, a simple story is meant to hide tragedies, scandals, or painful memories. Up until the present day, life was hard in the Ozarks for most people, even if you were living in town. Ozarkers constantly faced the hardships of living in such isolation, away from medical care and educational opportunities. Oftentimes, if it couldn't be grown or gathered, you'd just have to do without. Stories can often be misleading, like the commonplace notion of having a "Cherokee granny," or a small amount of Native American ancestry despite not having any real proof apart from the word of a parent or grandparent. Few know, though, how diverse the ancestry of most Ozarkers really is.

OZARK ANCESTRY

The Ozark people, much like their Appalachian cousins, are made up of a few large ethnic groups, mostly of European origin. These include Scots-Irish, British, German, and French. While many of these communities stayed with their own, others freely associated with different groups of people in the area, leading to families like mine, where all of the cultural regions' groups are represented. Many Appalachian hillfolk also intermarried with indigenous peoples of the Southeast, namely the Cherokee and Muscogee Creek. These diverse families created their own unique traditions based upon a mixture of various folk beliefs born from both the Old and New Worlds.

Take, for instance, Pennsylvania German (often called Pennsylvania Dutch) traditions that are found in certain Ozark communities. You might wonder how this is possible as we are so far removed from Pennsylvania. For the answer, we have to again go back to the source of our culture: the Appalachian Mountains. Many people don't know that the mountain ranges that make up the Appalachian region extend far north, well into Pennsylvania. In the early 1700s this region saw an increase in Protestant immigrants, mostly from German states like the Palatinate, fleeing religious persecution in their homeland.[5]

They were pulled specifically to this area by tracts William Penn published and distributed throughout the southern German states.[6] These pamphlets talked about his colony and the "holy experiment" of tolerance he had established there. Many people tend to associate the Pennsylvania Germans with the Amish or Mennonites, but these were just two of the religious groups who found homes in Pennsylvania. There were many others included as well, and not all of them were of German descent. The Religious Society of Friends, also called Quakers, were a group of English Protestants who settled in the same area and are often included in Pennsylvania German culture. It didn't take long for these new immigrants to head west into Appalachia, so reminiscent of their own mountainous homelands.

Over the next hundred years, Pennsylvania German families spread west and south through the fertile valleys of Appalachia. Many were seeking land to cultivate, others a deeper sense of religious isolation, and some were escaping constant conflicts with their Scots-Irish neighbors. Eventually, many of these families, now in the Southern Appalachia regions of Tennessee, North Carolina, and Georgia, took the opportunity to settle on land west in Arkansas Territory, newly opened up after the forced removal of the Osage. Here, their German folkways further mixed with those from other English and Scots-Irish families to become what we might call uniquely *Ozark*.

CULTURAL FINGERPRINTS

Our traditions of healing and folk magic bear the fingerprints of many cultural identities because they were passed down through diverse families and communities. Each encounter with outsiders became a new opportunity for fingerprints to be added. For instance,

---

5. Milnes, *Signs, Cures, and Witchery*, 4.

6. Milnes, 3.

we Ozarkers inherited our use of juniper in healing and magic from two main sources, the Scottish Highlanders and the Cherokee. In Scotland, the common juniper (*Juniperus communis*) was traditionally burned in cattle stalls to protect against milk-stealing witches[7] as well as used as an effective fumigation for illness and evil inside the home itself. For the Cherokee, red cedar (*Juniperus virginiana*) is considered a powerful tree alongside all the evergreens, which are said to have gained their medicine as a gift for being able to stay awake all nights of creation, unlike the other trees who are now cursed with losing their foliage in the winter.[8] The Cherokee, like the Highlanders, have traditionally used the smoke of the juniper to keep away illness and evil, as is related by ethnographer James Mooney:

> The small green twigs are thrown upon the fire as incense in certain ceremonies, particularly to counteract the effect of *asgina* dreams, as it is believed that the *anisgi'na* or malevolent ghosts cannot endure the smell; but the wood itself is considered too sacred to be used as fuel.[9]

THE LITTLE PEOPLE

Another crossover between the Ozarks, Cherokee, and people across Europe is a belief in fairies, or the Little People, as they are called here. The Little People are said to be trickster spirits of nature and fierce protectors of the land. They have towns and clans of their own, and even customs, medicine, and magic that they are sometimes willing to pass along to humankind. They are greatly angered by change, in particular when large boulders, hills, or ancient trees that house their villages are destroyed. Ozarkers are known to leave them gifts of food or drink to ensure the safety and prosperity of their vital crops. In particular, there's a tradition of always leaving some food out for the Little People on Christmas Eve so they don't become jealous by the merrymaking. In times of need, I've also heard of healers who petition the Little People for aid in finding the proper medicine for their clients. There are even some who derive their power from apprenticing with these spirits of the land. For example, I met a man who said that when he was a teenager, he fell asleep under the shelter of a bluff overhang that must have belonged to the Little People because when he woke up, he found he had the power to heal.

----

7.   Campbell, *Witchcraft and Second Sight*, 11.

8.   Mooney, *Sacred Formulas of the Cherokees*, 421.

9.   Mooney, 421.

The Little People don't fit very well into conservative notions of good and evil. They are said to treat the individual in a like manner as they were treated, meaning: be nice or you'll find yourself in a lot of trouble. For those who petition them with respect and kindness, they are said to offer gifts of material wealth, good crops, and powerful magical knowledge. But for those who approach with greed, or for the unlucky sorts who dare disturb their abodes, the Little People are known to set fire to farmland, make cows give bloody milk, and cause sickness in the home, just to name a few examples. Buildings built atop a town belonging to the Little People won't last long, it's said, and will soon burn down, flood, or tip over into a sinkhole. Respect for the Little People can be seen as the Ozarker's way of respecting the natural world itself. Many of the taboos surrounding the Little People situate them in areas of striking natural beauty, as with certain waterfalls or springs said to be protected by the Little People. Taboos against disturbing features of the landscape then act as an extension of the deep connection Ozarkers have to nature itself. To this day, I've met farmers who leave solitary trees or boulders alone in their fields, believing they belong to the Little People, or old-timers who refuse to cultivate stretches of woods near their homes despite the richness of the soil, believing the Little People have taken up residence in the trees.

It's always surprised me how belief in the Little People has encompassed both the liberal and conservative, old and young, rural and townsfolk alike. Often the staunchest church-goer still dares not disturb certain auspicious trees or rock formations for fear of angering the Little People. One woman I met who was a proud conservative Christian and member of the Republican Party said she left the Little People alone because they "protected nature and nature needs protecting." That's all she said on the matter. Later, when I spoke with her grandson, he said she had a birdhouse in her backyard nailed onto an old oak tree that she called her "fairy house," and it was believed by the family to be a sort of hotel for wandering Little People. This added anecdote didn't surprise me at all. I've encountered the same story over and over again, not only with the Little People, but with belief in magical traditions in general. In the Ozarks, a person can believe a lot of strange things about the world, and you only cross the line when you start airing your dirty laundry in public.

GERMAN OZARKS

Specific Pennsylvania German traditions I've found mixed into Ozark folkways include a connection to Powwow, or *Braucherei*, as it's sometimes called, a folk healing tradition brought originally from Germany but then mixed with various other practices found in the colonized New World. The most well-known work related to the subject is *Pow-Wows; or, Long Lost Friend*, a manuscript of household remedies, charms, and spells compiled and published in 1820 by German author John George Hohman. This book was traditionally very important to Pennsylvania German *Brauchers*, or healers, also known as Powwows.

The word powwow has a bit of a mysterious history. Some try and connect it back to the appropriation of certain Native American traditions encountered by German immigrants in Pennsylvania, but a more likely theory is that it is a corruption of the word power as heard and transmitted through mostly German-speaking communities. It's even theorized that the Ozark term power doctor traces its origin back to the same source of the word powwow. In many ways, the Ozark power doctor and the Pennsylvania German Powwow practiced the same form of healing, based mostly in the use of prayers, verbal charms, talismans, and amulets. The practices of the Braucher or Powwow are completely unlike any traditions that would have been appropriated from indigenous peoples of the time. Today, many people within this tradition choose to use the term Braucherei as a more culturally sensitive way to describe their practice. The origin of this word is almost just as mysterious, but some connect it to the German *brauche*, meaning "to use" or "to try."[10] You sometimes even hear folk healers in the Ozarks saying they will "try" for a person instead of an affirmative statement of, "I will heal you." I have tended to follow the lead of modern Brauchers and use this term in my work as well.

The tradition of Braucherei existed long before the publishing of Hohman's *Long Lost Friend*. The book itself is a collection of charms and remedies pulled from many other oral or written traditions from across Europe, including the famous *Egyptian Secrets of Albertus Magnus*. This tradition of healing found its way into Ozark culture with the Pennsylvania German families from the Southern Appalachian Mountains who eventually resettled west in the Ozarks. Some of them would have certainly brought copies of Hohman's work along with them. I know this because I've seen one, an old copy carried to Missouri by the family from their ancestral home in West Virginia. Randolph even includes a charm in his *Ozark Magic and Folklore* pulled verbatim right out of the *Long Lost Friend*.[11] Whether he actually heard the charm recited by one of his Ozark informants or whether he added it later for dramatic flair is up for debate.

10. Bilardi, *Red Church*, 22.

11. Randolph, *Ozark Magic and Folklore*, 286.

Another influence from Braucherei includes the use of "passes," or movements of the hands over the client's body, often close to the skin but not actually touching it, so as to adhere to conservative standards. It's believed in the Ozark tradition that the healer is able to deliver healing energies from their own body into that of their client through these passes. This tradition is also common amongst the Cajun and Creole healers known as *traiteurs* who, like the Brauchers and Ozark healers, have inherited many practices from a much older European folk magic tradition. In the case of the Ozarks, one origin for this practice—as related to me by a number of healers—can be traced back to the Christian tradition of laying on hands as a way of transferring the power of the Holy Spirit, as in, "Then Peter and John laid their hands on them, and they received the Holy Spirit."[12]

A BLENDED HERBAL TRADITION

You can also see cross-pollination from other cultures in Ozark herbal healing practices. I've known several herbalists who have had upward of a hundred plants memorized, including the names, medicinal value, and how to prepare them, all locked away in their minds for future use. A good deal of this knowledge came from Europe, alongside non-native plant varieties brought by colonizers as sources of food and medicine. A common example of this is yard plantain (*Plantago major*), which also carries the name "white man's footprint," as it was always carried with Europeans as a winter potherb and a useful medicine for all sorts of skin complaints. Other examples of medicinal plants now considered naturalized here in the US—meaning they aren't invasive and don't compete with native plants—include mullein and lemon balm (*Melissa officinalis*), both staples of any mountain herbalist's chest of remedies.

The vast majority of other plants would have been completely unknown to Europeans upon arrival. Knowledge of the medicinal value of these botanicals would have come directly through interactions with indigenous peoples. In the case of the Ozark tradition, the Cherokee and Muscogee Creek would have been the leading sources of botanical information while the culture was still developing in the Appalachian Mountains.

It's an unfortunate truth that little overlap exists between Ozark and Osage medicines, as the Osage had been forcibly removed from the area before hillfolk settlement. For the Ozark people, the merging of plant traditions would have taken place in the isolated Appalachian communities to the east. Here, families would have mixed their indigenous plant

---

12.   Acts 8:17 (New Revised Standard Version).

knowledge with European herbal preparation techniques, including the process of tincturing or creating a concentrated plant extract using alcohol. They would have then added in their own folklore, traditional prayers, and verbal charms that had been passed through European families for centuries to create their own unique system of healing.

CULTURAL SENSITIVITY

While many of our healing traditions here in the Ozarks might bear the fingerprints of other cultures, what was created is still a unique body of folk knowledge. For example, you can no more call Ozark traditions "German" because of the use of certain charms passed down from Braucherei than you can call spaghetti "Chinese" because the noodle originated in China. Ozark traditions are uniquely Ozark, for lack of a better term. Our folklore and practices exist as a blending of many different cultures and traditions. We have to take traditions for what they are and study them within the context of our present culture.

Origin stories aren't completely useless to Ozarkers, of course. Tracing the lineage of certain traditions often helps fill in what might be missing from our own record. Take, for instance, the use of wood taken from a tree that has been struck by lightning. In the Ozarks this wood is seen as a powerful source of natural magic. Vance Randolph mentions slivers of the wood being taken and made into toothpicks to magically cure toothaches.[13] Often the wood is worn as a protective amulet against getting struck by lightning while outside. Slivers can even be kept in the house to ward off insects. There's also a common taboo against burning lightning wood in your fireplace, lest you run the risk of lightning being drawn to the fire and striking your cabin. While there's a great deal of lightning lore that came into the area with Europeans, there's another possible connection to Cherokee culture. According to James Mooney:

> Mysterious properties attach to the wood of a tree which has been struck by lightning, especially when the tree itself still lives ... An ordinary person of the laity will not touch it, for fear of having cracks come upon his hands and feet, nor is it burned for fuel, for fear that lye made from the ashes will cause consumption.[14]

....

13.   Randolph, *Ozark Magic and Folklore*, 144.

14.   Mooney, *Sacred Formulas of the Cherokees*, 422.

Tracing this Ozark tradition back to an ancestral belief amongst the Cherokee might give us a little bit more insight into those folkways that have influenced our own, but we have to be careful about falling down the rabbit hole of "filling in the blanks." In the Ozarks, as more and more storytellers and healers have died without passing down what they might know, we've lost a great deal of the folklore and practices my ancestors held sacred. It's tempting when looking at similar practices to take pieces here or there and add them to our own tradition. In many cases this might be seem harmless, but we have to be aware of cultures that have been seriously damaged by this kind of appropriation, including many of the North American indigenous traditions, which are constantly being taken, misused, and abused.

It's not enough to just say, "Well, I've got a Cherokee granny!" (a phrase I've heard a lot while collecting stories). If you've ever lived in the Ozarks, you know that everybody says they've got a Cherokee granny, and they're all somehow dead. I used to immediately cringe when white informants started talking about their Cherokee ancestry, mostly because I've worked with people from Cherokee Nation, East and West, and have seen how destructive this flippant view of culture can be for them in their struggle against stereotypes and misinformation. Many people across the Ozarks likely do have some indigenous ancestry, but because they aren't participating in the cultural traditions of the group they claim to be a part of, everything they do in the outside world is falsely considered as something the "Cherokee" do, or something the "Muscogee Creek" do. This can be severely damaging to the work done in communities by actual cultural representatives. So, while someone claiming to be of indigenous heritage is off in deep woods spreading around the lie that the Cherokee use Plains-style war bonnets in their ceremonies, actual Cherokee people are struggling to keep their language and traditions alive amidst a culture that's been constantly trying to force them to assimilate for a few hundred years now. This is the story not only from my Cherokee friends, but from nearly all of the indigenous peoples of the United States and abroad. As much as I might weep for the lost traditions of my own culture, I can't even imagine what indigenous people have been forced to go through.

Over the years, in workshops and other events, I've made a point to talk about this very issue and how Ozarkers living in the modern world can combat our own appropriations and prejudices. It's important for us to remember that we can't sacrifice the value of one culture just to fill in some of the missing blanks within our own. This has been a hard lesson for me to learn over the years, but taking it to heart has meant embracing the ever-evolving power and strength of my own ancestors. Instead of blindly following traditions of the past, I let my work come to me in dreams and visions as a continuing revelation.

Folk culture in the Ozarks didn't halt when Vance Randolph first published his informant's words in print. It continued evolving, growing, and changing. Pieces that didn't work anymore were cast aside or allowed to slip into the shadows of forgetfulness. What worked was saved, treasured, and passed down through the generations. This process continues even today, and as a practitioner in the modern world, I'm constantly making these changes not only within my own work, but also for the culture as a whole. By embracing the heritage of power within myself, by listening to the voices of my ancestors and the ones calling out from the land itself, I no longer need to pick and choose from other practices to fill in the blanks within my own. Instead, I let the blanks stand as they are, as testaments of loss and reminders to future generations of the importance of sharing stories with each other.

Chapter 2

OZARK
TRADITIONAL
HEALING

OZARK HILLFOLK HAVE RARELY separated illness into what we today might call "physical" and "mental." To those who still adhere to more traditional ways, healing the body and the mind, or mind as spirit, as it is often referred, are always intimately linked together. You can't ever have one without the other. To a traditionalist, simple illnesses like fever, cough, or chills can also have a deep connection to a person's current state of mind, which will need to be healed right alongside the physical ailment. This connection often manifests in a folk healer's bedside manner. Healers are often seen as caregivers, and in the old Ozarks, healers would often live in the homes of their clients to keep an eye on them until their sickness had passed.

You rarely see that these days; people are more guarded about their private lives. But this hasn't changed the Ozark healer's approach to comforting their clients. Being at ease is seen as having an equal part to play in the healing process as the medicine itself. Healers today will often sit and talk with their clients before any healing work is actually done. They will find out if their client has had any life changes that might have contributed to the illness, or if they feel as though they might have been "goomered," or cursed. By having an intimate conversation with the person who is ill, the healing process is able to begin before any remedies are even mentioned.

This form of folk psychology or counseling still has an important role in Ozark healing today. One healer I met said she always made sure her client's house was in order before her healing rituals began. For her, if a client was constantly worrying about their spouse, kids, or how clean the house was, they wouldn't be focusing on their own healing process. A person who needs healing can't afford to lose any energy to unnecessary worrying. It's a shame that, for the most part, this sense of caregiving has been lost in our modern medical system, where doctors often see so many clients during the day that there's no time to have an intimate conversation with any of them. I am happy to see that with a resurgence of interest in traditional systems of healing, more and more people are beginning to take these more personal practices into consideration.

OZARK THEORY OF ILLNESS

Illness in the Ozarks is most often identified by its *source*, not where the illness sits inside the body. Meaning a fever, whether caught from some physical agent or as the result of a curse, will act the same way inside the body despite where it might have come from. A source, then, can include physical or magical agents.

PHYSICAL ILLNESS

Physical illnesses result from coming into contact with contagion from the outside world. Hillfolk in the old Ozarks weren't as oblivious to the existence of germs as we might think today. They knew there was some invisible, disease-causing agent and that certain methods could be employed to keep it away. These methods most often included the use of certain strong-smelling substances like asafetida (*Ferula assa-foetida*) or camphor, the crystallized essential oil of the camphor tree (*Cinnamomum camphora*). Both of these substances were thought to be able to ward off sickness with their pungent odors. Many of the old-timers I've interviewed bemoaned a childhood having to carry little bags of stinking asafetida around their necks in the wintertime to keep away coughs and fevers.

This system of warding off illness was commonplace throughout Europe until medicine advanced to include germ theory. In rural areas of the Old and New Worlds, this belief oftentimes remained in rural areas well into the twentieth century. Folk illnesses said to be of a physical origin include:

- **BAD BLOOD:** Euphemism for syphilis. Also sometimes refers to tetanus or "blood poisoning."
- **FLUX:** Severe diarrhea.

- **FLOODING:** Heavy menses or heavy bleeding during childbirth. Also used as an umbrella term for many unidentifiable gynecological issues.
- **HIGH BLOOD:** High blood pressure. Sometimes also refers to conditions caused by anger or stress issues. Sometimes used to refer to people with ruddy complexions.
- **LIVER GROWED:** Unknown illness affecting babies. It is characterized by lethargy, not taking to feeding, and a general state of poor health. Said by folk doctors to be caused by the baby's liver attaching to the lining of its body cavity. At one time the common cure for this illness was shaking the baby until it was believed the liver had become detached again. With modern medicine now more widely available, this folk illness has thankfully been relegated to tall tales and humorous anecdotes alone. Do not shake a baby.
- **LOSS OF COURAGE:** Euphemism for impotency or loss of sex drive.
- **LOSS OF NATURE:** Another euphemism for impotency.
- **LOW BLOOD:** Low blood pressure. Sometimes refers to anemic conditions or to those who are generally seen as being weak or sickly.
- **PILES:** Hemorrhoids.
- **SUMMER COMPLAINT:** A mysterious illness that usually only affects children, specifically during the summertime. Characterized by chills, fever, and severe diarrhea. Often considered an illness related to poor hygiene and contaminated food or water during the hot months of the year. Sometime misapplied to heat stroke.
- **TETTER:** Name given to many forms of itchy dermatitis. Usually applied to eczema, psoriasis, and ringworm.
- **THRASH:** Or "thrush" as it's commonly known. A yeast infection of the mouth that almost strictly affects children. Cured in the old Ozarks by visiting the local thrash blower, a specialized folk healer able to magically blow the thrash out of the child's mouth.

FOLK MEDICINE

Physical illnesses like the ones in the previous section are most often cured through the use of folk medicines, usually of a botanical nature. These remedies often come in many different compositions and preparations including tinctures, infusions, salves, poultices, oils, etc. Folklorists call this corpus of physical healing methods and ingredients *materia medica*. This type of healing is the domain of the "yarb doctor," one of several old names for specialized healers still sometimes heard throughout the Ozarks today. The yarb doctor specialized in healing with *yarbs*, the Ozark word for a medicinal plant. They were the herbalists of their day and took their healing knowledge from European folk sources as well as from interactions with indigenous peoples of the New World.

The Ozark Mountains are rich in biodiversity. Some folk herbalists have hundreds of individual plant varieties in their mental repertoires. These plants are chosen for their actions or effects upon the body. Many of the most valued plants have the action of being a mild to strong laxative or purgative. Mountain doctors have inherited much of their folk knowledge from systems of healing practiced in villages across rural Europe. One of these is the theory of the four humors. In this system, digestion is one of the most important functions of the body. It's what helps us expel toxins and illness. The sanguine humor is connected to the vital bodily fluid blood and the liver. In sanguine conditions, a person is defined by sluggishness and difficult digestion. Purgatives and laxatives, sometimes called liver tonics, were at one time very important in helping to cure this condition. The importance put upon digestion and blood in Ozark folk medicine gave rise to a few phrases for referring to specific actions of purgative plants like sassafras:

- **BLOOD THINNER:** Euphemism for a laxative.
- **BUILDS BLOOD:** Stimulating, helps with energy, helps with anemia.
- **CLEANS THE BODY:** Euphemism for a laxative. Also sometimes refers to a vermifuge, a medicine that kills internal parasites.
- **CLEARS THE BLOOD:** Euphemism for a laxative.
- **LIVER TONIC:** Strong plant laxative or purgative said to be able to clear toxins from the liver.
- **SPRING TONIC:** Strong plant decoctions taken for a short amount of time in the spring to "clean the blood." Usually a mild laxative like sassafras or a diuretic like dandelion root (*Taraxacum* spp.).

A great deal of our botanical and mineral medicines in the Ozarks rely upon the use of the four humors in some application. Each example in our *materia medica* has been long studied by folk doctors for how it affects certain organs and systems in the body. The old doctors favored a system of "cleaning out" the body using purgatives, laxatives, and emetics, more so than the majority of folk healers in the Ozarks today. In our modern world we tend to be a little squeamish around vomit and excrement, whereas many of our ancestors would have found them both a completely natural part of life. Purgatives will be mentioned more in chapter 7.

As we talk about these physical medicines, we have to remember that most everything in Ozark traditional healing involves a certain amount of magical invocation, even if it's just saying a quick prayer or a few words over an herbal infusion. Medicine-making might also employ a ritual, like pouring medicine through a "hole root," for example. These are chunks of tree root with a naturally occurring hole through some part of the wood. Because they are naturally occurring, these holes are believed to be portals to the other-world of spirits and the Little People. By pouring medicine through the hole, the healer is able to capture some of the magical power from that other place for use in their preparation. Hole stones, or hag stones, gathered up from Ozark creek beds are often used for the same purpose.

Rituals like these often go overlooked by healers when talking about their practices. For them, it might not seem like anything out of the ordinary to pour medicine through a hole in a root or to recite a few prayers while stirring medicine that is bubbling on the stove. From my own experience collecting stories, in several cases I've had stop my informants to ask them to explain their specific methods in more detail before moving on to new subjects. What has fascinated me the most is how diverse these simple acts of herbal preparation can be. For instance, some healers have very strict rules about how to stir medicines, either clockwise or counterclockwise.

One healer told me that medicines should always be stirred clockwise, or "sunwise," often considered a holy direction. "Counterclockwise," he went on to say, "is only for when you're wanting to hex someone!"

Another healer I met no more than two hours away from the first one said she always went counterclockwise because for her it symbolized removal or reversing the illness. Consider the horseshoe we discussed in the introduction; this is just another example of how different Ozark traditions can be from person to person.

MAGICAL ILLNESS

Magical illnesses are said to have a magical origin, or some might say they originate with the spiritual or mental. Often folklorists and academics will say this includes illnesses without a "natural" explanation, but for the Ozark healer, both physical and magical illnesses can be a part of the natural world. The source of these illnesses is often said to be from a witch, or a figure traditionally believed to use the neutral magic of the natural world for evil purposes.

In the old Ozarks, healers often cited witchcraft as the source of the majority of the magical illnesses they fought. These witches were often said to be someone close to the afflicted person, someone able to steal away a lock of their hair or fingernail clippings with which to work their malign magic. A vital part of the healing process was then to send the evil back to the witch, usually in a violent way. For example:

> *Ol' Bob thinks he might have been cursed, so he goes to the local healer who knows how to deal with these things. The healer determines that the witch is likely the old widow who lives down the road from Bob and he sets out to teach the old lady a lesson. The healer has Bob go out and steal a chunk of stone from the side of the widow's cabin and bring it back to him. The healer grinds up the stone, mixes it with some water, then paints it on a paper cutout that is made to look like the widow. He then has Bob shoot the cutout using a rifle loaded with a silver bullet, known to be the only weapon able to kill witches. The next morning Bob feels better and hears from his wife that the old widow down the street died mysteriously in her sleep.*

Today, stories like this one are just humorous anecdotes told for entertainment around campfires, but for many in the old Ozarks, witchcraft was a real fear. Sudden illness was often taken to be a curse thrown by some spiteful witch. Blame was cast not only on family members, but upon anyone in the community who was looked at suspiciously. These traditions have evolved greatly throughout the years as far fewer people now hold these outdated and more conservative beliefs about witches and witchcraft. Both of these terms are even being reclaimed throughout the Ozarks by individuals who look at the term witch in the same way many of the older generations might have used doctor or healer.

With this change in beliefs about witches, the sources of magical illnesses—which are still very much present in many cases—have also changed. Healers now speak more about the primal forces of evil or contagion as a source for illness. Blame is hardly ever put upon a single individual as the cause of magical illness. In my own work, when someone comes to me believing they've been cursed, I don't try and work against the person who might have cursed them. Instead, I seek to help my clients be cleansed and purified with the understanding that those who harm others always get what's coming to them in one way or another. There are also those practitioners working with a more neutral magic who have no qualms about hunting down and magically harming those who curse others needlessly. The Ozarks is still a wealth of diverse practices and I look forward to seeing how we evolve in the coming decades.

Common magical illnesses seen in both the folklore record—and even today, in some cases—include complaints like curses and hexes, but also other strange conditions like:

- **FEAR:** Poor or slowly degrading health that is traced back to a sudden, shocking experience. Today, this would in part be covered by experiences like PTSD.
- **GOOMERED:** An Ozark-specific word with no modern equivalent. Goomering is often seen as a much more powerful cursed condition than being spelt or wished. The goomer doctor is a specialized Ozark healer able to remove these hexes from their clients.
- **HAINTED:** "Haunted." Refers almost entirely to the presence of malign haints, or spirits, in a building. Certain objects can also be hainted.
- **LIVE THINGS:** A mysterious illness characterized by the feeling of having crawling animals inside your body. In the Ozarks, these animals include snakes, lizards, toads, salamanders or "ground puppies," cockroaches, or flies. The creatures are delivered into the victim's body when they unknowingly eat or drink the dried remains of the corresponding animal that had been secreted there by a cursing agent. This disease likely has a historical connection to the issue of internal parasites like tapeworms.
- **SPELT:** "Spelled." Another Ozark term for being hexed.
- **WISHED:** "Witched." An Ozark term for being cursed or hexed.

FOLK MAGIC

Magical illnesses require magical methods and ingredients, often grouped under the heading of *materia magica*, or simply put, folk magic. This is the domain of specialized healers like the power doctor who uses prayers, charms, rituals, and amulets in their healing work, and the goomer doctor, mentioned in the previous section, who specializes in removing curses or goomering off of their clients. In the old Ozarks, these two categories of healers were much more likely to have been accused of being witches themselves, often because the work they did made use of an invisible power that few laymen were able to comprehend. It was easier to just cry witch now and ask questions later, more often than not. For this reason, power doctors then and now are secretive about the work they do and how they gained the magical power they wield.

In the Ozarks, the word *magic* has always been associated with witchcraft, and therefore malign or evil work. Healers would have rarely used the word in describing the work they did, as opposed to today where folk magic is a very useful way of encompassing similar beliefs and practices of a supernatural variety. Old Ozarkers would have described the methods, medicines, and rituals of their local healers using very different terms. A healer might be referred to as someone who "knows things," or who has the gift. The work they did was called curing, helping, doctoring, or healing. Oftentimes, particularly if the healer was a preacher or other prominent member of the local church, what they did was just praying for someone, or lay on hands, as mentioned earlier.

Today this is very different, at least outside of the more conservative parts of the Ozarks. The word "magic" no longer holds such a stigma unless someone is talking about using the power to harm someone else, which is still held in suspicion by backwoods healers. Some gifted individuals even refer to what they do as magical healing, or natural magic, drawing connections back to the importance of nature in the work.

In a more conservative Ozarks of the past, the healer often had to talk around every illness and cursed condition with certain circumlocutions of language. It was vitally important that as a healer you remained in good standing, not only in the community but with your clients themselves. One mistaken use of the word "magic" around the wrong ear and the healer might be accused of working witchcraft from their home. It's easier with healers today, who often use the word "magic" freely with their clients. Others have lessened the use of the word completely and tend to incorporate terms like "spiritual healing" or "healing the spirit." These terms aim at the same goal as those referring to magical illnesses, but they do so in a more widely acceptable way.

Modern medicine would say it has since cured almost all of these magical ailments, either with chemical compounds or psychology. But as I've found in my own research, folk psychology, although not based in textbooks, serves as the basis for the work of many traditional healers. Even today, the healer often stands at the crossroads of the community. They tend to know everyone, and by nature of the work they do, they hear things few might choose to say aloud in public.

Take, for instance, the example of the medieval priest, who was often consulted for physical as well as spiritual healing. Much of the work they did was intimately connected to the sacrament of confession, a process often very similar to counseling. This same idea can be seen in the old Ozarks, where the local preacher often doubled as a local healer, not just because of their connection to the Divine, but because of their intimate position in the community itself. A little folk psychology can go a long way in the healing process.

Folk magic can include healing the body of certain ailments and cursed conditions, but it can also encompass the healing of certain situations; for instance, a power doctor working to magically bring in business for a client, take the anger out of a marriage, or break up a toxic relationship. Even these examples were traditionally seen as healing work because it was working for the betterment of someone's condition. Amongst more conservative Ozarkers, though, even these uses of the power were looked at with suspicion for treading a very thin line between helping and witchcraft. For many, toying with fate or matters of the heart should be left up to God and God alone. Again, this is less of an issue today; healers and other magical practitioners across the Ozarks are working in a variety of ways for their clients. As one healer once told me, "If someone's sick in love, the body's soon to follow," reiterating the idea that what happens in the spirit or psyche can greatly affect the well-being of the physical body.

GENDER AND HEALING

At one time, when the area was much more conservative than it is today, it was considered taboo for male healers to work on the female body. The healing profession, both from community healers and from country doctors, was a male-dominated field. Even the old titles for healers, like yarb doctor and power doctor, tended to only include males. Folk herbalism was the only area where you might occasionally see a male yarb doctor who had no problem giving out herbal remedies to whoever asked for one, but for the most part, male healers limited diagnosis and contact to men alone. "Women's work" was instead left to the "granny women," a specific type of Ozark healer that developed as a catchall for women who were gifted with the power to heal.

Characterizations of the granny woman vary based upon who you're talking to or whose folklore record you might be reading. From a man's perspective, a granny woman is often depicted as a grumpy old widow who lives on her own in the hills, and who is only consulted in times of dire need. She is often the first person to be accused of witchcraft in many of the old stories. In reality, though, granny women were often the only way Ozark women received proper medical care until the influx of modern medical centers, and even then, many of the incoming country doctors were ignorant when it came to "female troubles."

A granny woman was usually an older woman, but not necessarily a widow. Older granny women had successful careers as healers because they'd been able to survive so much in their long lives. Most of them were also considered skilled midwives, often because they themselves had birthed many of their own children. Sadly, the importance of the granny women—along with their remedies, rituals, and diagnosis methods—have, for the most part, been intentionally left out of the folklore record, of which most authors are male.

Today I often hear the term granny woman used by younger-generation healers, and it makes me smile that some of the old traditions are still alive. Healers in the Ozarks today don't usually have the same hang-ups surrounding gender as the older generations, unless they are part of a more conservative community. You now see healers working for whoever happens to walk through their door, calls them up on the phone, or sends them an email requesting healing knowledge.

This shift in perspective has even influenced how certain healing abilities are passed from one healer to another. In the old days, there were many taboos surrounding passing of the gift. For instance, a person could only pass their power from older to younger, and always male to female or female to male. Many traditionalists still hold to this view of the gift, but I've encountered more and more modern practitioners and healers working in a way that disregards many of the outdated gender norms and stereotypes. There are even many healers like myself who incorporate gender nonconforming, or nonbinary, gender identities into the work they do. For me, my nonbinary identity helps me connect on a much deeper level not only with people from all different backgrounds, but also to the neutral identity of the natural world itself.

THE HEALING PROCESS

Ozark traditional healing has historically been a very pragmatic system. When looking at material for both physical and magical illnesses, the key phrase is, "If it works, it works. If it doesn't work, find another way." The overall process could be rendered like this:

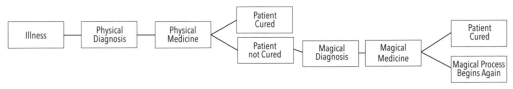

Healing flowchart

All healing work of course begins with an illness. The majority of the time, that illness was considered to have a physical cause, and therefore it could be cured through the various physical methods of folk medicine mentioned earlier in this chapter. An exception to this rule comes in the form of what the old-timers termed "madness," where more often than not, a magical cure was considered first. Diagnosis of a physical ailment was almost always done at home. I've encountered many an Ozark family who constantly used some old book of herbal remedies they found at a garage sale or had been passed down through the generations. *A Modern Herbal* by Maude M. Grieve was a popular choice for many, as was Dr. O. Phelps Brown's *The Complete Herbalist*. Modern choices might include any number of herbal or home remedy guides picked up at the local bookstore.

Diagnosis by the family was almost entirely based on empirical evidence. The body was observed, temperature taken, symptoms described, etc. As the diagnosis was centered on the home, likewise the cure was often found in the kitchen cabinet, in the garden, or in the woods. *Materia medica* of the cabin often included common botanicals like sassafras, goldenseal (*Hydrastis canadensis*), bloodroot (*Sanguinaria canadensis*), spicebush (*Lindera benzoin*), and many other specimens. These would almost always have been dried and used in infusions (teas) in the case of leaves and flowers, or boiled decoctions with roots and twigs.

Tinctures were sometimes made at home. These are strong plant extracts made by drawing out the active chemical compounds from the plant into an alcohol solvent. This is done to create a concentrated medicinal product and also to preserve the medicine for long-term use. In the old Ozarks, tinctures were only made if the family had some corn whiskey to spare. Otherwise, alcohol was saved for use without the plant matter added in. Oftentimes extracts, tinctures, and salves were purchased at the local pharmacy. Many an Ozarker has reported being slathered in Vicks VapoRub for everything from a torn muscle to the flu.

From here, the client either recovered or didn't. In the case of a lingering illness, a professional yarb doctor might be called to the home. Usually there was at least one within a day's hike. As dirt roads were cut into the hills and hollers to connect distant communities, local pharmacies became the place to receive a wide variety of medical diagnoses and remedies. An illness that stood up to even the most potent herbal preparations always made suspicions turn toward malign magic. Here the pharmacist or yarb doctor might recommend the family talk with someone with the gift.

In the modern Ozarks, this healing process often works in a similar way. People in the rural parts of the Ozarks have historically been known for their distrust of medical professionals. This isn't completely unfounded, as at one time the Ozark people fell prey to traveling charlatans or country doctors with little to no formal education. To this day, many people throughout the region only go to the doctor when they are seriously ill. This story isn't limited to the Ozarks alone, of course. Many places across the country have felt the burden of rising insurance costs and endless amounts of medical debt. Many people still consult herbal manuals or recipe cards with remedies written on the back, passed down through generations of people who had to make their own medicine. Today, we have fewer and fewer traditional herbalists left, so most people will make do with their own home remedies. Fewer still will consult someone in the know about magical illnesses.

While interest in traditional forms of healing has been on the rise over the past twenty years, there are still many small communities across the Ozarks whose healers died years ago, leaving behind no one to fill the void left by their absence. I myself often travel upward of a few hours to reach clients in isolated communities throughout the Ozarks. More and more healers I know are moving to online methods of healing, using Skype and other video conferencing programs. I myself will sometimes record a healing session for a client and have them listen to it while meditating. Like other modern healers, I believe that our intentions and healing power can travel across time and space and that the client need not always be present to receive what they might need.

It should be noted that modern healers choose to take a different approach from their older counterparts; they recommend their clients first seek professional care from a licensed physician before turning to the alternative treatments they provide. The healers I know see the work they do as a companion to modern medicine, not a replacement. These traditions of folk medicine seek to represent the other side of the healing process from just the physical. They provide care for the spirit of the client in a way that helps bolster their healing body.

MAGICAL DIAGNOSIS

As mentioned before, diagnosing magical illnesses is specifically the domain of the power doctor and, in the worst cases, the goomer doctor. These experts in the occult know exactly how to tell if an illness is from a physical source or from some malign curse. The method of diagnosis depends solely upon the healer's training, preferences, and so on. As I've said before, there's a different way of healing for nearly every healer out there. There are, however, some methods that are common in the folklore record, although the full details of the rituals and words involved are likely only known to the doctor themselves. Many of these methods are still in practice today amongst younger generations of healers.

LOOKING FOR TOKENS

This is probably the most commonly used practice to see if a magical illness is present. In the Ozark dialect, a *token* is another word for an omen or something auspicious. Tokens can be both good and bad, and there's a whole list of associations that are well-ingrained within Ozark folk culture. Common tokens include animal sounds, specifically owls and crows, which are always signs that death or severe illness are close behind. The scream of the screech owl is bad news supreme. To hear the screech owl means someone close to you will die within three days. Unless you "take off the cuss," of course, meaning you perform some counter-magic act. Such methods given to us by the folklore record include:

- When you hear a screech owl, throw some salt into a fire.
- When you hear a hoot owl, blow tobacco smoke in the direction of the sound, or clap your hands together loudly three times.
- If you see a witch make a strange gesture at you, turn out all of your pockets.
- If you drop a dishrag, throw a pinch of salt over your left shoulder.
- If you spill salt at the table, poor some water on it.
- Returning to your house immediately after leaving incurs bad luck, but this can be removed by exiting backward while saying, "Ten, nine, eight, seven, six, five, four, three, two, one, amen!"
- If a black animal crosses the path or road in front of you, take off your jacket or shirt, turn it inside out, and put it back on again. You can also say, "There goes (name of animal). Have a nice day!"
- When you feel the "chill" of a ghost, cross your arms across your chest and spin three times clockwise.
- When you hear a crow call, spit on the ground or flip your tongue over inside your mouth.

For the healer, to hear the cawing of a crow or hooting of an owl while administering medicine to a client is a clear sign that another magical practitioner is countering the work. I had a student once ask me if it was the owl that was bringing the curse or if it was just a messenger. My answer was that it's often considered an amalgam of both. As with most things in Ozark folk culture, context is key. We have to know whether the belief is a part of the old or modern Ozarks. In Ozark folklore, there was always a chance that the owl you heard was actually the person who originally sent the evil work, returned to the cabin in disguise to make sure everything went according to plan. A particularly effective, old-timey way of countering this malign magic was to shoot the owl with a silver bullet just in case it was a witch in disguise. Most people I've encountered who still keep an ear and eye out for these tokens have told me that the bird is just nature's reaction to the evil curse, like an alarm system, since certain animals are thought to be closer to the otherworld. I've encountered very few modern Ozark healers who still hold to the strict interpretation of these old tokens. I myself choose to be aware when certain odd things are happening during a healing ceremony, like a candle tipping over or popping sounds within the walls of the house, but my reactions are hardly ever as dramatic as shooting an innocent bird out of a tree for fear it's an enemy in disguise. Other traditional animal tokens include:

- Redbirds, whose tapping at a window signals something is amiss inside the house.
- The cry of the "painter," or cougar, who is said to call witches to their infernal meetings.
- Seeing a white deer while doing the work means evil is trying to interfere. This is a supremely bad omen, much like the scream of the screech owl.
- A rat or mouse found hiding under the client's bed might indicate a witch's familiar lying in the shadows, spying on the work of the doctor.

READING THE SIGNS

Another option for the healer is reading the signs of malign magic using ingredients from their bags of *materia magica*. These signs, in all respects, can also be called tokens, but I'll use the word sign here to differentiate them from omens read from the appearance of animal sounds or sightings, as mentioned in the previous section.

Reading the signs can take many different forms depending upon the specialty of the healer. Common methods include reading signs in fire, smoke, water, or animal entrails. Many of these methods were at one time performed in secret in order to avoid being associated with divination, a practice condemned by the old conservative Ozark culture. As the stories have shown us, though, most people won't ever openly question the methods of the healer during their diagnosis, and many activities normally seen as being taboo are often overlooked for the sake of healing. Few would want to risk a healer suspecting *them* of somehow trying to stand in the way of their work.

READING SIGNS IN FIRE

Fire reading comes in many forms, but all are centered on the healer's interaction with fire, traditionally in the form of a fireplace located inside the home of their client. One common method is to take small pieces of wood, usually from the pawpaw tree since it is considered a witch tree. Name each piece of wood for an enemy or someone you know who works evil magic, then toss them into the fire one by one. This ritual is repeated until one of the pieces of wood pops loudly, signaling to the healer that the person that piece of wood is named after was the one involved in the curse. Sometimes this rite is continued to verify if others were also involved. (Some healers name off everyone they can think of just to be sure. It's always a shock when the local kindhearted granny is named by a popping in the fire.)

A similar method uses matches. A matchstick is held up and named for a known evil practitioner or questionable person in the local town. Then the matchstick is struck only once, and if it lights, it is a sign that the named person is the culprit. If it doesn't light, the healer renames the stick and strikes again.

Vance Randolph tells of a certain fire ritual where a healer would go off into the woods at a certain time of night, build a large ring of brush and sticks, mutter some magical incantation, and then light the ring on fire. The witch would then be summoned magically into the burning ring, and the healer would be ready with a rifle loaded with a silver bullet.[15]

READING SIGNS IN SMOKE

Reading smoke trails is often used in conjunction with fire rituals. In this diagnostic rite, a pinch of dry plant matter is placed on a hot coal. The healer then reads the smoke trail. Things I've seen modern healers look for include the abundance of smoke produced, scent, and direction the trail goes toward. A good sign might be taken from an abundant amount of smoke that smells pleasant and goes straight up. A bad omen, on the other hand, might be shown in a little amount of foul-smelling smoke that spins or blows in all directions despite no wind being around. For this reason, smoke rites are almost always performed indoors, away from moving air.

The plants used in this rite are ones known for their sweet smells, like red cedar, or a species from the *Monarda* genus, usually all called horsemint, which can include beebalm (*M. didyma*), lemon beebalm (*M. citriodora*), and wild bergamot (*M. fistulosa*). Other plants commonly used include wormwood (*Artemisia absinthium*) and yarrow (*Achillea millefolium*.) Tobacco is also often used in this smoking rite, specifically what Ozarkers call old tobacco, *Nicotiana rustica*, as opposed to what is used commercially, *Nicotiana tabacum*.

Old tobacco has a long line of use amongst the indigenous people of the Southeast, from whom the European settlers would have learned about its healing and magical properties. From what I've been able to gather from Ozark stories and folk belief, the forces of evil never use tobacco, and it's often said that evil can't even stand to be around its smoke. For this reason, old tobacco is sometimes put onto a hot coal and used as a way to divine if evil is present and fighting against the healing work being done. In other cases, the crushed

---

15. Randolph, *Ozark Magic and Folklore*, 289.

leaves are sometimes slowly dropped into a fire and the direction the ash travels is seen as the direction of the source of evil.

Mullein is often associated with tobacco for how its leaves and flowers grow. They also share similar medicinal and magical uses. Mullein is sometimes used in place of old tobacco in these smoke rituals.

READING SIGNS IN WATER

Water divination comes in a couple of common traditional forms. First, a bowl of water is placed on the client's chest or stomach. Then a small twig or leaf is floated on top of the water near the center. The leaves of the spicebush are most commonly used. Other options are leaves from a witch tree like pawpaw, sassafras, or witch hazel (*Hamamelis virginiana*). The healer then says the name of someone they might suspect sent the curse and observes the direction the twig points. If the twig spins, the evil is said to be directly above the client. If it sits motionless, then another name is said and the ritual repeated.

This method is also sometimes used like a backwoods Ouija board to communicate with spirits of the dead. The medium first establishes which direction, clockwise or counterclockwise, is a "yes" and which is a "no," then asks their questions and observes which way the leaf spins.

Another method of water reading comes closer to traditional mirror or crystal ball scrying and is most often seen with more modern practitioners. A glass bottle, usually blue or green, is first filled with fresh water, often taken from a healing spring. The healer holds the bottle up to their eyes so that the both the client and a candle flame can be seen through the water. Then certain signs are read by how the light and water move together. One healer told me that whenever evil was at work, a black smudge would appear in her vision. If the smudge was outside the light, it meant she was successfully driving away the evil. If the smudge was around the client it meant the evil was nearby and trying to hurt them. And finally, if the smudge was on the person's body, it usually meant they would perish unless some powerful work was done as a countermeasure. I've read accounts of the famed Irish healer Biddy Early using a similar bottle divination.[16] This form of diagnosis likely has ancient roots.

---

16.   Gregory, *Visions and Beliefs*, 47.

READING SIGNS IN ANIMAL ENTRAILS

Rarely seen today, but once traditionally used by Ozark healers and witch finders, is reading signs inside animal entrails. This was almost exclusively done with chickens, specifically black chickens since they were often said to be connected to witchcraft. In this method, the healer would hold a live chicken by the feet and sweep its wings along their client's body. Usually this would be repeated a certain number of times—three or seven were often used, as these numbers were considered sacred because of their biblical connections. Then the chicken was taken outside and killed, and its body was cut open so that the healer could read the innards. Signs a healer might look for included any abnormal colors, specifically black, which would show that witchcraft had been transferred from the client to the animal's body during the sweeping.

The chicken was usually eaten if it wasn't infected with evil, or burned with asafetida if it was. Again, this is a rare form of diagnosis today, as few people keep chickens around anymore, and even fewer are able to kill them for the purpose of healing. I myself have only seen this rite performed once while on my travels across the Ozarks.

CARD READING

It should be noted that in the old Ozarks, card reading was seen as being a form of witchcraft and therefore condemned by more conservative communities. Card playing in general was often looked at with suspicion. This form of divination is widely used by healers in the Ozarks today, however. Even in more conservative communities you will find people consulting tarot readers to help with all manner of life's problems, though they would never admit to it.

A favorite used by many of the healers I've interviewed is the Lenormand, a system of cartomancy, or card reading, developed in France in the late eighteenth century and based on a divination system made famous by Marie Anne Lenormand. As it can be based on regular playing cards, it has become very popular amongst rural folk who might not have access to the tarot, but who can pick up a pack of playing cards at their local grocery store.

DREAMING

Dream interpretation is also used by a number of specialized doctors. This category includes both the interpretation of the client's dreams as well as the healer themselves dreaming up a remedy or dreaming of finding the magical source of the illness. What's more common is listening to the client recite their own dreams, then examining omens based upon the symbols described. This symbolism is most often derived from local folklore or from widely published dream dictionaries like Gustavus Hindman Miller's *10,000 Dreams Interpreted*. A few examples of dream interpretations from Ozark folklore include:

- "If a person dreams of ants, it has been known for them to foretell trifling annoyances."[17]
- "It has always been good to dream of milk because it means peace and plenty."[18]
- "To dream of snakes presages a battle with one's enemies."[19]
- "The vision of a black boat means an early death."[20]

Based upon what the images might tell a healer, they can then proceed either with a physical medicine or magical cure. When it's the healer doing the dreaming, they're usually working in conjunction with their spirit guides or guardian angels. One healer I met in Missouri said she had a "ghost guide," as she called him, who would visit in her dreams (or sometimes when she was alone in the darkness of her room) and tell her how to cure her clients. As we've seen with other examples of folk magic, this sort of spirit work is uncomfortably close to witchcraft for many more conservative people in the area. In general, though, most folks today will base the alignment of a healer on the works they produce in the world and whether the outcome of this work is ultimately for the sake of helping or harming.

SYSTEMS OF HEALING

How does the doctor determine what cure they should use based upon their diagnosis? There are a few yarb doctors who were, or still are, known for their use of certain medical systems, like the four humors mentioned earlier. Nowadays you might also encounter someone working within traditional Chinese medicine or even Ayurveda, a system of traditional medicine from India. There are several other options as well.

SYMPATHETIC MAGIC

The most common way of working is using the law of sympathy, a term said to have been coined by Sir James George Frazer in *The Golden Bough*, or "sympathetic magic," as it is

17. Parler, *Folk Beliefs from Arkansas*, 11363.
18. Parler, 11375.
19. Randolph, *Ozark Magic and Folklore*, 881.
20. Randolph, 881.

most often called. This law is further divided into the law of similarity and the law of contact or contagion. Frazer writes:

> If we analyze the principles of thought on which magic is based, they will probably be found to resolve themselves into two: first, that like produces like, or that an effect resembles its cause; and, second, that things which have once been in contact with each other continue to act on each other at a distance after the physical contact has been severed. The former principle may be called the law of similarity, the latter the law of contact or contagion. From the first of these principles, namely the law of similarity, the magician infers that he can produce any effect he desires merely by imitating it: from the second he infers that whatever he does to a material object will affect equally the person with whom the object was once in contact, whether it formed part of his body or not.[21]

To simplify, the law of similarity works on the principle that "like cures like." For example, in the Ozarks a boar's tooth amulet might be worn to help heal the toothache of the wearer. This theory lies at the heart of the old-style of Ozark healing, often even when the healer was using traditional herbal treatments.

There are certain plants, bloodroot for example, whose medicinal benefit was traditionally derived from its color. Historically, bloodroot was taken internally for certain blood disorders and to help clean the blood. This is no longer widely in practice as bloodroot contains sanguinarine, a toxic chemical compound that can kill human cells. The shape of the leaves, flowers, or roots were also often connected to a certain medicinal benefit. The common violet (*Viola* spp.), for example, has heart-shaped leaves and was therefore said to be good for the heart and also for use in love magic or other matters of the heart.

SPITE DOLLS

The law of contact describes the magical connection that exists between two or more people; for example, the healer and their client or the hexer and their victim. This magical thread will exist until it is severed or until the task of healing (or hurting) has been completed. This concept is most exemplified in the Ozark "spite doll," made to look like the person whom the hexer or healer wishes to manipulate. Outsiders have often called this

---

21. Frazer, *Golden Bough*, 11–12.

tool the Ozark voodoo doll. They likely have a common ancestry with other poppets in European folk magic.

The spite doll is traditionally made from paper, wax, or cornhusks in the Ozarks. A lot of practitioners I've encountered also order candles made in the shape of a man or woman from various online botanicas. In rural areas, people still most often use paper, cut in a general human shape and then colored or drawn on to make it look like their client or victim.

The connection between the doll and the person the doll represents comes through certain identifiers like fingernails, hair, or scraps of the person's clothing. These are embedded inside the doll or tied to its form, thereby creating a semipermanent link that can be manipulated. That is, unless the person is able to steal away their doll or cut the bond through certain magical means.

Healers often use these dolls to work remotely on their clients who might not be able to travel to see them in person. Others use the dolls for more malign purposes by sticking nails in parts of the doll's body or even burning the doll in a fire. Because of the connection made with their victim, it's said the person represented by the doll will feel the effects of such torture or fall into an unexplainable sickness while the all-important magical link remains intact.

METHODS OF CURING

The diagnosis process might show you where an illness or hex exists, but choosing the remedy or ritual is traditionally based either upon the idea of "like curing like," or what I like to call the "rock breaks scissors" method. When playing a game of rock paper scissors, each element is able to surpass other elements: rock breaks scissors, scissors cuts paper, paper covers rock. This same theory is often used in Ozark folk magic. The idea is that if you know the illness, you need only think of what might overcome that illness in order to find the cure.

In this way, illnesses—especially of a magical origin—are often given certain qualities like hot, cold, wet, dry, etc., much of which is derived from theories about the four bodily humors. Therefore, hot conditions, such as fever, sunstroke, rash, and inflammation, might be cured by cooling methods like soaking in a stream or using cooling herbs. Likewise, magical conditions like the dreaded live things might be cured in a similar way by perhaps petitioning the spirit of a bird to swoop in and magically eat the creatures found inside the client's body. Internal parasites in general are often cured magically in a similar way by working with these "spirit birds" that can fly in and eat the worms.

	WET	DRY
Hot	Sunstroke; heartburn; blood; blisters; eruptions	Fever; rash; skin irritation; inflammation; shingles
Cold	Congestion; diarrhea; indigestion; vomiting	Dry cough; chills; frostbite; sore throat; constipation

ILLNESS	MAGICAL CAUSE	MAGICAL REMEDY
Fever	"Heat" inside the body	Cooling the body, usually with water; purification in a stream
Congestion	"Wet" inside the body	Heating the body, usually with camphor oil or hot peppers
Live Things	Feeling lizards, snakes, insects, or frogs inside the body	Magical birds; raccoons; possums; rats
Toothache	"Worms" in teeth	Small magical birds

The ability to cure is often limited only to the healer's imagination, as I've been told. The Ozark healer is in a unique position of dreaming up (sometimes literally) a cure for anything that might come their way.

I once played a game with a healer I was interviewing in which he'd name an illness or condition and I'd have to name some magical force that would be able to beat it. For example, he said, "Fever!" and I replied, "A cold spring in wintertime!" Then he said, "Fear caused by a rabid dog!" and I replied, "A mean boar to scare away the dog!"

This went on for a while as we each tested the limitations of the other's imagination. Ozark healers are often said to be able to weave new creations from the stream of neutral magic that flows through the natural world. Healers and power doctors skilled in the use of prayers and rituals can magically overcome sicknesses and curses without ever picking up a ritual object or herbal medicine—they are able to cure using the power of their words alone.

PREVENTING ILLNESS

Any experienced healer will tell you that it's always better to prevent illnesses and curses from the very beginning than have to play catch-up later on. In the Ozarks, these methods of prevention fall under the name of "warding." Warding often puts people in strange circumstances because they tried to keep the hand of disease and magic away from them, like the old man I met who always had a pokeweed leaf (*Phytolacca americana*) in his right shoe. He told me that a pharmacist had told him it would ward off arthritis. I asked him if it worked and he said no, but that if he "kept on a-goin' it was bound to work someday."

Historically, wards against illness and malign magic were much more important in the daily life of hillfolk who were often surrounded by illness with no apparent cause. There's a theory in Ozark traditional healing, likely derived from similar beliefs from across rural Europe, that plants and minerals with a pungent, strong, or putrid stench are perfect for warding off illness and death. Like fights like, in that case. This is why the buzzard is widely considered a powerful healer in the Ozarks, as they are able to eat rotting flesh without becoming ill. Feathers of the buzzard are often kept in the house, particularly above the front door, to ward off illness.

A famous ward against illness of all kinds, both physical and magical, was asafetida. The resin of asafetida roots would most often be purchased by families from their local power doctor or pharmacist, as the plant isn't native to North America. Whole roots or powdered resin would be worn around the neck in little bags or placed outside the home over the doorframes of any entrance. Many old-timers have complained to me about being forced to carry around the bags of stinking roots as children; they can still remember the stares and giggles they got from other kids at school. But then again, the giggler could easily turn into the asafetida bag-wearer, especially in the winter when illness was said to be at its highest and most deadly.

Camphor crystals or oil were also purchased at the local pharmacy. At one time, they were widely carried in bags or placed in bowls of water around the house to clean the "bad air" that carries disease. Again, this ward derives its power from the pungent odor of the camphor. Camphor was also used as an effective fumigant for clearing out evil curses and even unwanted spirit entities.

Carrying the nuts of the buckeye tree is probably the Ozarks' most famous ward against illness and evil. This practice isn't limited to just the Ozarks; it can be found in many folk traditions across the country. The nuts are carried in a pocket or purse and are traditionally believed to have supreme authority over rheumatism, arthritis, and certain illnesses you might pick up at the local brothel. They are also said to be a strong defender against witchcraft, if you take care of them. A buckeye is never washed and is often oiled by rubbing it between your thumb and forefinger like a worry stone. This helps it keep its rich brown color and prevents the nut from drying out.

One fall, I collected about a hundred buckeyes that I was going to dry and sell to local New Agers for top dollar. Much to my shock, even though they were spread out on well-ventilated drying racks, every damn one of the buckeyes shriveled up and molded. A friend of mine was a skilled herbalist, so I asked her why they might have done that. She said I must have offended some local spirit by collecting them in such massive numbers. She also mentioned she'd always heard a buckeye could never be bought, only gifted, and it had to be a fresh one, allowed to dry naturally in a warm pocket. I took her words to heart and have never tried to collect that many again. But I still get upset when I walk through damn near every single flea market in town and they all have bushels of the things for sale, all in absolutely perfect condition.

In the Ozarks today, warding off illness has mostly been left to old wives' tales and home remedies. I've only met a handful of people who still use asafetida around the house as a ward against illness. The powdered resin is called *hing* and is used in cooking throughout the Middle East and the Indian subcontinent. As bad as the stuff smells, it has a wonderful taste when cooked properly. One old-timer I met on my travels got his asafetida from the local Indian grocery store. The old man would sprinkle some in hot water and breathe in the steam to clear out his sinuses whenever he thought he might be getting a cold.

I use camphor crystals in my salves and oils; it adds a nice eucalyptus scent and has a warming quality on the skin. I know of some old-timers who also still use camphor as a moth repellent in their closets and drawers.

Most people today ward off illness by boosting their immune systems with native herbal medicines, most of which make use of elderberries (*Sambucus nigra*), believed to have antibacterial and antiviral qualities.

Few people these days see the need for magical protection, but for those who do hold to a magical practice like myself, fumigation or smoke cleansing using plants held sacred to the Ozark hillfolk like red cedar, mullein, or yarrow is still a common practice used throughout the year.

Chapter 3

THE HEALER AND THEIR WORK

OLD OZARK COMMUNITIES OFTEN held multiple healers, many of whom were specialized in certain types of healing. There were often burn healers, blood stoppers, thrash blowers, wart charmers, love doctors, and an individual who knew how to fix your luck for the card tables. There was usually a generalist at hand as well, someone like a granny woman who knew some backwoods herbalism as well as the magical practices of healing. Together, these individuals often created a network of healers and, more often than not, they knew about each other, even if the wider community didn't.

Oftentimes, in order to avoid any associations with witchcraft, Ozark healers would work in secret and only by word of mouth. One old informant I met said his dad knew how to make charms for luck in gambling but worked in the strictest secrecy. He would make his clients swear to never tell a soul about where they got their luck, and if they did, they risked the damnation of their own soul. The old man told me his dad had a long career making gambling charms, so everyone around must have been too scared of him to ever say anything.

Established healers in some of the smaller communities in the Ozarks were not always known for their pleasant demeanor. I've heard stories about these overly serious individuals who would even work against other healers in the area like stray cats fighting over their territories. One old man I was told about was known around his area for being a "witch master" as well as healer. A witch master is like the goomer doctor in that they are said to be able to remove malign curses from a person's body or spirit. A witch master is also said to be skilled in hunting down and identifying witches. This man in particular was said to have identified many witches in his long career and managed to run all of them out of his community.

The informant who told me the tale said most people in town always looked at the witch master suspiciously because the people he ran off were almost always other healers or traveling doctors, card readers, etc. "He didn't take kindly to competition!" my informant said with a laugh. Healers often had to tread a very thin line between work that was acceptable and useful in their community and what might be called witchcraft. It's no wonder so many healers themselves were the first to accuse someone else of being a witch. I imagine it was a constant battle for a healer to practice such an important service while also dodging witch accusations.

In the Ozarks today, we have a much bigger problem than witchcraft accusations. Our troubles come every time a healer dies without passing any of their knowledge to someone still living. As more and more of these individuals pass away, more Ozark traditions are lost to the universe. In my travels collecting folklore, I was lucky enough to be able to gain the trust of many of these healers, and they chose me as a recipient of their knowledge. The story was all too familiar most of the time: the healer had kids, grandkids, and a lot of times even great-grandkids, but none of them wanted the power.

Oftentimes the power to heal is also a great burden. You have to be able to take a lot of people's pain onto your own spirit without much material gain. You have to constantly face people's laughter and disbelief while holding strong to the faith you have in yourself. It's not a path for everyone, that's for sure. Most people don't feel like they're cut out for the responsibility; others just want to distance themselves from their "hillbilly" upbringing or the "white trash" stereotype that goes along with so many of our Ozark traditions. For those few who do find themselves called to the path of the Ozark healer, there's a world of diverse practices and traditions to learn from.

OZARK DOCTORING

At one time, there existed many different types of healers, or doctors as they're often called. Some of the healers left to us by folklorists like Vance Randolph include yarb doctor, power doctor, goomer doctor, and granny woman, all of which will be discussed in greater detail later on in this chapter. It's a rarity to find any of the old terms used today outside of ever-diminishing pockets of very rural people still adhering to some of their ancestral traditions. Some still use the name "Doc" as a term of endearment for respected individuals in their communities, oftentimes a local healer. Most people I spoke to while on my travels simply used the word healer to describe individuals in their communities who still held these healing traditions. Others included newer terms not found in the folklore record like "mountain doctor," "field doctor," herbalist, and even psychic.

Use of the word doctor comes from interactions between hillfolk of the old Ozarks and traveling country doctors. These interactions would have begun first in the Appalachian Mountains, then continued as larger communities developed in the Ozarks. In the beginning, hillfolk had to rely upon the skills of their local healers alone until towns started popping up in the safer and more accessible valley areas. The pharmacist would have been the first medical professional brought in before an established doctor's office was ever built. Oftentimes the pharmacist was more highly trained than the country doctor themselves, and the pharmacist was certainly cheaper.

Distrust of medical professionals is common across the rural parts of the Ozarks. You can still find old-timers who have never once stepped foot inside a doctor's office. "I'd sooner bleed out facedown in pig shit," one informant told me angrily, "then go to one of them butchers!"

Most healers I've met today are very careful not to use the term doctor for themselves, lest the eye of the law fall upon them for practicing medicine without a license. Historically, while the healer might have had the backing of their community, the country doctor oftentimes had the law. There was a famous healer back in the early twentieth century known as the Wizard of Oto[22] who lived around Powell, Missouri, near the Arkansas border. He was a mysterious man who went by Omar Palmer, although few believed that was the name he was born with. He was said to have just appeared in the area one day and started healing people with highly effective herbal remedies, all for free. He got so popular that folks were traveling from as far as Chicago, Illinois, to see the healer.

Despite his good work, the law often came down against him for illegally practicing medicine without a license, and he ended up in jail a few times. Each time he was released he'd just go right back to healing people. Eventually he folded up the business in a sort of retirement, but he still occasionally practiced until his death, although in a limited way. To this day, no one knows where he came from or where he obtained his knowledge. Some

---

22. Andrus, *Wizard of Oto*.

say he was a failed doctor that was on the run for some malpractice crime. Others say that he had a religious conversion that led him to heal without charging. While the theories are numerous, the takeaway from his story is that healing can be dangerous work, especially if you come up against a country doctor who's got the sheriff on his side.

OZARK HEALER'S OATH

Practicing as an Ozark healer today comes with nearly as many rules and taboos as the regular medical profession. Traditionally, there hasn't been any Hippocratic oath apart from the golden rule: "Do unto others as you would have them do unto you." But, based upon what I've collected from modern healers and from my own work, I've been able to come up with my own Ozark Healer's Oath as a way of explaining the overall ethos of the practicing healer today.

HARM NONE

The first rule in the oath is a simple one: heal others to the best of your ability and don't leave them worse off than when they arrived. This notion comes with its own set of problems, of course. As we see with modern doctors, there are many who aren't trained properly and do end up harming their clients. In the old Ozarks, these quacks were usually run out of town by a mob. Folks in rural areas had little tolerance for someone not earning their keep in the community. The community only accepted the strange, and oftentimes questionable, power of the healer because they were a necessary part of life. If they didn't successfully heal others, the community was often quick to dismiss whatever respect had been built for them.

In Ozark folklore, this rule is the very thing that separates the healer from the witch. A healer was always quick to say that they harm none, unlike so-and-so on the other side of town who used their gift for cursing, stealing, and all manner of witchcraft. This was a useful form of protection for the healer, and as I said earlier, many times they were the first ones to accuse others of witchcraft, often as a way of distracting from their own questionable work. Most of the healers I've encountered today still abide by this principle in one way or another. Many of them exist in the neutral, or gray, area of natural magic, though. These healers choose to view their work as encompassing not only practices for the betterment of their clients, but also retribution.

I once met a man who was a traveling preacher in his youth, meaning he had no formal training at a seminary but was still invited to various rural churches to preach "from the spirit," as he said. He was a mystic by all accounts, and full of wisdom despite his impoverished upbringing. He was known around the area for having a Bible verse for every condition. He claimed no other medicine was needed and that God contained the entire universe in every letter of the holy book. Folks around the area would visit him for healing, blessing, or assistance with problems in their lives.

I had the opportunity to watch one session, but only with the understanding that I was there because of my own gift for healing. The man would sit facing the client. After a period of reflective silence, he would flip back and forth through the pages of his Bible, then let it fall open naturally to a page. He would then read verses from the page aloud. Sometimes it was only one, other times the entire page. I asked him how his practice worked exactly, and he just chuckled and replied, "God stops the pages, not me." He was widely respected and loved by his community, many of whom commented that the work he did was straight from God himself.

He told me a story about how some folks in his community were having trouble with a local fellow who was drinking himself stupid every night. For a while, the drunk was just an annoyance that everyone talked about before church or grumbled over down at the corner store. But soon he started getting violent and, sensing trouble ahead, the community decided to take action.

The man's dad asked the healer to say some verse from the Bible and curse the man to die or leave town. At first the healer refused, saying he "didn't ever do no harm to anyone and never would!" This was, of course, the correct answer in a situation like this—a healer should never play their hand too quickly. But the townsfolk started getting uneasy about the whole thing. The gossiping grannies started talking about how the healer should have done something. "It ain't right, keepin' all that power to yourself!" they'd whisper.

In the end the healer did do some work for the man, but he made sure everyone knew that the verses he was reading were so he would be healed of his sickness, not cursed to die. He read verses so that the man would get better, not worse. Folks were satisfied with what he did, save for a few overly zealous types who would just as soon blow the drunk's head off with a shotgun if it were socially acceptable.

What we can take from this man's story is that the work of the healer is oftentimes constantly coming up against the wishes of the community. This goes for the past and present alike. The healer is in a unique and often awkward position. The only information healers have to go on is what their clients might provide them, and healers are never sure if the client is telling the truth or not.

Take, for instance, one client I was working with to help fix her marriage. She came to me worried about her husband, who she said was becoming angrier and angrier in their arguments. She worried he was going to start getting violent with her. She requested that I bind his hands so that he would always say yes to what she had to say. This immediately felt uncomfortable for me; I never do work to control someone else's will or spirit. I suggested that we instead do some work to cool off his temper and help ease both of them so that they didn't fight so much. In the end she agreed, and the work we did seemed to help them both a lot.

A few months later I was at a local bar and a man walked up to me, asking if I was Brandon Weston. I was hesitant at first but answered yes. He said his wife had come to me about their marriage, and he wanted to thank me because whatever work I had done had really calmed her down. Then I noticed the fresh cut on the man's forehead near his hairline. "Did she give you that?" I asked. The man nodded and said she'd had a real bad temper as long as they'd known each other, but she seemed to have calmed down since visiting me.

For healers, it is a constant struggle to discover the heart of a situation or illness. Only when this core is found will the condition be truly healed. This work is constantly disrupted when people are dishonest or approach with anger and frustration, not realizing that the work they want at the time might not be what they want two days, a week, or a month later.

Healers today, while not dealing with the same troubles as those in our past, have their own set of struggles. I've lost friends and clients alike because I wouldn't do exactly what they wanted me to do. While I do often work in the neutral zone of magic, between what hurts and what heals, I still keep to the rule of harming none. I tend to believe that no one is too far gone to benefit from healing work. Humans today, just like our ancestors, can sometimes be hasty in our decisions and reactionary without fully thinking a situation through. While my beliefs might be inconvenient for many of my clients, others have later thanked me after I refused to do the destructive work they originally asked for.

HEAL ALL WHO FIRST ASK FOR HEALING

Another rule common among all Ozark healers, both past and present, is requiring the client to first ask you for healing. In the past, few healers went out advertising their gifts. Work was usually done by word of mouth alone. Part of this was to make sure the law didn't become suspicious, and it was also to avoid being associated with the selfish and greedy nature of the witch that was common to folk belief throughout the area.

In the rural Ozarks today, you still don't see many healers with websites or business cards. Nowadays, Ozark traditional healing is almost always done separate from your nine-to-five job, and almost always conducted from the home. In the rural areas, there still seems to be a fear amongst healers of being hassled by local authorities over practicing medicine without a license. This is a real issue in many places, where alternative medicine clinics are often shut down and the owners given hefty fines or worse—incarceration. Because of this fear, most rural healers still operate under strict secrecy and will often only work for clients who are a part of their family or whom they recognize from the community.

Outside of the rural areas is a different story. I myself have a website and business cards for the work I do. I see it as an updating of the old traditions, not as a replacement. So much of life for younger generations is found online. Whereas the Ozarkers of the past might have had local events, church, etc. where they would be able to come into contact with other people, the younger generations have far wider circles of friends, clients, acquaintances, etc. Even families aren't always in the same area anymore; many are spread far and wide across the country or world. One healer I met worked mostly through Skype, saying she started practicing in this way for her family who live across the country from her.

Through all of this is a core belief in the power of asking for help. In older times, this idea might have been a part of the mythic "quest for healing" found in many different folklore traditions. In this motif, a person falls ill. Then someone close to the person (dad, mom, wife, husband, etc.) will first try home remedies to cure the condition. But the old tales usually tell us that none of these remedies work. (And stories that go something like, "Once upon a time, Bill got sick with a terrible fever, so his wife brewed up some herbal tea and the man got better," don't often hold an audience in suspense.) When all the home remedies fail, the seeker of the cure will then go out to find someone they've heard knows things. These people are usually removed from society, choosing instead to live in the woods or out in a dark holler. It's far enough out that it requires the seeker to work a little bit to find the cure. This ritual all becomes an important part of the healing process itself. Those people who inhabit the ordinary world are forced to admit to themselves that something is terribly wrong in order to be welcomed into the extraordinary world inhabited by the healer. Usually these stories end with the healer giving the seeker the cure only after they complete some task as a symbolic gesture of sincerity.

In short, if you want help, you have to ask for it. This rule is just as important today as it was for our ancestors. The healing process always begins when you are first able to admit something is wrong.

TAKE NO MONEY

Taking monetary payment for healing services is a common taboo amongst more traditional Ozark healers. This can be traced back to the idea that the healer has a gift that isn't in their possession; they're said to only be "borrowing" it until they die. Therefore, it's believed that this gift shouldn't be used to make money. Along those same lines, the work of the healer should never be considered a profession. "You can get a job with your two hands, your two feet, your mouth, your head, but not with the gift," as one healer told me. In more traditional communities, this gift always comes from God, and therefore it should be used to heal all who ask for healing, free of charge.

Many healers today will publicly say they absolutely don't take any money from their clients, but most have found clever ways around this rule. One loophole I've seen is a client leaving money or gifts where the healer won't see them. This spot is often somewhere in the kitchen, like in a drawer or cabinet. The idea is that the healer isn't implicated in asking for payment, but just sort of stumbles upon the gift later on and is very surprised by the generous gesture.

This loophole isn't a development of modern healers. It was in use even in the old Ozarks, but not usually for money. Before heavy development to the region, most people were on a bartering system, so people tended to leave behind food, kerosene, tobacco, or other items the healer might need. Most healers today won't ever say anything if you don't leave something behind; they're usually too nice to make a fuss. But you might find their schedule suddenly full the next time you ask for a favor.

Some will have their clients offer a donation, placed between the pages of the healer's Bible. This is a way of blessing the money and showing God, who is always watching, that the money will be spent wisely. Along similar lines, healers might accept donations but never set their prices. They'll just leave it up to the client to pay what they can.

I observed one healer whose client asked how much he should donate immediately after the work was done. The healer started cleaning up the room we were in, ignoring the client's question completely. So the man asked again, this time a little louder. The doctor said casually that she "couldn't even say," as though they were guessing about the cost of rump roast at the grocery store. The man just looked at me and chuckled while the woman went to fixing herself some lunch. I smiled back, knowing exactly what was going on, and the man took some cash out of his wallet and stuffed it in the spine of the healer's open Bible.

These days you almost always see cash given as payment to a healer. As I mentioned earlier, in the old days payment would have been food, tobacco, or—in the case of a big ritual—maybe even a chicken or goat. In the more rural areas, you still sometimes see pouches of loose tobacco given, usually alongside some cash. I myself often use tobacco in my healing work and do have clients who like to give some as a donation, knowing it will go toward the healing of others.

In the modern Ozarks, there are a couple schools of thought among Ozark healers about charging for services. Some in the more traditionalist camp are still staunch believers that only witches and city doctors charge for this kind of work. Others say that the offering of a sacrifice on the part of the client has long been a part of the healing process.

I had mixed feelings about charging for my services for a long while. If people left an offering I'd take it, but I was always apologetic and uncomfortable about the whole thing. Then a healer I met gave me a different perspective. He said that the folks he saw for healing always wanted to give him something as a payment, even if it was just taking him out to lunch. I started to see this same thing myself. There was an impulse inside clients that made them genuinely feel that unless they gave some sacrifice, the healing wouldn't work. I couldn't help thinking about our ancient ancestors offering up blood and life in exchange for this powerful magic. This work has always had a price in one way or another.

DON'T CROSS OTHER HEALERS

I've found that this rule isn't as important across the board as some of the others, especially today, but it's still one worth mentioning. Traditionally, many Ozark healers have a taboo against healing someone who has recently seen another healer. This doesn't apply to city doctors, of course. Some modern healers have told me they have to know the name of the illness in order to heal it, so they encourage their clients to see a medical professional first. This is a good trick I've used on more than one occasion for people who I knew for sure needed medical attention right away.

A lot of traditional healers will still say they can't do work on a person where someone's already prayed or "done things." This belief can be traced back to a primal fear of crossing another healer, found throughout the old Ozarks. Making enemies of someone who has the gift is about the worst thing you can do for yourself. After all, the only thing separating a healer from a witch is how they use the magical power inside themselves. Not to say the healer will always turn to witchcraft to exact their revenge upon you, but you never know.

At the very least, a healer could shame you to the community, saying you're an uppity know-it-all that no one should ever visit—or worst yet, a witch yourself.

Today, the healers I've met in the rural parts of the Ozarks happily try to get along with each other. There's so few of us left that I commonly encountered excitement when a healer was able to meet someone else with the gift. In the more populated areas, it's often a different story. I've had more than one unpleasant encounter with healers or other magical practitioners who thought I was working in the wrong way. These sorts remind me of some of the old stories I heard from informants about healers claiming other healers weren't working in the right way, but that *their* cures were always effective. Childish, petty nonsense I say, and to stay out of all the trouble, I try not to take on someone else's clients unless I know I can work in a more helpful way. Even then, I follow the example of other traditional healers and choose never to gossip about whomever else my clients might have seen before me.

GENERALIST HEALERS

The older titles for Ozark generalist healers are rarely used today, apart from folks like myself trying to revive some of the old traditions. As I mentioned earlier, most people today use the words healer or doctor for individuals with the gift. In rural areas you also find other terms brought in, like mountain doctor or field doctor, both of whom might be considered folk herbalists akin to the yarb doctor.

The word "psychic" has come into wide use in the rural Ozarks for people with magical healing knowledge or for local experts in divination. In the old Ozarks, people would have said these sorts had the "sight" or "second sight," both terms still heard today.

What's more likely is that most people today won't know how to describe the work of the healer at all. They'll instead say something like, "You should go see Mr. Evers about that knee, he'll know how to fix you right up!" or, "Don't you worry, I'll have Granny pray for you." In both of these phrases is the coded idea that Mr. Evers and Granny know how to heal by other means than the local doctor. Oftentimes conversation is left at that, unless the would-be client is curious about the suggestion, in which case words like healer or even some of the old titles might be used.

The generalists are known for their wide variety of methods and broad knowledge of healing. This category includes what some might term the major healers of the old Ozarks, but oftentimes the specialists were more widely popular than the generalists.

YARB DOCTOR

Yarb is one of my favorite Ozark words. It refers specifically to a medicinal plant. For example, yarrow might be called a yarb because it is widely known for its ability to stop bleeding. The folklorists offer few theories as to the origin of the word. Some believe it has a Spanish root, as in the word *yerba*, an alternate form of *hierba*, meaning herb. This is possible, but not likely, due to the lack of Spanish influence in the Ozarks until the late twentieth century, when there was an influx of Latinx families to the region for work. It's more likely the word has older roots in rural dialects found across Britain.

The yarb doctor has mastery over the countless medicinal plants that grow in the Ozarks' hills and hollers. They are often called herbalists or naturopathic doctors today, and many of these traditional healers have sought out training online or through correspondence courses to help bolster their folk knowledge. Their skill lies in the creation of various herbal preparations including infusions, decoctions, salves, poultices, and many more that will be discussed in chapter 6.

The yarb doctor was, at one time, the first line of defense against illness in a community. When home remedies didn't work, the yarb doctor was first consulted before a magical cause was suspected. For this reason, the main difference between the yarb doctor and other healers has traditionally been that they rarely used any charms, prayers, talismans, or rituals in their craft. Their work focused on the intricate compounding of various plants, fungi, and naturally occurring minerals for their contained chemical compounds rather than magical quality. As stated earlier, though, the yarb doctor would likely have also prayed over their cures and remedies, believing faith and physical medicines to have an equal part to play in the healing process.

In my journeys across the Ozarks I've found this form of medicine the easiest to talk about with new informants. It always seemed like everyone I met had a handful of home remedies passed down through the generations. We live so close to nature here in the Ozarks that plant medicines are often a common part of many people's lives, not just those in rural areas. We even have a local organization called the Ozark Herbal Academy, located in Eureka Springs, Arkansas, that offers workshops and training classes for budding herbalists. They utilize not only traditional Ozark methods of healing, but also bring in healing practices from around the world to create a complex holistic system.

Because these plant medicines are so commonplace and popular amongst Ozarkers, they have historically been recorded by folklorists as the only methods of traditional healing that exist here besides some silly superstitions about prayers and amulets. Modern folklorists often put herbal medicines at the center of their research because of the possibility for more scientific trials with certain plant species. This is important work, especially considering the high biodiversity of the Ozark Mountain region. The goal of my research has always been to highlight the fact that these herbal medicines have existed alongside an equally complex system of magical healing that deserves studying as well.

GRANNY WOMAN

Traditionally, the granny woman, like the yarb doctor, most often used native medicinal plants in various preparations. As stated in chapter 2, this title was often applied by the community itself to any female born with a healing gift, especially those who were older in years or were widely known for their work as midwives. In the traditional culture of the old Ozarks, there was once a taboo associated with male healers doing what was often called "women's work," that is, working with gynecological issues, pregnancy, and birthing. Because of this, you often hear of male healers who were completely ignorant when it comes to even the most basic functions of the female body. The granny woman was then an essential member of the local community.

These powerful healers are often portrayed in male-dominated Ozark folklore as a grumpy old woman, usually a widow, usually with a lot of kids of their own. They were known to give out foul-tasting medicines and to perform strange birthing rites, like placing an axe beneath the bed of a woman giving birth in order to magically cut her pain. In reality, the granny woman would have known both herbal and magical cures for the many gynecological issues faced by the community, as well as proper use of fertility medicines and when needed, abortifacients, or medicines that would induce an abortion in cases of unwanted pregnancies. In the arsenal of the granny woman were rites and charms to ease the pains of childbirth and ensure the health of the mother. The rite with the axe beneath the bed is a common practice still to this day. I've talked with several women who vouched for the efficacy of this charm during their own deliveries. Many granny women were also skilled in areas of love and marriage divination, as well as knowing exactly how to ensure a husband didn't stray too far from the home.

The granny woman's gift also traditionally extended to other activities of the home, like milking and butter churning. These two are no longer relevant in most areas of the Ozarks, but at one time, producing good milk, butter, and cheese would have been a must on any farm, not only for the family's consumption, but also to sell in town. According to the folklore, witches are known to steal or spoil milk and butter with their malign magic.

The granny woman would therefore know exactly how to prevent this evil and also how to exact revenge upon the witch who was able to slip through. One old method told to me by a modern, proudly self-proclaimed granny woman, is to heat up an iron horseshoe until it's red hot, then drop that into the milk before you churn it. According to folk belief, the hot horseshoe will burn any witch who might have been waiting to spoil your butter.

POWER DOCTOR

The power doctor was once commonly contacted whenever a magical illness was suspected. These healers were skilled with a keen mind for memorizing charms, prayers, and rituals, as well as knowledge of making various amulets and talismans. The origin of the name is mostly unknown, although there are some convincing theories proposed by folklorists. One draws a simple connection between the word "power" and the power of healing itself. Another theory is that it the word shares an origin with Powwow, or the Pennsylvania German folk magic tradition. This is certainly plausible, as Pennsylvania German culture moved into the Appalachian Mountains and then west over time. More information about German folk traditions in the Ozarks can be found in chapter 1.

Unlike the yarb doctor and granny woman, the power doctor might only have made use of plants in a magical, not medical, way. Take, for instance, the plant often called poke-weed, pokeroot, or simply "poke." The active chemical compound in pokeweed is known to painfully slough off skin, therefore it was often used by backwoods doctors for rashes and other skin complaints. This remedy is not recommended for modern use. The yarb doctor used the noxious root as a bath for rashes and the infamous "seven year itch," a folk term applied to several different venereal diseases. The power doctor, on the other hand, used the same root but instead buried it in bags near the front door of a house to help magically ward off illness and evil.

The modern power doctors I've met have all been just as intimately connected to the natural world as their herbalist counterparts, sometimes even more so. Traditionally, the power doctor used plants and other objects found in nature in their work, like certain sacred stones or crystals, especially those with naturally occurring holes in them (often called hag stones), as well as feathers, bones, dirt, insect bodies, etc. The power doctor knew that the magic of the natural world flowed through all things in creation, not just the plants and animals. Everything was looked at as containing a spirit of its own, a magical power that could be harnessed by those born with the gift.

Although power doctors never called their work by this name, they were often skilled in folk psychology. The healer easily solved many cases of magical illness by providing a nonbiased ear to listen. Power doctors were often highly trusted members of their communities. For this reason, you often traditionally see preachers and other religious figures doubling as this kind of doctor. By the nature of the work they provided, they would know many of the secrets of their community. People brought with them all kinds of problems, and the power doctor, as with other Ozark healers, was expected to keep everything said under close guard.

As a part of my own practice as a modern healer, the key is still to just sit and listen to my client, then prescribe a cathartic ritual to release any built-up anxiety or tension. For example, let's say someone visits me with a condition linked to being hexed, but which is most likely sleep loss caused by stress at work. I would first listen to the whole story, making sure to ask pertinent questions that might drudge up some hidden aspects of the issue that my client might have avoided mentioning. Then I would prescribe a cathartic ritual, something simple yet powerful. I first prescribe passionflower (*Passiflora incarnata*) tea, a mild sedative, to be drank every night before bed. Along with this herbal remedy is a ritual, or a physical act they must do in order to intimately connect to their own healing process. This ritual involves the person drinking most of the tea, then taking the last few sips out to the backyard. They then dig a small hole in the ground, pour the remainder of the tea into the hole, and while they're pouring, they visualize that all of their stress is going deep down into the ground where it will be purified. They then fill in the hole with dirt and return to their house. They perform this rite for nine days, and afterward they are able to sleep again.

Another popular method involves spiritual or magical cleansing, either using smoke from burning tobacco or red cedar or a bath of various herbs and *materia medica*. In the case of a bath, the client is often instructed to continue with the same bath for a certain number of days before being completely healed. In the past and present, a good healer will make sure to watch for tokens, or omens, that will show whether the work was successful or not.

Ritual acts like this are common to power doctors and healers alike in both the old and modern Ozarks. The purpose of the healer is often to just listen to their clients and act as a source of unbiased advice. Rituals always help to seal in the lessons learned through conversation. The person who is ill then becomes an active, not passive, participant in their own healing process. It can be compared to being written a prescription by a doctor: the medicine won't work if you don't pick it up from the pharmacist, and you have to physically take the medicine before you can see results. Breakthroughs made by the healer during their diagnosis process always require integration on the part of the client. If they aren't willing to take the medicine, they won't be helped.

Many healers today who might have traditionally been called a power doctor choose to go by different titles. Some have even reclaimed the title witch in their practice, seeing this as another form of the power doctor, and I tend to agree with them. While historically the word witch would have been condemned by the more conservative Ozarkers, today it bears with it an identity that no other term can really cover. I myself still use the title power doctor because I'd like to see some of the old traditions return to use. Others might use spiritual healer, spiritualist, psychic, energy worker, or any number of other titles common today.

One title I've found common in many places around the Ozarks is "shaman." To many people's ears this word bears with it images of a host of wrongfully appropriated practices from indigenous peoples. We should always be mindful of *why* we might want to use terms like this, or others like "medicine woman." Is the desire to use these titles driven by a want to connect to some other culture? Is it to give more perceived legitimacy than other titles would? Both of those terms are commonly heard across the Ozarks and I will say, as much as they might make me cringe, the people I've met who used these titles were genuine healers and not trying to play a character. For them, like with the word witch, these other titles encompass so much for them that no other word will do. However, I still try to preach the good word of going back to our *own* titles instead of co-opting those we might not deserve.

GOOMER DOCTOR AND WITCH MASTER

Traditionally, the goomer doctor and witch master were very similar in their work to the power doctor. In fact, many power doctors doubled as witch masters and vice versa. Like the power doctor, the goomer doctor and witch master both made use of *materia magica* in the form of charms, prayers, and rituals in all their work for clients. But, unlike the power doctor, these healers specialized in removing goomering, or curses. The goomer doctor and witch master were called upon in the direst of circumstances, when no other medicines—magical or physical—were working. The goomer doctor was said to be able to see the signs of witchcraft on a person, and they knew not only how to remove these curses, but also how to turn the spell back around on to the person who sent it in the first place.

The weapons of the goomer doctor were prayers, rituals, and purgative plants. Prayers were most often taken from the Bible, sometimes also combined with folk exorcisms from household books like the *Long Lost Friend* or the *Sixth and Seventh Books of Moses*, a much rarer find, but still around the area, mostly from contact with Southern Conjure and Hoo-doo. Rituals included purifications using water or smoke, repurposed household items like string for tying up or catching the hex in knots, pegs of wood for plugging the hex into a hole bored into a tree, or knives for magically cutting the hex off the body. (These rituals are talked about in greater detail in chapter 7.)

The use of purgatives and emetics might seem odd, but in the old Ozarks, the first sign of bodily sickness was often seen in the signs of poor digestion. Using emetics and laxatives were a way for Ozarkers to clean out toxins from the systems of the body. These methods were also taken as being useful for releasing any curses or hexes caught inside the body. One illness commonly cured by purgatives was live things, much more common in the old Ozarks than today. Live things was one of the worst hexes a person could catch, defined by the sensation of animals crawling on the inside of the body, usually snakes, toads, lizards, or insects found in the Ozarks. The most effective cure was using purgatives or strong laxatives to physically cleanse the body. There was likely a real-world connection between these live things and actual internal parasites like tapeworms that would have been very common amongst rural people in the old Ozarks.

For the goomer doctor of Ozark folklore, healing a client ultimately meant killing or harming the witch that sent the evil spell in the first place. This was seen as the only way to ensure no further magic would be repeated. Ozark folklore provides us with many ways of killing a witch, but the most common ritual involved the goomer doctor or witch master making spite dolls (as mentioned in chapter 2) of the witch, then physically manipulating the doll in a number of ways. Identifying items like hair, fingernail clippings, spit, clothes, or even pieces of the witch's house were embedded or tied to the spite doll to create the sympathetic connection needed for the witch master to magically manipulate their target.

Once created, the spite doll is given a name, either of a living person or sometimes simply put, "the witch who sent this curse," and can then be hung up and shot through the heart with a silver bullet, as the folktales tell us. More commonly, spite dolls were burned, drowned, or crumpled up and buried. This ritual was performed quickly, as there was a belief that if the witch found their own doll, they could reverse the healer's work. After the work was completed, folklore tells us the person named by the spite doll would then turn up dead or seriously injured and the curse would be broken.

In the old days, people assumed to be witches were often: orphans, blacksmiths, widows, widowers, people with mental illnesses, people with disabilities, LGBTQIA+ individuals, outsiders in general, adulterers, people who are overly grumpy, or just the person the witch master happened to claim was a witch that particular week. The work of the witch master would have targeted these individuals specifically, oftentimes ending in terrible violence. As the pockets of rural culture became less and less isolated, there was an evolution of these practices, aiming work instead at the *idea* of the witch, or a representation of the evil of the world itself, rather than a real-world person. You can see this even today amongst some of the more traditional healers. Their work now focuses on the witch said to live "over the mountain," or "across the holler," as you often hear, instead of an actual person within their community. The blame is instead removed to a different location.

WORK PERFORMED BY HEALERS

To put the work of the four historical Ozark healers into a more easily understandable form, here is a table detailing which practices were traditionally performed by each classification of healer. Please note, as I've mentioned before, that healers of the past and present have all worked in very different ways from each other. This information doesn't represent 100 percent of practices, but it does represent the majority of healers as described in the work of folklorists like Vance Randolph and others.

DOCTOR	MATERIA MEDICA	MATERIA MAGICA	RITUAL	PRAYER	AMULETS
Yarb Doctor	Yes	No	Yes	Yes	No
Granny Woman	Yes	Yes	Yes	Yes	Yes
Power Doctor	Rare	Yes	Yes	Yes	Yes
Goomer Doctor	Purgatives	Yes	Yes	Yes	Yes

SPECIALIZED DOCTORS

In addition to the healers mentioned in the previous section, there are several specialized doctors who focus on treating one kind of affliction alone. You do occasionally see crossovers with healers, as in the case of a power doctor who also specializes as a "blood stopper." More often than not, these specialized healers are standalone experts, whether they have many techniques for a single goal or, as with the "thrash blowers," a single yet very effective method of healing. Like the more generalist healers in the previous section, these specialized doctors are far less common these days than they once were. Many of the informants I met on my travels had stories about relatives who could blow the fire out of burns or a neighbor who could charm warts off your hands, but I only met a couple of these specialists who still practiced. Because of the dwindling number of healers in the Ozarks, their role has, in many cases, merged with that of the generalist.

BURN DOCTORS

In the old Ozarks, one important specialized healer was the burn doctor, said to be able to blow or charm the fire out a burn or wound. Common belief once said that if left untreated, the fire that caused the burn would snake its way into the bone, where it would sit as a permanent pain for the rest of the person's life. Because of this, it was believed that the fire must be removed from the burn as quickly as possible. The burn doctor was often either born with the gift for blowing the fire out of burns or was passed the power by another healer. There were once many methods for drawing the fire out of a burn, but the most common was a combination of verbal charm and blowing action. A well-known charm used throughout the Ozarks to this day goes:

> There came three angels from the east,
>> One brought fire,
>> Two brought frost,
>> Out fire! In frost!

This charm would fall under the classification of non-biblical verbal charms. While there are three angels mentioned, the charm itself is not a verse taken from the Bible, nor does it contain overt biblical imagery. Angels, of course, are associated with goodness and the gift of healing. Even today, angelic forces are often petitioned by healing charms to bring their power, or the power of the Divine, to earth for a certain purpose. I've even met several healers who said they received their own gift from an angel that once appeared to them. The east is also considered a holy direction in Ozark folk belief (more information about directions can be found in chapter 7).

This charm can be classified as a reversing or canceling charm, meaning the fire that is brought into the burn by one angel is then canceled out by the frost brought in by the other two. In the old rites, the healer would recite the charm over the burn, usually under their breath to conceal the secret words from their client. Then they would blow three times across the burn. This entire action of reciting the charm and blowing on the burn was often repeated three times.

Many of my informants who had experienced this form of healing themselves told me they felt instant relief from the charm and no blistering or further pain ever occurred. A few others reported the burn and pain disappeared overnight, as they slept.

WART CHARMERS

Wart cures, including those held by the specialized wart charmer, could easily fill an entire book on their own. There were once thousands of charms, rituals, and remedies in use across the Ozarks to help magically remove warts. Likewise, each wart charmer usually had their own individual way of taking the affliction off their clients. There were wart blowers, whisperers, cutters, knotters, spitters, singers, and—my favorite—wart buyers.

My great-uncle Bill was a wart buyer. Whenever he was around, usually at family reunions, you'd see him wander around asking people if they had any warts. If you did, you'd say yes and he'd give you a penny or dime, say "Thank you," then walk away. The warts he bought would then disappear overnight. I always wondered where the warts went after he bought them. In some tall tales, the charmer is able to throw the warts onto their enemies, but I never imagined my kindhearted Uncle Bill doing that.

There are other, more benign methods for getting rid of the warts after the healer charms them off their client. Some say the healer puts them in small pieces of bread and then throws them in the river. The current is said to take the warts off into the otherworld with it. The most powerful river would be one flowing west, said to be the "land of sickness" in Ozark folklore. The wart charmer can also simply pick up a toad and transfer the warts back to the creature. As many Ozarkers have been told as children, toads are a known originator of warts. A much more common belief today is that the charmer need not do anything, as they are said to be made immune to warts by the power of their gift.

Wart charmers today are even fewer in number than many of the other specialized healers. Their sacred duty has been replaced by wart-removing medicines easily purchased at the local pharmacy. Besides my late Uncle Bill, I've encountered only one other wart charmer, and they included these methods alongside their work as a generalist healer.

THRASH BLOWERS

As mentioned in chapter 2, thrash, or thrush, is a yeast infection of the mouth that used to be very common amongst Ozark children. It's a rare problem these days, but it was once so widespread it warranted its own variety of specialized healer. The thrash blower was almost always an individual who gained their power by the simple fact that they had never once seen their father.

The thrash blower could be either male and female and any age. Some blowers employed certain prayers or Bible verses as a part of their healing work; others chose to leave out the formality. Regardless, all shared in a common ritual of blowing into the mouth of their client a certain number of times. It was usually as simple as that. After blowing, the thrash usually cleared up within a day or two.

This ritual was often used in conjunction with certain herbal cures as well, though rarely prescribed by the thrash blower themselves. After forwarding their client to a skilled thrash blower, a granny woman or yarb doctor would also gave out mouthwashes made from strong astringent plants like green oak leaves, cinquefoil (*Potentilla reptans*), or witch hazel as a remedy.

BLOOD STOPPERS

Blood stoppers were once the most widely important of the specialized healers, as they dealt so often with the deadliest of injuries. Nearly every Ozark community once had a blood stopper of their own, if not one locally who could be called upon in a hurry. The blood stopper could be anyone with a charm for stopping blood and a little faith, or they could be considered a healer who was born with the innate power to stop a bleeding wound.

Charms for this work were often passed down in strict accordance with certain rules and regulations to ensure the charm remained effective and didn't "die." Some blood stoppers were known to use the famous "blood verse" in the Bible: "I passed by you, and saw you flailing about in your blood. As you lay in your blood, I said to you, 'Live!'"[23] There are many even today who swear by the healing power of this simple verse and always make sure to have it written down and in their pocket, just in case.

Other healers used different charms, of which there are more than a hundred examples, and some chose to combine these verses with certain rituals like blowing across the wound a certain number of times or marking the wound with their thumb in the sign of the cross. Rituals of the specialized healers were often much simpler than those of the generalists. A common belief I've found is that the specialized healers were often thought to have an inborn ability to heal and needed no other outside methods than just extending some of

---

23.   Ezekiel 16:6 (New Revised Standard Version).

their power, usually through words or breath. One informant I met told me her dad could stop a bleeding wound by just saying, "Stop!" and letting out a swift puff of breath across the wound.

—

Although the methods of both the generalists and specialists are very diverse, at their core all Ozark healers of the past and present are individuals who are held away from their communities while at the same time being such an important part of them. Because of their gift, gained either at birth or through apprenticing with an elder, Ozark healers were often looked at with great suspicion as being someone closer to the Divine than the rest of the community.

To this day, there's a common story amongst the healers I've met of isolation from the world around them. This isolation is often not a choice made by the healer themselves. One older woman told me about how she lost many of her friends at church when she gained her power to heal in adulthood, inherited from her grandmother. She said that once word got out, people started treating her differently than before. People would feign a smile around her more, as though the sight of them being a normal person might enrage her. People also started asking her for advice about issues she had no experience with, like the cattle rancher who called her wanting advice about intestinal worms that were running through his cows. Healers of the past and present are often linked by this presence they have in the world around them. It seems to draw in certain types of people and repel others. I've found this even in my own work as a healer.

Healers in the Ozarks today are few and far between. There are too few to widely use the old terms mentioned above. These are of interest to us today as folklore, mostly. With this work, though, I'm hoping to revive some of these titles for a wider use once again, as they are such a unique part of our cultural heritage. Most people with a gift or power today will call themselves simply a healer, or sometimes you hear spiritual healer. More and more people are reclaiming the word witch and other variations of the old practitioners of magic, like wizard, sorcerer, conjurer, etc. You can see the use of the word witch even in the rural areas, which shows me the times are indeed changing for the better.

GAINING THE POWER

TRADITIONALLY, HEALERS IN THE OZARKS have gained their gifts in a number of ways. The most common include by birth, by apprenticing with spirits or entities of the magical otherworld, or by apprenticing with an elder (but not always older) healer. Many of these same origin stories can be seen throughout the Ozarks today. Of the healers I interviewed, the majority believed they were born with some innate gift or power that manifested within them at a certain age as a calling.

Being born with the gift doesn't always mean you will become a successful healer. Likewise, not being born with the gift doesn't mean an ordinary person can't gain some power of their own. In many cases this magical ability can be learned from reaching out to the otherworld of spirits or the Little People, and they can teach as well as any elder. As with many aspects of Ozark traditional healing and folk magic, there are nearly as many origin stories as there are healers. Everyone has their own unique connection with the power residing inside their own spirit.

What is often common to all the stories is that the gift inside the healer is a manifestation of the neutral magic of the natural world. This magic is almost tangible in many cases, and can be born within certain special individuals, picked up at random, or passed from an elder who currently holds the power or the otherworldly source of the magic itself. Because this magic is seen as something tangible, it can also be lost. Many healers I've met believed that when they passed this power to an apprentice, it would be like pouring water from one jug to another. The magical gift they might have held their entire lives would then be lost forever for them. Others have told me that the power can be "used up" if the healer uses it for hexing or stealing from others, as in the case of the witch.

In the more traditional folk beliefs of the Ozarks, the witch is said to be able to gain their magical ability in the same exact ways as the healer. The witch is said to sometimes be born with the power, especially if one of their parents was a witch. Likewise, they can learn their witching ways from an elder or through a ritual connection to the evil forces of the otherworld, including demons, devils, and Satan himself, in many cases.

The only difference, then, between the witch and healer is said to be how they choose to use this neutral power. In the folkloric depiction of the Ozark witch, they choose to use their power to hex others, as well as steal, maim, torture, and all manner of action that would result in the general harming of another person without due cause. Today, more and more Ozark healers now identify with a gray or neutral form of healing that exists somewhere in between the more conservative notions of good and evil. The few conservative healers I've met said they didn't believe in the witch as a physical person, as in the old legends, but instead as a symbolic representation of evil and sickness in the world that they were constantly in battle with.

BORN WITH THE GIFT

Being born with the power to heal is the most common origin story here in the Ozarks. In the old days, healers were almost always born "in the caul" or "under the veil," meaning they were born with the amniotic sac fully or partially covering their head at the time of birth. This was often considered a sure sign they'd been given the gift. In the modern Ozarks, I'm starting to encounter this phenomenon once again as home births have become increasingly popular. This is another example of how certain folk beliefs that were once thought to be dead can make a resurgence.

Besides being born in the caul, there are other auspicious conditions that might point to a child being destined to become a healer. Note that while the following examples appear widely in folklore, they are rarely ever seen in the Ozarks today.

BORN ON CERTAIN HOLIDAYS

The most powerful of these holidays include May Day (May 1), Midsummer (summer solstice), Halloween, and Christmas Eve. The magical associations of these holidays can all be traced back to the European folk beliefs Ozarkers brought with them to the region. These dates were all once connected to the belief that at certain times of the year, the veil between this world and the otherworld is so thin that it allows certain magical beings through. It was often said that a baby born when this veil was thin would enter into our world with certain powers and abilities others weren't born with.

BORN AS A RELATIVE DIES

The exiting of one soul from the world as another one enters was once seen as a moment charged with magical energy. This belief was heightened even more if the baby was born at the exact time of death or if the person dying was a healer. Often this belief extended to babies born on the death date of a relative, however distant in the future. This shouldn't be seen as a form of reincarnation; rather, the general belief is that the soul of the baby and the soul of the dying relative are able to meet on the road, so to speak, and the elder is then able to pass some wisdom down before continuing their journey.

BORN AT MIDNIGHT

In Ozark folklore, dawn, dusk, and midnight are three times during the day when the veil between our world and the otherworld is thin. As with certain holidays, this thinning of the veil allows for the transferal of certain magical abilities to babies born at these times.

BORN THE SEVENTH CHILD

As with many other folk beliefs, Ozarkers inherited this example from their European ancestors. The belief is that the seventh child born into a family—son or daughter—would be born with certain healing abilities. The belief can be traced to associations with certain sacred numbers, seven being sacred because of associations with the seven days of creation in the Bible, seven archangels, seven days of the week, etc. Sometimes you'll see this belief extended and it's actually the seventh child of a seventh child that is destined to be a healer.

APPRENTICING IN THE OTHERWORLD

Gaining the power to heal through encounters with otherworldly beings ran uncomfortably close to the path of the witch for many people in the old Ozarks. Traditionally, healing ability was seen as a gift from the Christian deity alone. A well-respected healer could either be born with the gift or learn the gift from a churchgoing elder. All other paths were seen as temptations into witchcraft sent by the devil.

While many hillfolk might have told stories about encounters with spirits of the land, Little People, and even ghosts of ancestors, these stories were left to fireside gatherings and were never seen as an actual source of knowledge or wisdom; that was left up to the Bible alone. For many of the more conservative Ozarkers, all this business with spirits and the Little People reeked of Paganism, and was therefore almost always associated with evil and witchcraft. For this reason, many healers who did gain their power in this way often kept their stories secret as a way of protecting their work.

In the old folklore, you also sometimes see healers claiming an angel visited them with healing knowledge. This is often a sincere belief on the part of the healer, but other times their stories bear more resemblance to visitations by spirits of the land or ancestral ghosts than the traditional depiction of an angel. While I certainly don't know what was in the hearts of the healers who shared stories like these, I question whether angels were used intentionally as a way of masking the exact source of their power. Or perhaps it was simply a person's way of describing their encounter with the otherworld in terms that would be more understandable or acceptable? Regardless, more often than not, a healer of this type was able to practice without any trouble. After all, angels were often sent to humankind with knowledge all throughout the Bible.

On my own journeys, I've met several modern healers who obtained their power through otherwordly encounters, and all of them are considered upstanding citizens in their local communities. One healer I spoke to said she was taught her healing prayers as a child by a "fairy man with hair shining like the sun," as she described him. I asked her about the old belief that the Little People were connected to witchcraft and she smiled and replied, "If it teaches you goodness, then it's good." I often encountered this sentiment on my travels, and I've met healers who were given the gift in a variety of ways. This is a wholly modern way of looking at the supernatural world, however, and it wouldn't have been the same for the more conservative generations of the past.

LITTLE PEOPLE

In Ozark folklore, encounters with the Little People are often related as cautionary tales more than anything else. The Little People were often seen by more conservative Ozarkers as tricksters, akin to demons, who often waylay innocent travelers by lulling them to sleep for long amounts of time, or tripping them on stones or vines cleverly hidden across the trail. For most, the Little People were at best mysterious and fickle creatures who were to be appeased or exorcised, depending upon your own level of piety. At worst, they were sometimes seen as servants of the devil himself sent to terrorize and tempt humankind.

Appeasing the Little People was often a part of the daily and yearly rituals on the Ozark homestead, although few hillfolk would ever actually admit to such traditions. Gifts of food and drink (usually alcoholic) were often left outside the home at certain times of the year, especially holidays associated with merriment, like Christmas Eve, so that the Little People wouldn't feel left out of the festivities. Similar food offerings might also be left for the Little People whenever work might disturb the earth, as during planting in the spring and harvesting in the autumn. It was often seen as being easier to appease the Little People from the beginning rather than apologizing later on after your crops failed, your goats stopped giving milk, and your family fell ill. Even today, there are many Ozarkers who still leave out gifts for the Little People. As one man told me, "I'm not superstitious, but you never know, and I'd hate to be on their bad side."

Tales of being offered magical power by the Little People aren't rare, even in the conservative Ozarks, but are usually relegated to stories for teaching and entertainment. For example, tall tales where the protagonist is able to trick one of the Little People out of some of his treasure using their sharp cunning. These stories are often akin to the "Jack Tales," where Jack is seen as a trickster and is able to wiggle himself out of any situation using his mind. For Ozarkers, tales featuring the Little People were almost always used to dissuade listeners from having encounters with these tricksters—or to give them a way out of the situation if they weren't so lucky. Stories about being gifted power from the Little People almost always featured witches, as it was often believed that only a witch would try and gain any knowledge from these pagan devils. Healers who did receive their gift in this way kept their stories secret, for the most part. Even in the folklore record, we only have a handful of these tales and they are often told as humorous anecdotes, not as serious histories.

The modern Ozarks are a different story altogether. Today, as the fear and panic surrounding the dangers of witchcraft have almost completely died out (save for a few more conservative communities), healers and magical practitioners are now able to share stories about the sources of their power. I have a theory that many more healers of the past likely also gained their powers in this same way, but they were unable to be truly honest with the community around them. We're more fortunate today because people are able to share their stories more openly.

The stories I myself have collected represent a wide variety of beliefs surrounding the Little People as well as other spirits of nature. Common to all of these tales is a similar process: the potential healer first finds themselves out in nature. This is most often out in the deep woods, not in your local park. The Little People are said to prefer the quiet of untouched forest areas, usually around large land features like big boulders, bluff outcroppings, or natural springs. In several stories, the protagonist becomes lost in the woods, unable to find the trail back home. While scrambling to orient themselves again, they usually stumble upon either a clan of Little People or a solitary wanderer. Fearing the power of this otherworldly being, the healer will kindly ask for directions back to the trail—sometimes they give the spirit a compliment, as in one story where the healer I interviewed said she "told the little man he had a very smart red coat." The spirit will judge the healer's character in this moment and decide if they might be deserving of some magical power or if they should be lost even deeper in the woods.

A person of good character will be offered not only the path home, but also often the gift of healing knowledge or a certain spell. If they accept, the spirit will sometimes give the power all at once by handing the healer an object representative of their gift. I've only ever seen one of these, however; it was an ordinary walnut to me, but the healer I spoke to said it was given to him by the Little People and contained all the magical power he would need, so long as he kept it always with him. Others have told me stories about similar otherworldy objects but were fiercely protective of these gifts, believing that the power would disappear if anyone ever saw the container.

The Little People will almost always ask for something in return. Common examples I've encountered in my research include asking the person receiving power to abstain from marriage or sex, most often for the rest of their lives. Alternatively, it might be a simple request to never take money for services, which has come up with several healers I've encountered. Other exchanges are a bit darker, as though they were plucked from one of Grimms' fairy stories. In one case, the healer I met lost a tooth to the Little People, and another told me he lost the vision in his left eye in exchange for power. Often it's not that dramatic, and the Little People are seen as playful beings who offer up a game in exchange for magical ability, as in this folktale:

There's a story of a woman who wanted to gain the power to heal others around her, so she went to a certain old oak tree where she'd heard the Little People lived and fell asleep on the ground, surrounded by its thick, gnarled roots. When she woke, she was encircled by hundreds of people that looked just like humans, except they were all only about a foot tall. Their leader approached and greeted the woman warmly, asking what it was she wanted from them. The woman replied that she only wanted the same power he had. The chief smiled and proposed a game of shape-shifting.

"Whoever is able to best the other," he said, "will win the game."

"And if I win?" the woman asked.

"I will give you the power you want. But if I win, you will stay here and serve us for the rest of your life."

The woman agreed to the terms and the game began.

First, the chief rushed forward in the shape of a bear with claws and teeth that crashed down on the poor woman. The woman escaped in the shape of a mosquito. The chief pursued the insect in the shape of a bat, but the woman swooped down on him in the shape of a swift hawk. The chief tried to escape in the shape of a fast boar, crashing through the woods, pulling up entire trees with his tusks, but the woman surrounded the boar in the shape of a great wildfire. Just as the chief was about to burn up, he made himself into a toad-stranglin' rain that put out the wildfire instantly. But the woman just made herself into a rushing river that fell down the mountain. The chief pursued on in the shape of a trout, swimming through the river, but the woman snapped him up in the shape of a big ol' wolf. The chief escaped the wolf's sharp teeth in the shape of a grasshopper that flew off into the woods, but just as the grasshopper touched the ground, WHAM! he was caught by the woman as trapdoor spider, who might be small but is the fastest hunter in the forest.

With the game finished, the chief of the Little People laughed and cheerfully accepted defeat. He hadn't played a game that good in many, many years. As a reward for winning, he gave the woman the power she sought, giving her only one stipulation; that she would return once a year to play the game with him again.

It's interesting to see that the gift almost always comes to healers because of their kindness or respect for the natural world. Many believe this love is an inborn trait of those who are destined to heal. While the Little People have traditionally been seen as tricksters, many have seen them as fun-loving and sometimes even kind. I've heard stories of children who were led out of the dangerous forest by the Little People; the Little People disappeared as soon as the children reached the path to town. If we look to the old tales as our guide, we might see a pattern of thought emerge. Where respect for the natural world dwindles, the Little People and other magical spirits are turned into devils and tricksters whose sole purpose is to hurt or mislead humanity. But in cases where the Little People are seen as protectors of the land or gift-givers, their stories and traditions change. We then see farmers avoiding cutting down a section of forest, believing it to house a clan of Little People; altering building projects in order to avoid disturbing a boulder belonging to the Little People;

or even believing that the Little People can offer powerful healing knowledge to those who are kind and respectful to nature.

"INDIAN GUIDES"

Many of the old Ozark traditions were born from interactions with indigenous peoples while still living in the Appalachian Mountains. As Ozarkers moved west, they took to lands previously occupied by several indigenous groups including the Osage, and earlier than that, the Caddo, and earlier still were a group indigenous peoples called the "Bluff Dwellers." Legends about these ancient peoples began to pop up as a result of hillfolk stumbling upon prehistoric bluff shelters that were, at one time, commonplace across the region, especially in the Arkansas Ozarks. Sadly, there are only a few of these sites still remaining intact. They have suffered a great deal of pillaging and looting by hillfolk and archaeologists alike over the past two centuries.

These ancient peoples entered into Ozark folklore in a couple of ways. One was alongside other tales of hidden treasure and hillfolk stumbling upon caches of ancient gold or gems. The other was in relation to traditional healers, who were sometimes said to have gained their abilities through encounters with "Indian guides" found within these ancient bluff shelters. This belief isn't just relegated to the past, though, and I myself have heard a number of healers claim that some kind of knowledge was gifted to them by these spiritual entities, as in this tale:

> She was a normal looking woman, by all accounts. Just by looking at her, I wouldn't have thought she was a healer or mystically inclined at all. I met her through another informant, who told me she was someone I'd want to talk to. She had a husband who did some farming but earned most of the family's money as a car mechanic in town. She had two sons, both in high school when I met her. At first we talked about healing plants and home remedies, but then the conversation shifted quickly as the healer talked about her gift of praying. She said when was about twelve years old, she went out walking in the woods one day in the summertime. As she was walking along, she all of a sudden heard a voice, like someone trying to get her attention. She immediately became scared, wondering who might be there, secretly watching her. She called out into the woods and the voice replied, "Come closer!"
>
> She could tell the reply came from an old oak tree nearby, so big she couldn't even wrap her arms around it and touch fingers. The girl walked cautiously over to the tree. "Why are you hidin'?" she asked, standing a few feet away.

"Come closer!" the voice replied.
"Are you inside the tree?" the girl asked.
"Come closer! Listen!"
The woman then walked closer, despite her better judgment, and put her ear to the
bark. Then she could clearly hear something moving around inside the tree. She kept
on listening and said the voice sang healing songs to her.

After telling me the story, I asked the woman how exactly the voice in the tree had given her the power to heal. The woman looked confused and just said, "The Indian man just *gave* it. I can't explain it simpler than that!"

Other stories of encounters with these guides run in a very similar way as was recounted to me. Many of them also share characteristics with stories of the Little People. With these so-called "Indian guides," though, there hardly ever seems to be an exchange made between the spirit and the healer. It is more often than not a true gift. The healers I've met with these guides seem to have first heard the call of the spirit, then listened to its voice or song through a medium like a tree, or in other cases a boulder, and were then granted some healing knowledge or magical ability. This power, as with the Little People, is hardly ever herbal knowledge, but instead focuses on certain verbal charms, prayers, or songs that the healer memorizes and then uses in the outside world.

Why people call these spirits "Indians" I haven't been able to tell, apart from their location in proximity to certain ancient bluff shelters, which is often the case. While in many cases a healer might add a connection to some indigenous heritage in order to legitimize their practices, this seems to be a rarity, at least amongst the healers I've spoken to. All have been fully convinced that the spirits they were talking to were somehow related to the ancient peoples of the Ozarks. There might be a possible connection to the use of "Indian" spirit guides in Southern Conjure and Hoodoo, often identified with the Black Hawk tradition. This tradition goes back to certain Spiritualist churches of the late nineteenth, early twentieth century who used mediums to channel certain "Indian guides" of their own. One of these was traditionally the figure of Black Hawk, who lived from 1767 to 1838 and was the leader of the Sauk Nation. These "Indian guides" were believed to be able to give their mediums certain magical and healing abilities. For more information on this tradition, see Jason Berry's *The Spirit of Black Hawk: A Mystery of Africans and Indians*.

While many people today might be exposed to a wider variety of practices like Hoodoo and Spiritualism, Ozark hillfolk traditionally would not have had such interactions. This has led me to believe that the healers I've met with their own "Indian guides" can be seen as a part of a wider category of Ozark folklore that's centered around the mysterious bluff dwellers as a source of possible magical knowledge akin to the Little People and other spirits of nature.

Many of the sincere healers, even with their "Indian guides," still practice in a way that doesn't seek to borrow or appropriate from actual indigenous cultures. In most of the cases I've encountered, the healing rituals or words gifted bear no resemblance to anything that might have been picked up from actual indigenous sources. This runs opposite to the white "medicine men" or "shamans" I've also encountered, who not only claim dubious Native ancestry but also appropriate and utilize highly visual symbols and rituals in a way completely disconnected from actual indigenous traditions. For example, using made-up versions of the "sweat lodge" in healing ceremonies.

GHOSTS AND OTHER SPIRITS

Spiritualism as a practice has not been unknown to the Ozarks. In fact, Fayetteville, Arkansas, was once a hub of Spiritualist activity around the turn of the twentieth century. More information can be found in Stephen Chism's *The Afterlife of Leslie Stringfellow*. For rural Ozarkers, however, the practice was otherwise unknown. Hillfolk hardly ever used the word medium outside of humorous anecdotes about city folk. People in the rural areas instead chose to talk about this subject using their own terms like "the sight," "the second sight," or someone who could "see things," always meaning spirits of the dead or the land.

For the more conservative hillfolk, interactions with the spirit world were never seen as something upstanding citizens would ever participate in, and for some it stunk to high heaven of witchcraft. For this reason, stories of healers and other magical practitioners who derived their gifts from interactions with the spirit world were rare in the old days. These individuals chose instead to keep their practices secret lest the eyes of the community fall upon them as being a witch.

The rare few whose work did center around communicating with the spirit world all knew how to operate within the boundaries of this more conservative Ozark culture. These mountain seers, as they were often called, operated by being able to sense the spirit world either by sight, sound, touch, smell, or a combination thereof, and then interpreted their findings to the world of the living. They were mostly consulted to read death tokens and to make sure the dearly departed were happy and not destined to become troublesome haints. On rare occasions, they might also be asked to help clear out poltergeists causing a ruckus in a local cabin or barn.

Long before Spiritualism reached the Ozarks, hillfolk derived their beliefs about the spirit world and those who could see it from much older European and indigenous traditions. There's a great amount of suspicion when it comes to spirits, though. Being of conservative Christian stock, the average Ozarker wouldn't ever admit to believing in ghosts. It was once widely believed, despite evidence to the contrary, that when you died you went to Heaven or Hell; there was nothing in between. Ghosts were then seen as a force that went against God's laws and were often immediately dismissed from conversation, held in great suspicion, or left to spooky fireside tales around Halloween. Someone who could see and communicate with the dead was then often held under more scrutiny than any of the other healers.

As I've mentioned before, this belief doesn't generally apply to angels. I often still include them under the name spirits, as most traditional Ozarkers won't ever consider them ghosts, but instead as separate spiritual entities. I've met several well-meaning, kind, gentle, praying grannies who claimed to have an "angel guide" of their very own who taught them how to heal or gave them words to pray. Whereas our ancient ancestors might have used words closer to spirit in their day-to-day lives, at some point the more conservative Ozarkers began to believe that while ghosts and spirits were considered agents of the devil, angels were entirely different. In all respects of the word, an angel might very well take on all the characteristics of a spirit guide or disembodied helper, but by their very nature, they were often seen as being completely unlike the spirit. They were considered creatures of God, and therefore were open to all who chose to interact with them. In the Ozarks today, the distinction between angel and spirit is only seen in the more conservative areas, where healers might still need to operate within a more conservative Christian culture.

This category also includes what folklorists might like to call the *genii locorum*, a Latin phrase for "spirits of the place," or land spirits. These are considered by folklorists to be protectors of certain trees, rock formations, waterfalls, etc. Many of these spirits would later become spirits that also watched over the farm and home as humankind moved indoors.

In Ozark folklore, the Little People are examples of these land spirits, and they are often what healers are referring to when they tell stories of encountering the spirit of a bluff who gave them healing knowledge, for example. Oftentimes, though, the issue becomes more complicated. Some Ozarkers who still believe in these land spirits will separate them from the Little People completely. For them, the Little People are civilized like us, while the land spirits are wild entities who are even more unpredictable. Similar distinctions have always existed in the Ozarks between the hills and the town. The town is seen as the seat of civilization—at least to those who live there—whereas historically, the hills were the wilderness and the people living there were backward, strange types who should be avoided at all costs. For the most of the hillfolk, however, this worldview is just the opposite, and it's really the townsfolk who are so strange.

Ghosts and spirits of the dead were also often known to impart knowledge in return for a mortal performing a certain favor. In the case of the ghost stories I know, this most often includes taking a message of love and tenderness back to the ghost's family. Or, as in the case of one story in particular, the spirit of a certain bird-shaped pillar of stone on the edge of a river communicated with a healer that they wished for a bucket of ripe blackberries to be brought and smeared all over the rock's surface. The healer did this immediately and was gifted with three healing songs they had been using for almost twenty years.

Magical power often comes from the ghosts of former healers themselves who weren't able to pass their gift to someone before dying. As the legend goes, if a healer or witch can't find an apprentice to pass their power to before they die, it will sit in their soul and turn them into a haint until they are able to give it to someone. The task is made even more difficult as the healer will also have to find someone with the sight. In some folktales, these haunted healers or witches will wander the land in anger and frustration, attempting to hurt anyone they meet. As soon as the power leaves them and enters into another person, their soul will be at peace at last. This is an old belief not often found in the Ozarks today, where finding a worthy apprentice is a serious issue for many healers. Some still believe, though, that even if they can't find an apprentice in this life, they'll have a chance in the next one.

EXPERIENCES IN NATURE

Another unique road to power often found in the modern Ozarks comes in the form of receiving the gift through communion with nature. It might seem overly simplistic, but one of the beautiful aspects of Ozark healing is its simplicity. Many healers have found at least a portion of their power from just meditating out in the woods or next to a stream. Certain locations of grandeur including tall bluffs, vast cavern systems, and even waterfalls are particular favorites, as they are seen to contain ancient magical energies.

One healer I met learned a very powerful song from sitting and listening to a babbling brook. She told me that if you just "listen long and hard enough, the healers of nature will sing to you." This peaceful, animistic view of the world provides a pleasant alternative to the rigorous sacrifices of other healing paths. By simply allowing the world to speak, healers are able to receive the vital information they might need. This story must be similar to those of our ancient ancestors, many of whom were said to have found healing medicines by listening to the soft voices of plants themselves.

For many Ozark healers today, being out in nature acts as a way of replenishing their energetic stores after depletion through magical rites. Even for the mountain herbalist, being on the land is an important part of their work. Harvesting medicinal plants in the wild is widely seen as a superior source of medicine than those bought in the store or online. There's some truth to this, as many of the plants found through other sources might be subjected to chemical pesticides. One granny woman who helped me identify many different varieties of medicinal plants warned me against harvesting around roads as the plants "suck up the exhaust and aren't fit for medicines anymore." This deep connection to nature as a powerful, living entity lies at the heart of many Ozark folk beliefs.

ANIMAL GUIDES

For Ozarkers past and present, magical forces aren't just found in the plants and landscape elements; they can also be learned from interactions with wild animals. The following is a story I once heard:

Once upon a time, there was a woman whose daughter fell deathly ill with a bad stomach. She could hardly keep any food down, and even water wouldn't last long inside of her. The mother feared her daughter would waste away before she got help, as the closest doctor was almost a day's journey away. In a fit of dismay, the mother ran out of her cabin and into the woods to find some medicine. She knew what sassafras looked like, but there wasn't any growing around the house. She ran in circles, desperately trying to remember what medicines might be around her.

Then she heard a rustling nearby in the low shrubs. She crouched down and slowly moved in the direction of the sound, fearing it might be a bandit waiting to jump out. As she moved closer, she saw a raccoon foraging for some wild berries. The woman held her head and tried to calm her nerves. Then she heard the raccoon throw up from eating the berries that must not have been fit for eating. After throwing up, the raccoon walked over and ate the leaves of the horsemint, then the spicebush, then he dug up and ate some blackberry root before walking off into the woods.

The woman didn't know the names of these plants, only that the raccoon had eaten them and seemed to feel better. So, she ran off and plucked the leaves, dug up some of the root, and rushed home. She boiled them down together in a pot and then fed her daughter the liquid. Within a couple of days, the girl was back to eating, and after a few more, she was completely better.

A farfetched story for some, even for me, and I love a good tall tale. This isn't an isolated case amongst many Ozark healers, though. There's an old belief that our ancient ancestors learned about their medicines in this very way, by observing the habits of animals. This is connected to the idea that animals are closer to nature than humans, and therefore are able to know the healing qualities of the plants. "They can see the medicine within the plant," as one healer told me. Some of these animals are looked at as being spirits of nature itself, not just ordinary wildlife. They are often able to communicate this healing knowledge to humankind, or at least to those who have eyes to see it.

I once met a man who claimed his dog could smell out morel mushrooms, a big business in the Ozarks still to this day. He claimed he could take the dog out to any forested area and come home with a bushel full of mushrooms. While several of his siblings and a cousin or two were able to verify the story, I never saw the fruits of his dog's talent, nor did anyone outside his family. The man just scoffed at the doubters saying, "If they got damn pigs that can sniff mushrooms, why not my dog?" Perhaps we don't give animals enough credit. Maybe they can sniff out good medicine for us and for all these centuries, we've just been ignoring their messages.

These knowledgeable animals often act as companions for the healer, providing them with good medicines and other rituals for many years. In many of the folktales of the old Ozarks, though, these animals bear an uncomfortable likening to the witch's familiar, or an animal thought to be under the magical control of a malign practitioner. I've never met a healer who had a familiar of their own, although many of them found deep companionship in their household pets. Whether or not they were gifted some healing knowledge from these cats and dogs is unknown to me, but it wouldn't be surprising.

For the healers that find sources of knowledge in the animal kingdom, their practice is just another extension of the natural magic of the world around them. This deep relationship often manifests in the use of animal helpers during certain rituals; for example, the power to call in the spirits of certain birds to take out internal parasites, or using a magical version of the squirrel to come in and dig out a curse housed deep inside the soul of a client. Rituals like these are based on a sympathetic connection between the real-world actions of the animal and a proposed magical benefit. Birds in the wild make quick work of gobbling up worms from out of the ground. Likewise, the gray squirrel, a common sight across the Ozark hills, is known for its constant digging up of food stores that are then reburied in other locations. This form of magic relies heavily upon simple observations of the natural world that would have been commonplace for rural Ozarkers who spent much of their time outdoors. In the modern world, we might well take this as an example to watch and interact with animals and plants a little more mindfully.

ILLNESS AS A TEACHER

Many healers of the old and modern Ozarks have traced the origin of their gift back to a deadly sickness of their own. By surviving this initiatory experience, the healer is then able to use their new knowledge to help others in need. This sickness need not be deadly but is usually characterized by a strong fever in the old tales. This fever is often accompanied by strange visions, sometimes of ancestral spirits or angels who come and offer advice or healing songs. The afflicted then recovers over the course of a few days, sometimes with the help of another healer, one who is able to recognize that it's no ordinary fever, but a test of the will and the faith of the afflicted. After recovering, the healer doesn't normally recognize themselves as a healer at first. In the stories I've heard, the healer often resists the power for a time until they are haunted by the fever visions during waking and sleeping hours. At long last, the healer then accepts the gift and often goes off to study with an already experienced doctor. On rare occasions, the newborn healer will naturally know the words and songs needed or be guided by an invisible force toward certain medicinal plants in the forests that had previously been unknown to them.

A similar initiation also often occurs with near-death experiences. I've been able to see this common thread within several healer stories. An ordinary person has a brush with death, usually when very young, and then is brought back to life miraculously, often through the intercession of an ancestor or other divine being. They then find themselves with knowledge or the ability to heal that was previously unknown to them. Often this healing ability comes with the sight, or the ability to see spirits of the dead, who will continue to assist the healer on their path. I've heard healers of this kind referred to as miracles in their local communities, as they were not only able to survive death but also return with a sacred gift.

Often the would-be healer might choose to induce an artificial state of illness through stressing the body. This is a path usually taken by those who want power without having to wait around for a divine call. In Ozark folklore, this is often another path the witch takes to gain magical power, but today there are those who use these moments of stress to gain more insight about themselves and the otherworld.

These induced initiatory experiences often begin on an auspicious day of the year when the veil is said to be thin, almost always at midnight. The stressor will most often imitate a real-world illness. The most common stressors are heating or cooling the body. On rarer occasions, suffocation or constriction might also be used. Heating comes in the form of sweat baths or saunas, and cooling in the form of lying out in a stream in winter or sitting underneath a waterfall. Extreme temperatures can cause the body to go into a state of distress, which may lead to hallucinations and eventually death. The healer pushes their body until they are able to receive a gift from an entity that appears from within the vision, then they bring themselves back from the brink of death just in the nick of time. I do not recommend attempting either of these dangerous methods.

Suffocation and constriction most often go together in the form of burial in the ground. This is a tricky path and no doubt many a novice has died by self-burial out in the Ozark wilderness. It was recommended to me to always do this work in pairs, just in case. In this ritual, a person buries themselves in the ground, usually at midnight. Often they are naked throughout the process, or they wear clothes that will later be burned ceremonially. In some cases I've encountered, the face was left out of the dirt; in others, the one seeking knowledge was fully covered by dirt and was given a bamboo pipe to breathe through. The person remains buried for the duration of the night. At dawn the healer will then dig them up and rush them to wash in a nearby spring. The visions they saw while buried are held as knowledge from the otherworld of spirits soaking into their body. The entire process mimics a dying and resurrection sequence where in the end, the person buried is considered to be reborn into the world, forever changed. Modern healers often use this process to remove deadly curses from their clients. Because of the morbid nature of the ritual and the risk of complications, it's used only in the direst of circumstances.

APPRENTICING WITH ELDERS

Passing the gift from one healer to another is probably the most widely used form of transferal in the Ozarks, both past and present. As said previously, there's a common thought amongst healers that you don't want to die with the power still inside of you. This gift, this healing ability, is thought of in terms of a living being or a tangible force. It can be lost, and it can be given away. The power rests inside your soul and if you don't pass it to someone before you die, it's said to die with you.

Passing the gift is sometimes as simple as passing along a secret verbal charm used for healing, or it can be as complicated as the actual transferal of all of the healing power in one's body to a living apprentice. Traditionally, both options have come with a set of taboos that must be adhered to in order for the power to be passed successfully. These taboos often vary from healer to healer so that following the word of the elder becomes a vital part of the initiatory experience. Here are a few of the most common taboos collected from Ozark folklore:

- The gift can only be passed from male to female or female to male.
- The gift can only be passed older to younger, younger to older.
- The gift, or a verbal charm, can only be passed to a certain number of individuals (usually only one or sometimes up to three) before it is completely gone for the original holder.
- Verbal charms have to be passed down orally. They can't be written. If they are written down, the charm is considered to be "dead."
- Verbal charms can be said only once to the apprentice. They must repeat the charm in full back to the healer. If they fail, this is a sign they aren't meant to receive the gift.
- Sometimes the gift can only be passed to blood-related family.

As I said earlier, while these rules are common to recorded Ozark folklore, there are few healers today who abide by them all. I've met several healers who do still say they have to pass their gift to someone younger and someone of the opposite gender. Today, the notion of passing across genders makes for interesting discussion with individuals of different gender identities. Nonbinary healers who don't identify with traditional gender roles, for example, have said they can pass their power to whomever they please without any strict adherence to the old rules.

Most of the time, healers have a great desire to pass their gift to someone, especially the old-timers. Their kids and grandkids often aren't interested, so they must throw the old taboos out the window and look to someone outside their own home to be an apprentice. I've been passed many verbal charms in this way just by being a listening ear; it always seemed to have given those healers a great amount of relief knowing someone was going to use their gift and it wouldn't just go to the grave with them.

Very few healers I've known would seek to test their apprentices in any way. Instead, they opt to just get to know these budding practitioners. There often aren't a lot of complicated questions or initiation processes. Most of the time, an elder picks an individual who shows a natural inclination toward healing or the natural world in general. Maybe they like going out and picking medicinal plants with their granny. Maybe they have a religious leaning and enjoy going to church, praying, or reading the Bible. Or it could be that the person is just interested in what the healer has to say and how they do their work. This interest shows the healer that this is someone to keep an eye on.

In the event that an elder decides that their power should go to a certain individual, the healer will usually just have them answer a simple "yes" or "no" to the question of receiving the gift. The healer might tell them about the responsibility that will fall onto their shoulders and the fact that they too will have to seek out someone to pass the power to one day. With everything in agreement, the healer then starts the process of giving away their verbal charms, most commonly passed down orally from healer to apprentice. Botanical knowledge and any rituals used by the healer usually come after. Because verbal charms are almost always held in the memory alone, the healer is quick to pass these to their apprentice for safekeeping, especially in cases where the healer is elderly and prone to forgetfulness.

In other cases, especially with healers who hold to the belief of the gift as a tangible force within their own soul, they might choose to pass their power in a more ritualistic way. One example is of a healer who blew three times into the mouth of their apprentice, each time transferring a third of the total amount of their magical power. Alternately, as I saw in one case, they might hug them tight then release, the idea being that through this intentional physical contact between the healer and the student, the power can be transferred in full.

With the rite of transferal complete, the healer almost always continues to teach their apprentice for many years still, especially where folk herbalism or the use of certain rituals are involved. Elders will usually "learn up" their students from the time of initiation until the healer dies. I've talked to several former healers, meaning those who passed all of their power on to a student, who relished the release as though they were retiring from a very long and arduous job. The burden was no longer with them; they could now just sit back and relax. There are mixed opinions about what happens to these former healers after taking on a student. Some believe that as a healer, they can pass their power to however many people they want. Others believe there can only be one apprentice. For these healers, transferal of their sacred power is like pouring water from one jug to another. Although there are countless beliefs about transferring this power, there is a common consensus amongst most of the healers I've met that the elder healer doesn't remain the same after transferring their power. Whether or not they retain the gift for themselves, they often enter a state of retirement and no longer see clients.

LEARNING FROM THE BIBLE

For many Ozarkers of the past, acquiring the power to heal from the Bible itself was seen as being equal to—if not greater than—apprenticing with an elder. This type of learning was often still considered an inborn gift or calling, but the prayers and rituals would be derived from the text of the Bible rather than through the passing of knowledge from one keeper to another. In the much more conservative Ozarks, healing from the Bible was seen as akin to the calling to become a preacher or missionary and was most often held in high regard by the community.

Reading the Bible was once strictly the domain of the educated preacher. For the mostly illiterate community, going to church and hearing the text read aloud was just as good as reading the book themselves. The first hillfolk to the area would have already had many verses memorized, especially the Psalms, which had been passed down orally for centuries before. These verses were often memorized by setting them to music, as with the case of the *Sacred Harp* and *Lined-Out Psalmody* traditions of Appalachia. Up until the Ozark people became more widely educated around the turn of the twentieth century, gifted individuals would have used memorized verses alone in work centered on healing illness and dispelling evil forces.

As reading the Bible became more common for people, the Bible itself took on a different role in the community. For many gifted with the power of prayer, the Bible became a source of all the healing a person might need. The book itself often became a talisman against the forces of darkness. There are many old tales about people being saved from a bullet to the heart because of the Bible they carried in their breast pocket. There are even tales of hauntings where a terrible poltergeist is stopped in its tracks by a Bible-wielding granny. Even those with a different calling, the power doctor for example, might use the Bible to help with everything from creating a healing ritual to divination. As with Pennsylvania German communities and their *Long Lost Friend*, for many Ozarkers the Bible became a powerful source of arcane knowledge, second to none.

Historically, Ozark religious belief was almost entirely Protestant Christian, with the exception of a few Catholic enclaves that developed in the bigger towns. Of course, this is very different today, where you have centers of many different religions spread across the area, not only Christian. But the major influence upon the old traditions was a form of Protestantism that was born within highly isolated communities. This isolation gave rise to the idea that anyone with a calling could preach, minister, or heal, despite their formal training. Often times the one and only qualification was being able to read, but you sometimes even hear stories of illiterate individuals blessed by God with all the words of the Bible already written inside their hearts. These preachers usually drew the biggest crowds at annual revivals and were often consulted for healing or the laying on of hands.

Because traditional Ozark religion was based so heavily upon the individual's relationship with the holy text and God, it was seen as natural to have Bible healers spring up in local communities. The calling was akin to that of the preacher themselves. Bible healers used their holy book for everything from healing to casting out evil spirits, love magic to divination. Some used a form of bibliomancy, or divination using a printed text, in their diagnosis of an illness or situation. The healer would usually sit facing their client with a Bible placed on their lap. They prayed over the work being done, namely that it would be successful and quick. Then they took the Bible and flipped through the pages randomly and only stopped when they felt like God was stopping them. With eyes closed, they pointed to a verse. The healer then read this verse, sometimes aloud, sometimes only to themselves, and based their diagnosis upon what words were there. Sometimes the reading pointed to a certain ritual that might need to be performed; other times the verse would be read over a glass of water or herbal medicine that the client would then drink, receiving the healing words into their body. The latter form is common to see even today; Bible healers often whisper words from the Psalms and other texts over their concoctions as a blessing.

Some Bible healers kept a cache of verses memorized or underlined in their Bibles for very specific illnesses or conditions. For example, the famous blood verse Ezekiel 16:6, said to be able to stop the bleeding of a wound. There's also a famous fever-breaking verse: "The Lord will turn away from you every illness; all the dread diseases of Egypt that you experienced, he will not inflict on you, but he will lay them on all who hate you."[24] This verse has the added benefit of sending the illness back to the supposed witch who might have sent it in the first place. This sort of reversing or sending back work is still common amongst more than Bible healers, the idea being that the work is a sort of karmic retribution. The healers themselves, unlike witches, aren't throwing any malign spells, but only causing the magic that infected their client to be returned to its sender.

There are countless examples of these magical verses in the Bible. In the old days these verses were often passed down from healer to apprentice like other verbal charms. For healers who looked at the Bible as the greatest teacher one could have, these verses would be discovered while reading the text under the influence of the Holy Spirit, said to be able

---

24.   Deuteronomy 7:15 (New Revised Standard Version).

to guide the healer to find the exact verses they needed. These verses were almost always immediately marked or underlined for future use. If you're lucky, you might inherit a family Bible full of these marked verses. I even found one at a garage sale once. Being the kind of person I am, I took the Bible up to one of the people who was having the garage sale and asked her if she knew that the book was out on a table with some others.

"Oh it's just an old Bible. Thought someone might need it more than me."

I asked who the Bible belonged to and the woman said it was her husband's grandmother's. Then I showed her the many underlined verses scattered throughout the book. There was even written commentary in some of the margins and an occasional name list here and there. "Don't you want to keep it?" I asked, confused by the woman's nonchalance.

"If you want it so much, just take it!" she replied in the Ozark way of combining both annoyance and politeness.

Well, I did take the Bible, but I gave the woman a few dollars for it. I couldn't just stand there and let some poor granny's hard work go to waste. Bibles like that are often considered sacred by Ozarkers past and present. This isn't just because of the words contained in the book itself, but because of the energies put into the book through constant reading and use over many years. These books become infused with this energy, and those with the gift can sometimes even feel it radiating off them.

I spent the next few days reading through what Granny had marked down. A lot of the verses were common ones used for healing, protection, and reversing hexes. Then there was the list of names. It's not unusual even today to find grannies writing prayer lists in the margins of their Bibles. Most of the time these lists include prayers for their family, friends, and special cases, like the town drunk. This list in particular interested me, though. There were six names listed and all but two were crossed out. None of the other lists in the Bible had any names that were crossed out. Then, out to the side, right next to the list, underlined in black ink: "And this water that causeth the curse shall go into thy bowels, to make thy belly to swell, and thy thigh to rot: And the woman shall say, 'Amen, amen.'"[25] I shuddered as I read the words. I'd discovered Granny's spite list. These special lists are also sometimes found in old Bibles and were often ways for healers to perform acts of retribution or revenge while still maintaining their pious position in the community. "All words in the Bible are holy," as one praying granny told me. "God himself healed and cursed!"

----

25. Numbers 5:22 (King James Version).

THE BURDEN OF HEALING

It's important to remember that having this magical gift was often seen as a burden upon the healer, and it still is. It was often called the healer's "cross to bear" in the old Ozarks, meaning a burden that the person would carry in life, but which would grant them a greater reward in the afterlife. Being a healer has always been hard work. Illness doesn't abide by the calendar and can spring up any day, any time. The burden of the healer was often very similar to that of the city doctor, except the healer never got paid what they were worth. Not receiving a living wage for their work often meant the healer had to be supported by members of their own family, or they needed to hold down a full-time job in addition to hearing everyone's problems at all hours of the day or night. It's no wonder to me why we don't have many accounts or stories from the old healers. For many, this inborn gift became more like a curse and an overwhelming burden they had to carry around with them until they were able to pass it to someone else.

I've found in my travels, though, that you rarely see a bitter healer. The healers I've met, although often suffering greatly from poverty and ill health themselves, still wore a smile and tried to help anyone who showed up to ask for healing. For these healers—and I count myself amongst them—the gift is still a burden, but the reward attained from being able to help your family, friends, and community with problems that had no other solutions is a wonderful blessing and well worth the effort.

I often think about those healers of the past whose lives must have been unimaginably difficult compared to ours today. In my life, my one worry is often being able to balance my work and a relatively normal social life. It's nothing compared to what healers in the old Ozarks would have faced. Rampant poverty aside, healers were often the first targets of violence from the community. One healer I met told me about her great-grandpa, who was also once a healer for the same community. As the family legend went, he was working on healing a woman in town with a bad fever. Her husband was out of his mind with worry, but the healer tried to calm him down as best as he could. The medicines the healer gave worked for a few days, but the sickness returned worse than ever and the woman expired in her sleep before anyone could be called to the house. Without knowing this, the healer woke up and went about his daily routine. Pretty soon though, there was a knock at his front door. On the other side stood the dead woman's husband with a revolver. He shot the healer and fled into the woods but was later found by the local police. The healer survived, but he bore the memory as a disfiguring scar (and likely also PTSD) for the rest of his life.

This story and all of the others from healers across the Ozarks are a vital part of the history of this work and tradition. The burden of healing is often overlooked in the folkloric record, mostly because healers were unlikely to air such grievances to a stranger. From personal experience, a healer is often looked at by the community as someone who has been completely healed themselves. This is miles away from the truth—the healer is often just as broken as their clients.

An important lesson I learned early on in my work was to take time to heal myself. I constantly have to remind myself of this, even today. Many healers view the illness and other conditions removed from their clients as tangible energies. In my own practice, I make sure that after every client I see, I take time to wash my body off. I also usually do a smoke cleanse of my workroom. Just like a doctor might sanitize their hands and examination rooms in between patients in order to prevent the spread of physical illnesses, psychic or magical illnesses for the healer can also be dispelled. Through the use of spiritual baths, smoke fumigation, and other rituals, the healer can help to remove these unwanted energies before they affect their own bodily system. By doing these cleanses in between my clients, as well as scheduling one day out of the week to perform deeper healing work for myself alone, the burden of the gift doesn't feel like a burden so much anymore. In this way, I'm able to become my best self so that I can be fully present for those in my community who are in need.

Chapter 5

BASICS IN OZARK HEALING

THE METHODS AND PRACTICES of Ozark traditional healing are so varied that it would be near impossible to include them all in just one work. As I've said before, there are as many healing traditions as there are healers. The practice of folk healing is always highly specialized; it depends on the preferences of the healers themselves and who taught them. There are, however, some common elements from both the folkloric record and my own collected stories.

First, we should look at the baseline methodology behind this traditional form of healing and magic in the Ozarks. This is the foundation upon which the entire healing process is built. This foundation, as has been mentioned in earlier chapters, has traditionally been held together by a sense of simplicity. This simplicity pervades most areas of Ozark folk life, from religion to healing. This simplicity was historically born from the idea that there was very little an Ozark family might need besides food on the table, a roof overhead, and some whiskey from time to time. This simplicity has also greatly influenced our healing methods. Medicines were, and still are, hardly ever purchased at the store, but instead are found on the land or grown alongside vegetables in a garden. Likewise, our magical healing methods still often employ repurposed household objects like string, knives, brooms, etc. instead of creating or buying specialized implements.

Our healing tradition was born out of necessity above all else. There was a constant fear amongst hillfolk about inevitability of falling ill while the nearest doctor was hours away. This made developing home remedies and finding someone local with the gift all the more important. This simplicity of ingredients and practice is what first drew me to this tradition so many years ago. Ozarkers have historically had a distrust of things in life that are overly complicated. "If the same idea can be said using one word, why use two?" as one old-timer told me. Likewise, for many healers of the past and present, if a ritual can be performed just as effectively with a length of ordinary string, why use some complicated, esoteric ingredient or tool? Folk magic in the Ozarks has always been considered the work of the common people, born from the simple connection between the individual, their home, and the natural world around them.

HEALING METHODOLOGY

While the work of the healer might seem overly simple from an outside perspective, there are many considerations that are taken before the healing process even begins. The timing of a ritual can be equally as important as the medicines themselves. This timing has historically followed the moon cycles, signs of the zodiac, and certain hours in the day. Within the ritual itself, the number of times an act is performed or a prayer is said also has an added benefit for the healing process.

Many healers in the Ozarks still abide by these old beliefs on timing. They are seen across many different cultures, and many have their origins in European folk belief. I once asked an older healer why she believed these timings were so important. She told me in a very matter of fact way that "any healer out there with the gift can heal. Timing, location, spirit helpers, all of them things just add power to the work." A modern equivalent could be made with some of the medications prescribed by doctors today; some have to be taken at a certain time of the day, a certain number of doses might be used, or sometimes you have to take it before or after you've eaten. All of these factors are in place to ensure the medicine performs in the most effective way for the one taking it. In the same way, when a healer takes their client out to wash three times in a river before dawn when the moon is waning, those processes have a specific purpose for the exact work that was determined by the healer.

NUMBERS

Numbers in Ozark healing are usually taken from biblical sources, commonly three, seven, or twelve. They can also be compounds of these numbers, like six, nine, or twenty-four.

Three refers to the Holy Trinity, but it also comes to us from ancient Indo-European numerical systems that honored the triad as a sacred number. The number seven has connections to the seven days of creation and the seven archangels. It can also refer to the seven directions, which have traditionally been honored and employed by many Ozark healers during their rituals and in daily prayers. Twelve often refers back to the twelve apostles or the twelve tribes of Israel. It also has connections to the months of the year and the twelve signs of the zodiac. In numerology, twelve represents $1+2=3$, which also symbolically connects the number to the triad or trinity.

These sacred numbers are traditionally used in several ways. The most common is in counting out ingredients for use in an herbal preparation or amulet. In this way, three different types of plants might be used in a certain concoction, or perhaps even three roots from one plant. Likewise, a protective bag to hang up near the front door to ward off evil might include seven thorns, three nails, and twelve mustard seeds. The addition of even one of the sacred numbers enhances the overall power of the work by connecting it back to the Divine. Adding three leaves of a certain plant, for example, not only includes the power of the plant itself, but also the strength and ability of the Christian trinity as it is invoked through this sacred number. Christian healers often invoke the three holy names of the Father, Son, and Holy Spirit (or Holy Ghost) in their work, making a direct connection to the Christian trinity. Others not of a Christian inclination often still invoke the ancient triad using other phrases like "Maiden, Mother, and Crone," or even "Body, Mind, and Spirit," as I heard once.

Many healers today still hold on to this idea of sacred numbers, even if they themselves no longer hold any of the religious beliefs that they come from. For example, I met an herbalist who always made her concoctions using three, seven, or twelve types of plants, depending upon the situation. I asked her if she felt it added anything to the medicine to align with certain numbers, and she said it was what her granny taught her to do, and it always worked.

Another healer who used ritual bathing in a river as a part of his healing practice told me that washing three times "makes sure to get the front, back, and sides," of his clients but also "blesses them on all sides of their bodies." A similar ritual I've seen amongst several others invokes the power of the healer to bless their client inside and out, top to bottom. In this way, the entire body of the client is seen as being covered by the magical work being done.

DIRECTIONS

Directions have their own sacred identity, just like numbers do. In traditional Ozark cosmology, there are seven directions: north, south, east, west, up, down, and center or middle. These directional associations are based in part on Cherokee traditional belief that also values the number seven as highly sacred, but the directions have connections to European folk traditions as well. In the Ozarks, some of these directions have specific associations. The east, for instance, is considered the direction of healing and goodness. This idea can be traced back to Christian cosmology, which identifies the east as a symbol of the resurrection of Jesus Christ. Ancient churches had their altars situated so that the priest and the entire congregation were facing east, a tradition still followed by many branches of Christianity. This association has many more ancient roots as well. The east is the direction of the rising sun, a symbol of rebirth and renewal. For this reason, east is often used in Ozark healing rituals for cleansing and purification, specifically washing in a river as the sun rises.

West, the direction of the setting sun, is traditionally associated with death, decay, and illness. Ozark healers often throw all the evil and illness they pull out of their clients into this direction. In one ritual I observed, a healer took their client to a part of a river that was flowing west. They magically sucked the client's illness out using an egg that was rubbed on the client's skin three times from head to toe, then thrown into the river so that the illness would be carried into the west. This place in the west is seen as the source and dwelling place of the demonic and monstrous forces of the world. Traditionally, the west was considered a witching direction. Witches were said to pray facing the west and to call upon certain powers or entities from that direction to aid them in their work.

North and south traditionally had few associations with white Ozarkers, but those of mixed ancestry often incorporated Cherokee beliefs into their own system. In this way, north represented a cold realm of unhappiness and wet illnesses. This land was governed over by frogs, toads, salamanders, turtles, and all creatures considered to be cold in nature. From this land, wet and cold illnesses were believed to descend to the earth to torment humankind. Often healers would invoke warm or hot entities like a fiery wind, for example, to scare these illnesses back to the north, where they came from. The south was associated in a similar way as the east, and it was often considered a direction of peace, good luck, and healing.[26]

The direction "up" or "above" is often associated with Heaven in Christian cosmology, but it also holds the healing power of light and the sun. The sun is often still invoked today

---

26.   Irwin, "Cherokee Healing."

as a heating and drying force to do battle against cold and wet illnesses. The sun is also a source of the dreaded heatstroke, which would have affected my Ozark ancestors greatly, as they spent much of their days working outside in the fields. A common practice was to petition the sun with gifts of tobacco, and sometimes grains or corn, before work to keep its rays from shining too brightly. Traditional Ozark healing prayers and charms often employ imagery of the sun or sunlight in their verses.

Opposite this direction is "down" or "below," which is traditionally associated with Hell, much like the west. It is also associated with underground monsters like the gowrow, described in folklore as a giant lizard with two long tusks coming out of its mouth. This beast is known to eat cattle and any unlucky spelunker that happens to tread into its lair. The Ozark region has what's called karst topography, meaning that because it's mostly soft limestone beneath our feet, underground caves are constantly being formed as aboveground water seeps in through sinkholes and dissolves out the rock. As one geologist described to me, "We're all standing on Swiss cheese that could collapse at any minute!" The situation of caverns collapsing into sinkholes is a common occurrence throughout the Ozarks.

For many who still hold to the traditional beliefs, the direction down is looked at as encompassing these vast cavern systems. These caves are often associated more with a realm of danger and mystery than the fiery Hell of Christian cosmology. Witches were traditionally believed to have their infernal gatherings in caverns alongside the creatures of nighttime and death like crows, owls, wolves, coyotes, panthers, and the gowrow, of course. Others look to these caves as the home of the Little People, who are traditionally believed to be sources of magical and healing knowledge. Whereas in the past most Ozarkers feared what lurked in the darkness below their feet, today many of the magical practitioners and healers I've met consider these caverns as sources of sacred power in the world lying in wait for someone to discover them.

The directions down and west are often used interchangeably. I've heard healers send the illness they took out of clients "over the mountains into the west" as well as "down into the deepest, darkest caverns." Up and down often also refer to the direction the work is being done. For instance, cutting rituals where a knife or axe is drawn over the client's body so as to magically cut off an illness or curse. These rituals are always performed in a downward motion, considered the direction of removal. This is opposed to upward, which is associated with adding or building up, as in certain rituals for prosperity and luck where a healer might apply an oil meant to draw money on the skin of their client from feet to head.

The last of the cardinal directions to mention is the center or middle. This is traditionally the name given to this world, the world that humankind occupies. This direction can also include the otherworld or the spirit world, often depicted in Ozark folklore as a mirror image of our own where ghosts, land spirits, angels, Little People, and other disembodied entities dwell. Today, healers who work with this direction often do so using trance or rituals involving different states of consciousness in order to shift one's viewpoint from this world to that other place. Traditionally, only those with the second sight were able to see this otherworld, except on rare occurrences. Certain natural features are considered to be doorways into the otherworld, and at certain times throughout the year the veil between worlds was considered thin, like on Halloween.

Another specialized direction that should be mentioned is the crossroads. This is traditionally seen as a man-made intersection of all the directions. It can be found by the healer at the intersection of two roads or created using chalk or cornmeal. Because the crossroads is the combination of all sacred directions, it is often seen as a sacred stage upon which gifted individuals can perform powerful rituals for healing and hexing alike. In the old folklore, illnesses—in particular, warts—were often discarded at a crossroads using certain rituals. In one, a person would rub each of their warts on a penny, then leave the pennies at a crossroad. It was believed that the next person to come along and pick up the pennies would get all the warts.

DIRECTION	ASSOCIATION	COLOR	INHABITANTS
North	Negative; cold, wet illnesses	Blue	"Cold" creatures: frogs, toads, salamanders, etc.
South	Positive; healing; peace; good luck	White	Angels; guiding spirits
East	Positive; healing; power	White/Red	Angels; guiding spirits
West	Negative; illness; death; evil	Black/Brown	Witches; demons; illness-causing spirits
Up	Positive; Heaven; the sun	White	Angels; god; saints
Down	Mixed	Black	Witches; demons; monsters; Little People; magical spirits
Center	Positive; humans; spirits	None	Humankind; spirits; ghosts; ancestors

DIRECTION	ASSOCIATION	EXAMPLE WORK
Upward	Growing; adding; influencing; building	Anointing the body; climbing rituals, e.g., "As this tree grows tall …"
Downward	Removal; banishing; cleansing; clearing	Cutting off an illness; sweeping a curse off the body; washing

MOON CYCLES

Traditionally, one of the most effective ways for Ozark healers to harness the magic of the natural world in their own rituals was to work with the cycles of the moon. Ozark hillfolk always used to keep an almanac around to be able to monitor not only the moon cycles, but also the zodiac signs for each day. This wasn't just the domain of the healer; the cycles of the moon were also often watched by farmers. Planting with the moon was believed to ensure that a farmer was able to get the most from their seeds and produce the finest crops around. Generally speaking, it was believed amongst hillfolk that the brighter the moon, the more influence its energies had over things aboveground. Crops bearing fruits that are aboveground were planted when the moon was waxing, or growing brighter. Belowground crops like potatoes and peanuts were planted when the moon was waning, or growing darker. Likewise, harvesting fruits and vegetables was done during the corresponding time period.

In Ozark healing and folk magic, the waning moon has associations with work that aims at decreasing or making something smaller. A common cure during this timeframe is the removal of warts. An old cure goes something like this: first, cut a potato in half and rub the white part on your warts. Then, during the waning moon, bury the potato in the ground and say, "As this potato rots, so let my warts rot away." As the moon fades, so too will your warts. The waning moon can also be used for any situation where you want the outcome to be lessened or decreased. That goes for removing sickness, hexes, curses, and other malign magic.

Opposite is the waxing moon, seen as a time for work intended to build, strengthen, or grow. Love work is often done during this time, so long as the work is aimed at increasing love—or increasing the number of one's lovers, perhaps. Also done at this time is work for prosperity or growing a business. One modern ritual involves placing a person's hair in the roots of a flowering plant during the waxing moon so that as the plant and the moon grow, so too will the health of the one whose hair was planted.

In general, the full moon itself is a powerful time of increasing and growing. Rituals for powerful healing are often performed at this time. Opposite is the new moon, reserved for work aimed at severing curses, hexes, or breaking strong bonds.

Working with moon cycles is as widely used today in Ozark folk magic as it once was for my ancestors. Practitioners from all walks of life use this specialized timing to add a little extra magical energy to their work, not just for healing. Many know, for instance, that the waning moon can be used to decrease the power of another with the gift, just as the waxing moon can be to strengthen and grow that same power.

If you find your enemy running their mouth against you, repeat this ritual that was once taught to me. Do this when the moon is waning; two or three days after the full moon is best. First, take a small square of paper and write the name of your enemy three times horizontally in the center, one on top of the other, like this:

NAME

NAME

NAME

Then fold the paper in half—any way will do—and sew the two edges together using black string. At midnight, take the sewn-up paper outside and bury it in the ground, preferably at a crossroads or in a graveyard. Repeat these words while filling in the hole with dirt: "As the moon's light fades, so too let the words of my enemy disappear." Soon you will find your enemy's influence in the world lessening by the day.

MOON PHASE	ASSOCIATION	EXAMPLE WORK
New Moon	New directions; severing or breaking bonds	Removing malign magic; cutting bonds and contracts; severing ties with an enemy
Waxing	Building; increasing; growing	Bringing in new business; looking for love; drawing luck and money to the home; bringing in health after illness
Full Moon	Strength; increasing; growing; protecting	Protection; divination for the diagnosis of an illness
Waning	Decreasing; lessening; removing	Healing illness; healing warts; decreasing power of another

TIMES OF DAY

In Ozark folk practice, the liminal spaces of the dawn and dusk have been traditionally held as the most auspicious times to do magical work of any kind. Rituals for cleansing might have you wash in a river at dawn on a Sunday in order to wash the sickness away. Likewise, some work might have you go to the woods specifically at dusk and pick a certain plant that will be used in the healing work.

Dawn is almost always associated with a fresh start, a new day, and the cleansing of sickness or evil. Dusk has traditionally had associations with divination and the "darker" processes of healing. By dark I don't mean evil, but rather those rituals associated with the unknown, particularly those that petition the spirit world for aid. In these rituals, a healer might send their client into the woods at dusk to retrieve a certain plant or ingredient because it is believed that at this time, spirits of the plants are able to speak louder to humankind. This is connected to the idea that the dawn and the dusk both represent times of the day where the veil between worlds is thin, allowing healers to heal more powerfully and seers to see things with more clarity.

In the beliefs of a more traditional Ozarks, nighttime was often associated with true works of evil. It was believed that witches and other practitioners of malign magic worked in the dead of night, usually midnight, 2:00 a.m., or 3:00 a.m., depending on whom you asked. In this more traditional cosmology, the hours of the day can be divided between the world of humankind, the otherworld, and the world of evil or witches. Dawn and dusk are then seen as cusps between the human world and the neutral otherworld, both on the same directional plane. The daytime hours between dawn and dusk are ruled by humankind, and alternately, the hours between dusk and the next dawn belong to the creatures of night and evil entities.

These associations have evolved over the years as fewer people now hold to the same conservative views of good and evil. For many magical practitioners in the modern Ozarks, the division of the day is a little bit different. Dawn and dusk have for the most part retained their traditional values; dawn is still seen as a time of spiritual and magic rebirth, whereas dusk is seen as a time of introspection and diving into the dark mysteries within oneself. Daytime is often reserved for works of healing and illumination. I perform all of my general cleanses and healing work during the daytime, but I know that for serious works of removing curses and other deeply rooted illness, dawn is still the best time to work.

The nighttime isn't just for more malign magic anymore; it is now widely used for works of mystery, especially those that involve trance, divination, astral projecting, and communication with spirits. I once asked an Ozark spirit worker why she always worked at night and she replied, "I don't know about others, but at night I'm less prone to distraction. The spirits come to me faster and are clearer."

I like to think of the darkness that comes with nighttime as a blank canvas upon which many wonders can be drawn. Much of the work I do takes place at night. In the darkness I'm able to delve deeper into issues my clients might hold within them than during the daytime. Just like that healer said, there aren't as many distractions to get in the way of discovering the truth.

TIME	ASSOCIATIONS	INHABITANTS	EXAMPLE WORK
Dawn	Veil thin with otherworld; peace; tranquility; healing; purification; rebirth	Inhabitants of the otherworld; angels; guiding spirits; ghosts; seers; Little People	Washing away a curse in a river or burying an illness at a crossroad
Daytime	Time of humankind; day-to-day life; work for illumination	Humans; mortals	Regular healing work
Dusk	Veil thin with otherworld; diagnosis; introspection; letting go and breaking bonds	Inhabitants of the otherworld; angels; guiding spirits; ghosts; seers; Little People	Releasing a painful memory into a river or letting a spirit fade into the otherworld
Nighttime	Divination; mysteries; trance; diagnosis; finding answers; calling for aid from the spirit world	Inhabitants of the otherworld; angels; guiding spirits; ghosts; seers; Little People	Trance journeying to find the source of illness with a client or petitioning the otherworld for aid in work

ZODIAC

In addition to the moon cycles, the zodiac has long been used in the Ozarks to offer advice on healing, farming, and day-to-day action. Even modern copies of the *Old Farmer's Almanac* will tell you all about the "best days" for things like planting aboveground crops, planting root vegetables, cutting your hair, cutting your nails, proposing marriage, etc., the idea being that on each day, the moon is ruled by a certain sign of the zodiac and each sign is favorable to a certain kind of work, whether that that magical, medical, or mundane. For example, planting is generally best when the moon is in a water sign, like Cancer, Scorpio, and Pisces, or on earth sign days like Taurus for root vegetables. Harvesting is best on fire sign days like Aries, Leo, and Sagittarius, or air sign days like Gemini and Aquarius in cases where the plant will keep producing. Pruning back hedges and trees is always done on fire days when the moon is waning, as it is believed that this will help slow the grow-back.

Just as the days are governed by certain signs, so too is the body itself. Each part on the "Man of Signs," or "Zodiac Man" as he is sometimes called, is associated with a different sign. Healing using the Man of Signs goes back to the Middle Ages, when doctors developed the theory that a body part should never be interfered with when the moon is in its corresponding sign. For example, work on the eyes should never occur on an Aries day, as that sign governs the head and therefore, the eyes. Work instead should be offered on the day that is opposite to the certain sign. In the case of Aries, that sign is Libra.

Healing theories like this one seeped into Ozark folk culture by way of the almanac—many of which still print an image of the Man of Signs in every copy—and the local pharmacist. To this day, many Ozarkers keep an almanac around to determine the proper timing for specific work.

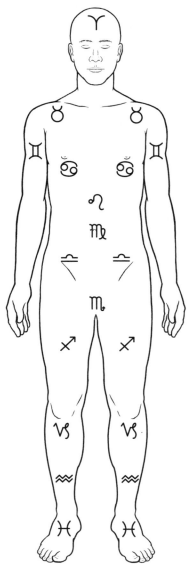

Zodiac Man

SIGN	ALMANAC ASSOCIATION	ALSO RULES	OPPOSITE SIGN	ILLNESS
Aries	Head	Eyes; nose; blood pressure; teeth	Libra	Pimples; headache; migraine
Taurus	Neck	Throat; shoulders; ears; glands	Scorpio	Sore throat; goiter; hemorrhoids; mumps
Gemini	Arms	Shoulders; lungs; nerves; arms; fingers	Sagittarius	Chest congestion; asthma; cough; pneumonia
Cancer	Breast	Chest; sides; organs; bile	Capricorn	Colds; sinus congestion
Leo	Heart	Stomach; spine; upper back; spleen	Aquarius	Heart disease; fevers; heatstroke; inflammation; stomach; upper back
Virgo	Belly	Intestines; gallbladder; pancreas; liver	Pisces	Constipation; diarrhea; bowels
Libra	"Reins," or Buttocks	Lower back; kidneys; buttocks	Aries	Kidney disorders; urine retention; lower back problems; hip problems
Scorpio	"Secrets," or Genitalia	Pelvis; bladder; rectum; ovaries; womb; genitalia	Taurus	Venereal disease; overactive bladder; issues with reproductive health
Sagittarius	Thighs	Legs; hips; groin	Gemini	Hip issues; leg issues; cramps; rheumatism
Capricorn	Knees	Shins; bones; sinew; nerves	Cancer	Skin complaints; all types of dermatitis; joint issues; rheumatism
Aquarius	Legs	Ankles; calves; lower blood vessels	Leo	Circulation in lower extremities
Pisces	Feet	Toes; soles	Virgo	Issues with feet; corns; bunions; colds; chills; stomach pains

While many healers in the Ozarks today might still try to adhere to the best days for work, sometimes the task just needs to be done quickly. Oftentimes, work can't wait a week or two for the best day to swing around again. Following the zodiac adds power to the work, but it's not generally seen as being necessary. It's like traveling in a boat—going with the flow is most efficient, but sometimes you've got to travel against the current. You can still do the work, but you'll need more energy to travel in that direction. The same can be said with healing work. It's always easier going with the flow of nature and following the signs of the zodiac; going against the grain takes more power to complete the task.

The zodiac moon signs not only rule the physical body, they can also be used for various other conditions and tasks. In these cases, work is often done on the day of the corresponding sign, not the opposite. For example, work with dreams and divination is best done when the moon is in Pisces. Working against certain other signs might also need to be done. Take Taurus for example. Taurus is an earth sign known for its work in grounding, protecting the home, and working against signs whose corresponding planet is Mars, like Scorpio, known as a sign for vengeance and cursing. Ozark healers who specialize in removing hexes might work with a client when the moon is in Taurus for this reason.

It should be noted that this extension of the zodiac is followed almost exclusively by modern practitioners, specifically those with a leaning toward astrology. In the old Ozarks most healers and folk magicians would have known the Man of Signs alone, and that was because this information was widely distributed in the almanac. Horoscopes, also often printed in almanacs, would have been consulted by a handful of individuals, but this was often looked at as being akin to witchcraft in more conservative circles. Planting and healing by the signs, however, was widely viewed as being a scientific and modern method of medicine despite its ancient roots in the same system of astrology.

Many healers today use these extended zodiac correspondences on a daily basis in their work. I once noticed while talking to a certain healer that he had filled his farmer's almanac with a lot of green and red dots. I asked him what they symbolized and he replied, "The green ones show me the best days to do gambling work."

"And the red days?" I asked, pointing to the page.

The old man smiled a toothless grin, then answered, "Them days are for my enemies."

The chart below will show you the extended zodiac correspondences that I managed to collect from across a number of informants who were themselves magical practitioners. From my reckoning, these correspondences aren't wildly different from what you might find in modern published resources on astrology. This work represents a modern evolution of work passed down from the old Ozarks. The zodiac is just as important for many hillfolk today as it was a hundred years ago. This modernization of zodiac use to include an expansion of other information makes me hopeful that many other Ozark folk traditions can follow suit and be brought successfully into modern practice.

SIGN	PLANET	ELEMENT	WORKS AGAINST	ASSOCIATION
Aries	Mars	Fire	Venus and the moon	New projects; business ventures; buying; courage; strength; vengeance
Taurus	Venus	Earth	Mars	Hearth and home; stability; security; healing relationships; family work; prosperity; comfort
Gemini	Mercury	Air	Jupiter	Divination; luck; gambling; communication; astral travel
Cancer	Moon	Water	Mars and the sun	Increasing love in family and relationships (waxing); breaking bonds in relationships (waning); cleansing; blessing; purifying; protecting; divination
Leo	Sun	Fire	Saturn and the moon	Fighting obsession (waning); increasing passion / sex (waxing); protection; prosperity
Virgo	Mercury	Earth	Jupiter	Cleansing; consecrating; dedicating; employment; initiation; communication; trickery
Libra	Venus	Air	Mars	Marriage work; contracts; partnerships; legal matters; leases; divorces; strengthening relationships (waxing); breaking relationships (waning)
Scorpio	Mars	Water	Venus and the moon	Self-defense; protection; exorcism (waning); banishing; death / rebirth; fertility; necromancy; wrath; vengeance
Sagittarius	Jupiter	Fire	Saturn	Studies; education; religion; spirit work; divination; long-distance travel
Capricorn	Saturn	Earth	The sun and the moon	Banishment (waning); masculine energy; career ventures; evil eye; authority; discipline; boundaries; separation
Aquarius	Saturn	Air	Mars and the sun	Influencing others; attracting friends; dreamwork; diagnosis; revealing secrets; authority; discipline; boundaries; separation
Pisces	Jupiter	Water	Saturn	Dreams; trance; divination; personal development; illusions

PLANETARY SIGNS

For healers in the Ozarks today, the planets also play an important role in their magical work. Each sign of the zodiac corresponds to a certain planetary sign. Modern practitioners might use a table of "planetary domiciles," like the following table, to determine these signs. Just like each sign of the zodiac has certain associated qualities, so too do each of the seven planets. These associations come to us from the works of a long line of astrologers that stretch back to our most ancient beginnings. Many practitioners have gone beyond the traditional seven-planet system and have added Uranus, Neptune, and Pluto as well. The following table keeps with the much older system of seven planets, which in my experience is much more popular amongst modern Ozark astrologers.

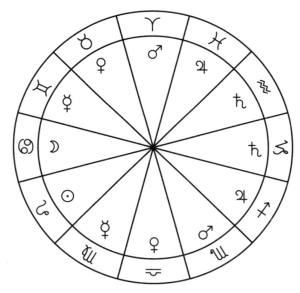

Planetary Domiciles

While the modern Ozark practitioners I've met all learned these correspondences from published guides on astrology and astrological magic, for me they represent the traditions of the new Ozarks and should be mentioned as a part of our ever-evolving system of belief. In many cases, modern healers and practitioners are making strides in applying these ancient traditions to a very Ozark setting. One example is with the zodiac and planetary correspondences of our native plants, most of which aren't mentioned in the books of traditional herbal astrology. Many of these correspondences that I've gathered will be listed in the next chapter.

PLANET	ZODIAC SIGN(S)	DAY OF THE WEEK	ASSOCIATIONS
Sun	Leo	Sunday	Wealth; prosperity; protection
Moon	Cancer	Monday	Dreaming; divination; emotions; astral travel; subconscious
Mercury	Gemini/Virgo	Wednesday	Healing; communication; connection to others; trickery; deception; illusion
Venus	Taurus/Libra	Friday	Love; healing/forming relationships; harmony; physical pleasures
Mars	Aries/Scorpio	Tuesday	Wrath; vengeance; physical energy; strength; will; drive; vitality; competition
Jupiter	Sagittarius/Pisces	Thursday	Politics; law; faith; optimism; opportunity; knowledge; enlargement; expansion
Saturn	Capricorn/Aquarius	Saturday	Relationship to authority; organization; self-discipline; boundaries; limitations; restrictions

LOCATION

Ozark healers of the past and present alike have also traditionally taken into consideration where their rituals are to be performed. Certain works often require certain settings if they are going to be successful. While many healers today might have a designated room in their home for healing work, healers in the old Ozarks often had to make do with what they had. The kitchen table was most often the site of deep healing conversations and rituals for old Ozarkers. Cleansing baths were easily taken down at the river, whose current was seen as a powerfully magic force on its own, able to carry sickness far away from the one afflicted. The natural world was often the setting for these old rituals. Ozark healers picked certain groves of trees, bluffs, caverns, waterfalls, and other auspicious sites for their specific connection to the spiritual otherworld. Many of these sites were looked at as gateways into that other place, or spots where the veil between worlds was thin enough to allow extra healing energies to seep through which could then harnessed by the healer.

Much of the work done by the healers I met on my own journeys was done outside in nature, if at all possible. A common belief across informants is that the natural world itself is able to add its own magical energies to the work being performed. By choosing sites where these energies are at their highest, the healer is said to be able to heal in a much deeper and more effective way. For example, one healer I met would always take her clients out to a small cavern on her property for their sessions. Her gift was "singing in the spirit," as she told me, meaning she had the ability to weave magical energies using her voice alone. She told me the darkness of the cavern allowed her clients to sit with themselves, free from distractions, and that her "spirit songs" were much more effective there than anywhere else.

Other healers might use certain natural springs or even individual trees in their work, believing these features are able to play their own part in the healing work at hand. Another healer I met who healed by passing eggs along the skin of her clients to suck out the illness taught me to always find an "egg tree" to use with this specific work. At the end of her cleansing rituals she would always throw the egg that sucked out her client's illness against one specific tree. She explained to me that she had made a deal with the tree that if it cleansed the illness from her clients, she would make sure it was taken care of and not chopped down or trimmed.

The belief in these site-specific sources of magical energies connects the paths of modern healers back to the roots of Ozark healing itself. This work is centered on the relationship between the individual and the natural world. For many Ozarkers, this is a deep connection to all living and even nonliving things in nature. Trees, bushes, rocks, rivers, caverns, and even cliffsides are still given individual characteristics and even names, like the bluff I heard one old-timer refer to as Ol' Grandad, or the ancient oak tree one healer I met named Albert. For many Ozarkers the natural world isn't dead, like many city folk would have you believe, but alive with spirits and personalities that are as diverse as our own. This belief harkens back to the animism of our ancestors who saw an individual spirit in every aspect of nature. I'm happy to say this connection is still alive within many Ozarkers today, not just our healers.

SPIRIT HELPERS

Ozark healing rituals are often performed with the help of entities from the otherworld such as spirit guides, ancestral ghosts, and even the Little People. Just like working with specific numbers, timings, zodiac days, and even sacred sites in nature can add extra amounts of magical energies to the work being done, having a spirit helper can also make a ritual much more powerful. Traditionally, more conservative Ozarkers would have looked at this work with great suspicion, as the spirit world was most often associated with witchcraft and bedevilment.

Healers who did work with helpers would have had to hide their practices with the utmost secrecy. Often petitioning prayers to these helpers would have been said under the healer's breath or behind their hand so that their client wouldn't be able to hear their words. This technique was often said to avoid inadvertently passing your power onto someone else, but it was also an effective way of hiding what was being said itself.

In the old Ozarks, spirit helpers often went hand in hand with a witch's familiar, said to be an animal or spirit who assisted the witch in their infernal rites and who could be sent out to spy on people in the community. These associations likely did develop from encounters with healers who had spirit helpers that they named as a part of their work. The associations with witchcraft came from a misunderstanding on the part of the community about the nature of the spirit world and the work of the healer in general. Many great healers in the Ozarks lost their lives to this strict view of the spirit world.

Traditionally, spirit helpers have taken the form of familiar animals like cats, dogs, squirrels, rabbits, crows, owls, and—in several folktales—even a spectral turkey. Some healers still identify their household pets as helping spirits or familiars. More commonly, spirit helpers for modern practitioners embody the word spirit more than for our ancestors. For some they might appear as ancestral guides, for others as radiant angels. Some healers even claim to be able to see the Little People and use their vast healing knowledge in their own work. For many of the healers I've met over the years, the form of their spirit helpers is seen as a deeply personal part of their calling and work.

The forms these helpers might take are as varied as stories about how they were found. In many of the stories, as with those involving the Little People, healers have claimed they were out in the wilderness when they first encountered their spirit helpers. Often this encounter is also when transferal of power occurs. The entity (or entities) who makes a connection with the individual often follows them home to help them in their future work. In this way, the spirits of nature have an invested interest in seeing the power they gave put to good use instead of being abused. Spirit helpers often also take the form of ancestral guides, or the spirits of departed relatives. These sometimes visit the healer in visions and dreams, or in the case of those with the second sight, they might appear at any time to offer healing knowledge and other useful information. One healer I met worked with many members of his departed family tree, a great number of which he had never met. He told me his house felt crowded with all the spirits gathered for a visit, but that having them there was a great comfort. The healer said one spirit in particular, a great-grandpa, was useful in finding lost items. He told me that whenever he lost his car keys he'd ask the spirit for help and would quickly find them.

The healer utilizes their spirit helper in a number of ways. For some, the spirit might bring rituals or lessons on how to make certain amulets to the healer in visions and dreams. For others, the spirit is able to add some of their own power to the work being done. Others are simply guides, or spirits that walk with the healer and offer them useful advice, omens of future events, and even words of warning. These guiding spirits might become fierce protectors for their wards, especially those who work against spirits of darkness and other malign entities.

Not all of the Ozark healers I've met have these spirit helpers, but there are many who do. It's not seen as a requirement of the work, but it is viewed as a possible side effect of how the healer gained their power in the first place. For those who were passed their gift by an elder, the spirit of this teacher often becomes a guide for them after dying. In other cases, the healer might not work with spirit helpers at all, but instead choose to view their own power as sufficient for all the work that they want to perform.

REVERSING AND SENDING BACK

Negating and reversing malign magic is an important aspect of the healing process both in the old Ozarks and today. These rituals usually involve specific healing methods like counting down, tying off, or cutting, all of which will be mentioned in greater detail in chapter 7. A specialized technique seen both today and in the folkloric record is washing a client's clothes. In this ritual, a healer will have their client take off all their clothes. Then they will boil the clothes outside, often with cleansing herbs like yarrow or horsemint (*Monarda* spp.), in the case of influences coming from haints and other spirits. After the clothes are boiled, the healer will dry them out and return them to their client, now free of the curse.

Often reversing a spell employs the same ingredients that the sender used in their work in the first place. For instance, a person might go to a healer convinced they've been cursed by one of their enemies. The healer then performs a diagnosis, and if the cause of the trouble is determined to have a magical source, they might divine for the ingredients the malign worker used to create their sympathetic connection with the victim. These items are often personal effects stolen from the victim themselves, like hair, fingernail clippings, spit, urine, etc. Other times it's a scrap of clothing, a photo, or even just the victim's full name written on a scrap of paper. Because the healer isn't able to steal away these items themselves, they might instead use a verbal charm or prayer that directly targets the items they divined and calls upon magical forces to destroy the ingredients, rendering the work null. Often these magical forces come in the form of the healer's spirit helpers, but they can also be other entities like angels, ancestral spirits, or even divine figures like saints.

In their diagnosis, a healer might find that a person's hair was snipped one Sunday morning in church as they snoozed away in the pew. In their reversing ritual, the healer would then use a prayer to call upon a certain magical force—a bird for instance, since birds are small and are known to collect items like hair. These spirit birds would be sent out to collect their client's personal effects and bring them back to the healer. Sometimes these spirits are told to bring the item into a sealed container. Bottles of water are sometimes used, as are eggs, walnuts, and acorns. During the ritual, the healer determines at a certain point that the sealed object is now filled with these personal effects, and it is burned or buried to safely destroy the items. Often the containers will undergo a specific transformation when they are filled. In one ritual I observed, the healer used a clear glass bottle filled with spring water, then corked. At a certain point in their ritual, the healer shook up the bottle and the water inside immediately turned black. This was a sign that it had been filled with the "spirits of the ingredients used," as I was told.

Returning malign magic back to its sender often also involves the healer performing certain rituals in the reverse order that someone cursing their victim might use. For example, through the diagnosis process a healer might determine that someone had been using a spite doll on their client. The healer would then make a spite doll of their own, dressed in scraps of their client's clothing and usually filled with identifying ingredients like hair and nail clippings. The belief common to the majority of healers I've met who work in this way is the more personal the items, the better and stronger the sympathetic connection. Once the doll is made, the healer sits with their clients and disassembles the entire doll piece by piece, throwing each item into an open fire. In one such ritual I observed, the healer began the process with the words, "As I take apart this spite doll, so too may the spite doll used on _____ be taken apart, burned, and destroyed." After all the parts are destroyed, the doll itself is burned.

Once the malign magic is successfully reversed, it's believed that the original sender themselves will suffer in some way. For some healers, the thought is that the sender of the curse will now receive the same curse they tried to send out. Others hold to the idea that the sender will somehow be worse off than their victim. In all cases, when work is reversed and not just sent off into the west, for instance (the location of evil and sickness in Ozark folklore), it's believed that the sender will suffer some sort of retribution for what they did.

What I've found most interesting has been talking to individuals who themselves work with cursing or hexing other people. Some work in a way that might exempt them from such retribution, as with one healer who often kept around a "spite list" with individuals locally and abroad whom she felt needed someone working against them. She told me that she always adds a certain protecting clause to her spells by saying, "Let _____ be broken, bound, and brought down, only as much as Fate will allow." In this way, she viewed the work she did as assisting Fate, not trying to work against it, which many view is the source of great trouble. By adding her clause, this healer was able to still seek the revenge she wanted, but was still able to work within a sense of universal order.

RITUAL PURIFICATION

Cleansing illnesses or curses off of the body has traditionally come in a number of ways. In the old Ozarks, a healer might simply take their patient out to a river and wash the sickness off their body. In other cases, a person might be smoked or fumigated using burning plants like red cedar or asafetida. These cleanses were often used on their own or alongside other rituals and remedies. Even today, cleansing work is usually performed when a specific illness or curse can't be identified. This ritualistic purification is sometimes seen as general upkeep for the spiritual body.

WATER

Water is highly symbolic of cleansing and purification. In the old Ozarks, this association was often traced back to the sacrament of baptism, as well as the Cherokee ritual of "going to water."[27] Ozark healers still see water as a medium by which all evil can be removed and carried away. For this reason, moving bodies of water like rivers and streams are most often used in the Ozarks.

A simple ritual might involve a person wading out into a stream, facing so that the water is flowing away from them, then dunking themselves under three times. This ritual act not only washes off the evil or illness, it also allows it to be carried away by the current of the water. The most auspicious setting would be a river flowing west, since that is often seen as the location of sickness and evil. Ritualistic washing is almost always performed at dawn, symbolizing renewal and rebirth. In this way, a client might be reborn in a very similar way as the first time: cold, wet, and with a new light shining ahead.

---

27. Kilpatrick, "'Going to the Water.'"

Moving water is sometimes replicated with a bath. In this sense, though, a bath doesn't mean a soak, but the pouring of water over the head, usually three or seven times. This not only connects with the idea of moving water, but also the downward direction of cleansing and purification. Sometimes a bowl is placed at the client's feet before being washed with the water. The water collected in the bowl is then taken out and poured onto a tree or into a stream, thereby creating the sympathetic connection, either with the strength of a growing plant or the cleansing nature of moving water.

Besides a simple bath of spring water, healers often add certain plants associated with cleansing and healing. These include native plants like mountain mint (*Pycnanthemum* spp.) and sassafras leaves, both associated with cleansing and purification, as well as horsemint, used in baths to cleanse off the influence of ghosts and often used after funerals or wakes. Non-native plant species like mint (*Mentha* spp.), rosemary (*Salvia rosmarinus*), or basil (*Ocimum basilicum*) are also commonly used today for their aromatic and cleansing properties.

Historically, Protestant churches in the Ozarks often baptized congregants many times throughout their lives. For these churches, baptism was seen as a cleansing act as well as a reconnection to the Divine. Usually annual revivals were paired with a mass baptism of anyone who asked to be dunked. This interesting tradition likely has ancient origins in both indigenous traditions of water purification as well as European connections to the healing power of sacred springs and rivers.

SMOKE

Frequent fumigation of a house has been used in the Ozarks past and present as a way of cleansing not only bad air and illness, but also lingering evil influences, ghosts, and other magical conditions. Our native red cedar is the most popular fumigation plant by far, used in all cases of sickness or malign magic. In the old days it was either thrown directly into the fireplace and left to smolder or put into a hot cast-iron skillet and then carried around the house. This skillet method was also frequently used with other fumigants like sulfur powder and asafetida. Today these noxious odors are left for work outdoors alone, replaced by more fragrant smokes for use inside the home.

Tobacco, both *Nicotiana tabacum* and *N. rustica*, is the second most widely used smoke for clearing out negative spiritual or magical influences. Traditionally, shredded tobacco was put on hot coals carried in a big metal spoon, or smoked directly from a pipe, then blown around an area. In the old Ozarks, tobacco was particularly powerful against witches "lighting," or landing, on the roof of the house in order to creep inside and suck the life out of a person who was sick in bed. In a protective ritual, the healer would go outside the cabin, light up a pipe, then walk around the entire house three times, clockwise, while smoking. After finishing their rounds, the healer would return to the front door and listen for tokens or omens that would show whether the witch had departed or was still hanging around. If the omens were negative, the ritual would be repeated until the signs were seen as being more favorable or until the healer opted for a stronger rite.

A simplified version of this ritual can be found amongst Ozark healers today. In this modern example, the healer still circles the house while smoking tobacco, but the belief surrounding the practice has changed. Healers no longer believe that a physical witch is perched on the roof waiting to sneak inside the house; instead, they take the ritual as a way of guarding from any evil influence that might try and affect the work being done.

RELEASING

Herbal purgatives and emetics include plants that induce a purgative action, either through vomiting (emetics) or through defecation (laxatives). Most have heard of the vomit-inducing ipecac plant, but in the Ozarks there are other naturally occurring purgatives that were used in both naturopathic and magical ways. In the old Ozarks, purgatives were commonly prescribed by yarb doctors to cure stubborn illnesses or to release curses. There were also some purgatives that were seasonal. Sassafras, for example, is still taken as a spring tonic by Ozarkers. Part of its action is as a mild laxative, so it helped release built-up toxins in hillfolk after a winter spent eating food poor in vitamins and minerals. Diuretics like dandelion and Solomon's seal (*Polygonatum biflorum*) roots were also popular in the springtime for this same reason. While hillfolk have a much better diet these days, many people still swear by the ability of sassafras tea in the springtime as a ward against illnesses throughout the year.

The main action of all purgatives, be they emetics or laxatives, is the action of releasing built up toxins from the body. This action can be applied to known medical conditions like worms or constipation, but purgatives can also take on a spiritual quality of releasing curses, hexes, or stored up negative influences. One such magical illness that still uses purging as a cure is live things, mentioned in chapter 2. This has traditionally been seen as the worst of all Ozark curses and manifests as the constant sensation of crawling insects or other creatures on the inside of a person's body. The most effective cure is a magical purgative cooked up by someone with the gift. One healer I spoke to said she hardly ever saw cases of live things anymore, but when she did she would always warn her clients not to seek their own releasing medicines.

"People would go off to the drug store and pick up a strong laxative or some ipecac thinking that would clear 'em out," she said. "This just emaciates the body though. Magical cures from a healer are the only way to get rid of 'em.'"

Historically these cures would have used strong emetics and laxatives, like mayapple (*Podophyllum peltatum*) root or black gum (*Nyssa sylvatica*) tree bark. Both mayapple and black gum are highly poisonous in large doses and are not recommended for modern use. Today healers will make emetic concoctions using Indian tobacco (*Lobelia inflata*) leaves or Culver's root (*Veronicastrum virginicum*), but even these produce many unpleasant side effects.

Other magical illnesses don't require such extreme purging. Some healers I've met specialize in releasing rituals and will use them for almost every physical or magical illness they might encounter. One healer prescribed sassafras tea, a mild laxative, as a panacea or cure-all for everything from fevers to hexes. He would always pair drinking the tea and washing in a river. Sometimes the client would make themselves vomit into the river to complete the releasing action of the ritual. Other times they were just washed, letting the sassafras cleanse them on the inside and the healer cleanse them on the outside.

In my own work, I repeat a practice I observed from several other healers. In this ritual, I take my client out to a river and give them an infusion of native plants like mountain mint, horsemint, and sassafras to help cushion their stomach and fortify their body. Then I give them a large amount of water to drink followed by some more tea made from sassafras and slippery elm (*Ulmus rubra*) bark, which has a slimy texture to it and usually induces the person to vomit into the river. Afterward, I wash them in the current, then give more of the native plant infusion to help calm their stomach.

While releasing with purgative plants has traditionally been a part of Ozark folk healing and magic, I want to warn my readers that these are powerful medicines and should only be used with a professional healer who specializes in this practice. As I said before, some of the plants that were traditionally taken as medicines are actually poisonous in large doses. Another example is pokeweed, which is poisonous unless cooked properly. Traditionally, pokeweed greens are boiled, then strained and boiled again in a fresh pot of water. Some people do this a third time; others strain the greens and then fry them in a skillet like spinach or kale. The toxins are very potent unless cooked properly. Historically, pokeweed has anti-inflammatory and mild laxative qualities, as well as a host of contained minerals and vitamins. The root should never be used, as it is highly poisonous when consumed. If pokeweed root is handled with bare skin, it can cause severe contact dermatitis.

All purgatives must be given in the proper dosage by a trained healer—otherwise you risk doing serious harm to yourself or your client. These plant medicines were traditionally accompanied by several days of dieting, rituals, and prayers in order to strengthen the body for the purging rite. This form of healing is almost always done before dawn (because of its associations with renewal and rebirth), and always during the waning moon so that the influence of whatever the client is purging out will grow weaker and weaker. A final ritual is sometimes performed on the new moon itself to kill the evil once and for all.

Chapter 6

HERBAL
HEALING
METHODS

THE MEDICINAL BENEFIT OF PLANTS within the Ozark *materia medica* is derived from a combination of folk belief and a good amount of trial and error. The vast amount of this plant knowledge would have originally come from interactions with the indigenous peoples of the Southeast. This exchange of knowledge would have been essential for Europeans trying to survive in the New World. Many brought plants of their own with them from their homelands. Some of these include species like plantain (*Plantago major*) and mullein (*Verbascum thapsus*), both of which are still an essential part of herbal knowledge to this day. The European settlers would have also brought certain herbal preparation methods with them, namely tincturing, whereby a plant extract is made by soaking plant matter in alcohol for a certain amount of time. Tincturing allowed herbalists to create much stronger plant remedies, and it preserved the plants they grew and harvested in the wild for much longer than drying.

Herbal healing methods in the Ozarks were traditionally derived from methods brought to the New World by the European settlers. This system of medicine would have been based on a simplified or "folk" version of systems like the theory of four humors, spread through the common folk by famous herbalists like Nicholas Culpeper, who wrote and practiced herbal medicine in the mid-seventeenth century. In my own journeys I've even met herbalists who swear by *Culpeper's Complete Herbal*, still in print to this day. It's also not uncommon to see herbalists today who have trained in non-Western medical systems like traditional Chinese medicine or Ayurveda. While these systems might influence the healer's diagnostics and application of medicines in the modern Ozarks, historically the work of the yarb doctor or mountain herbalist was done on an empirical basis. Medicinal formulas and individual ingredients were often memorized based upon their observable effect on the body, not because they fit into a larger system of medical theory.

HERBAL PREPARATIONS

In Ozark traditional herbalism, plants and remedies were noted by healers for their qualities, often derived from the four humors system, which divided medicines into hot vs. cold and wet vs. dry. Illnesses were seen as also seen as having these qualities, and the remedies to cure them were seen in plants of a nature opposite to that of the illness itself. Plants that have a hot or spicy taste, like spicebush, might be used to cure a winter cold. It was generally thought that a cold illness could be remedied by heating the body. Likewise, an illness caused by an excess of heat in the body, like a fever, might be cured using what we call diaphoretics today, or medicines that make the body sweat. This sweating action was believed to help the body cool off, thereby eliminating the fever. Other methods often included soaking in a cold stream or using plants with a cold nature, like one of the mountain mint (*Pycnanthemum*) varieties.

Ozark herbalists today take their methods of healing from a wide variety of sources. You are just as likely to see an herbalist working in the old four humors systems as you are to see someone trained in chemistry who studies the pharmacological value of native plant chemical compounds. Ozark herbalism isn't such a uniform system as it once was. Some might see this as a shameful degradation of a traditional culture, but I view it as moving and evolving with the times. There were traditional herbal medicines used by hillfolk of the past that have no place in the modern world today. Bloodroot, for example, was traditionally used as a topical remedy that removed warts, blemishes, and even skin cancer. The active chemical compound in bloodroot is sanguinarine, which is known to kill animal cells. Because of this, applying bloodroot to the skin may destroy tissue and lead to the formation of a large scab called an eschar. Applying escharotic chemicals like bloodroot to the skin can be disfiguring; used orally, it can lead to the development of premalignant oral leukoplakia, which can develop into oral cancer. For this reason, most modern herbalists don't recommend using bloodroot in any application.

There are many other examples of plants used in the past that I wouldn't recommend for today. Some of the older healers I've met are fiercely stubborn about using the old remedies in their work, but the vast majority hold to the belief that remedies must always be able to evolve and grow. Or, as one healer told me, "You've got to move with the times." Healers today recognize that they are oftentimes no longer the preferred source of medicine for most people in their communities. Folk healers are being held to higher and higher standards by the wider medical world, and for good reason. Just having a little plant knowledge isn't enough. One herbalist I met early on in my travels told me she always kept around a book of herbal contraindications and drug interactions because she found so many of the people she was seeing were on some kind of medication. This is an excellent example of how we can bring folk practices into the modern world. As healers, we have a responsibility not to leave our clients worse off than when they arrived. Ensuring this might mean keeping up to date not only with our own practices, but with the wider medical world as well.

Ozark herbalism is still based on a number of traditional herbal preparation methods. Most would have come from herbal traditions of Europe, but there are a few that would have been introduced into the practice by indigenous peoples of the New World, like scratching. These herbal preparation methods were traditionally paired with prayers and other verbal charms for added magical benefit. Oftentimes a simple ritual, like stirring an infusion three or seven times, might also have been used to allow the healer to connect spiritually or magically to the remedy. Today, many herbalists still employ these same preparation methods in their work, along with many more rites, rituals, spells, prayers, songs, and other magical healing practices as well.

POULTICES

Poultices have their origins in the earliest form of herbal healing. The preparation is simple: it requires only the wetting and crushing of certain medicinal plant matter, then an application directly to the skin. The contained chemical compounds are introduced into the body through contact with an open wound or through the pores. This system of healing is not only quick and effective, but it can also be employed by those with only the most rudimentary healing knowledge.

In the Ozarks, poultices are often moistened with oils or fats to help keep the skin from drying out. It's also common to see poultices—or "wraps," as they are sometimes called—used on a wound or skin complaint for several days, with both the herbal matter and bandaging replaced each day. It is thought that certain herbs and minerals have a "drawing" action, so leaving the poultice on the skin of the client helps aid with drawing out any infection or "pizon" (poison) from the wound.

Poultice making is one of the simplest preparations we have. First, take a small amount of an herbal plant mixture and place it in the center of a square of cheesecloth, gauze, or clean fabric. The size of the poultice will correspond to the size of the affected area of skin. Tie the bundle up so that no plant matter will fall out. Then wet the bundle with hot water, oil, or even alcohol, so long as it is at least 40 percent ABV. Knead the bundle until the plant matter is soft and you begin to see green liquid coming through the cloth. Apply the bundle to the affected area. The poultice can be held to the skin by hand, or you can tie a length of cloth or gauze around the bundle and the affected area. Traditional poultices and wraps included plants like plantain for bug bites, stings, and rashes; yarrow to staunch bleeding; and camphor for chest colds and coughs. Other poultice plants used by modern herbalists include:

- Arnica (*Arnica montana*) for burns, cuts, bruises, aches, pains, and inflammation. Please note this is for external use only—the plant is toxic if taken internally.
- Calendula (*Calendula officinalis*) for sunburns, burns, poison ivy, rashes, and bug bites.
- Cayenne pepper (*Capsicum annuum*) for inflammation and arthritis.
- Comfrey (*Symphytum officinale*) is wonderful for all dermatological needs.
- Yarrow (*Achillea millefolium*) for topical analgesic and antiseptic properties. It also helps staunch blood.

A traditional and related method is called a compress. In this method, herbal matter is steeped in hot water until a strong tea, or an infusion, is made. Gauze or cloth is then soaked in the warm, strained tea and applied to the affected area.

INFUSIONS AND DECOCTIONS

Infusions and decoctions are both words for what most might just call "making tea." For an infusion, you allow plant matter, fresh or dried, to steep in water that is just under boiling temperature for a certain amount of time. This steeping process draws out the essential oils, pigments, and other medicinal chemical compounds into the water. The liquid can then be taken internally or used as a wash on the skin. The medicinal compounds are absorbed into the body through the mouth and stomach (or through the pores, in the case of washes). Infusions are most suited for light plant material like leaves, flowers, and stems, or what is generally called foliage by botanists. Spicebush tea, which uses the leaves of *Lindera benzoin* to aid with high blood pressure and sinus congestion, is a good example of an infusion.

The process for a decoction is similar, except this time the plant matter is boiled in water for a certain amount of time. Decoctions are normally used for harder plant material like roots, bark, and fruits. The boiling process would normally destroy the sensitive essential oils in foliage matter, but with decoctions the boiling is needed to help break through the hard plant material and release the medicinal compounds. A common Ozark decoction is sassafras tea, made from boiling the roots of the sassafras tree. Sassafras tea has long been used as a spring tonic in the Ozarks, drank every day for a few weeks, usually in April, in order to strengthen the liver and digestive system, thereby protecting from future illnesses throughtout the year.

TINCTURES

Tincturing originated with the first distillation of alcohol by Babylonians of Mesopotamia around 1200 BCE.[28] It's truly a work of alchemy, although it's easily done at home by amateur herbalists and professionals alike. The basic process involves leaving plant matter, fresh or dried, in alcohol for a certain amount of time so as to draw out the contained chemical compounds and essential oils. In the past these compounds were often seen as the "spirit" of the plant, and the alcohol was seen as the solvent, drawing out this spirit. After a given amount of time, usually a couple weeks, the alcohol is then strained off and kept in dark glass bottles or in a cabinet away from sunlight. This process is assuming you already have a source of alcohol to begin with. Many hillfolk in the old Ozarks—and a few still today—use their own homemade moonshine for their tinctures, while others choose store-bought.

A few questions might arise when looking at the tincturing process for the first time; one might be whether dried or fresh plant matter is best. Usually with infusions and decoctions, either will work just fine, but with tinctures, dry material seems to do better than fresh. This is partly because in dry material, the essential oils are already somewhat stabilized and thus easier to extract.

Alcohol is the other key component, and I've found it doesn't really matter what alcohol you use; the only thing that makes a difference is the ABV, alcohol by volume, or the percent of the alcohol you use. Most modern herbalists use a 40 percent ABV, which includes most vodkas, gins, whiskeys, tequilas, brandy, etc. It's easily available and gives you a lot

28. Levey, *Chemistry and Chemical Technology*, 36.

of flavor palettes to choose from. The higher-percentage alcohols make for a foul-tasting tincture, but they are useful when trying to extract from barks, roots, resins, and other hard plant material. I find using 40 percent ABV and just leaving it longer also does the trick.

The basic process of tincturing is simple once you've procured your dried plant material and alcohol. For a quart of herbal tincture, take a quart glass jar and fill it one-quarter full of dried and crushed herbal matter. This can be a combination of different medicinal plants; just make sure it doesn't exceed one-half of the jar. Then fill the jar the rest of the way up with your alcohol, seal, and put it away in a dark cabinet. From time to time, make sure you shake your jar to ensure the maximum amount of herbal matter is exposed to the alcohol solvent. Leave your jar for two to three weeks, then strain, bottle, and keep in a dark, cool location. I use my tinctures for up to a year before discarding.

Tinctures are a much more concentrated herbal product than infusions and decoctions, so caution should always be taken with dosage. Most tinctures are taken in small doses, maybe ten to thirty drops depending upon the plant used, two to three times a day or as recommended by an herbalist. An herbal professional should always be consulted before adding any herbal medicines into your daily routine.

A widely used bitters, or tincture, mentioned by Vance Randolph is a spring tonic made from letting wild cherry (*Prunus serotina*) bark and dried cherries soak in a bottle of whiskey, then straining off the liquid after a few weeks.[29] Bitters are a common remedy in the Ozarks, used mostly for stomach complaints, but also employed for colds and fevers. They are also popular spring tonics. The bitter goes back to European herbalism, where bitter plants were used in after-dinner cordials for settling the stomach and preventing gas. The association of bitter-tasting plants and medicine transferred to the Ozarks, where granny women and yarb doctors are known to spout wisdom like, "If it tastes bad, it must be good for ya!"

SALVES AND OILS

Herbal salves and oils are created for the purpose of absorbing plant chemicals through the pores in the skin. In the Ozarks, salves made from animal fats mixed with medicinal plants were once popular remedies for aiding conditions like sunburn, dermatitis, poison ivy rash, insect bites/stings, coughs, colds, and for sore or aching muscles.

---

29.   Randolph, *Ozark Magic and Folklore*, 106.

Salves and oils are created using the same methods, the only difference being that salves are generally solid at room temperature and oils remain as a liquid. Both involve the slow heating of plant material in a fat or oil for a certain amount of time. The low temperature is necessary so as to not burn the volatile oils inside the plants. After the prescribed amount of time, the oil or liquid fat is strained off. When using animal fats, no wax needs to be added to stiffen the product, as fats normally solidify on their own at room temperature. For salves using oil, a little beeswax is usually added to help the solidifying process.

For making salves and oils at home, I've found a Crock-Pot to be a wonderful tool. It allows the oils and fats to heat gently, thereby avoiding scorching or burning the herbal matter. For a simple salve or oil, first choose the medicinal plant or plants you want to use. A good salve for many different skin problems uses the common weed called plantain. Take thirty-two ounces of solid fat or one quart of liquid oil and add it to your Crock-Pot. For fats, leave on high until the fat is completely melted, then turn to low. For oils, leave your Crock-Pot on high until warm, then turn to low. Add half a cup of dried and crushed plantain leaves. Other medicinal herbs can be added as well, just don't exceed half a cup of dried plant matter. Next, cover with a lid and let sit on low for two to three hours. Turn off your Crock-Pot and let the oil come to room temperature. When using fats, or if you want a liquid oil, you can strain and jar or bottle the product right from the Crock-Pot (once cooled sufficiently, of course). If you're making a salve using an oil, you'll need to stiffen the mixture using one-quarter to one-half cup grated beeswax, depending upon how stiff you want the salve to be. I usually add only a little beeswax and then test how stiff it becomes. If it's not stiff enough, I'll take and heat the salve to liquid again and add some more wax. When sealed properly in airtight jars or bottles, salves and oils generally have a shelf life of up to a year before the fats turn rancid. A small amount of vitamin E oil can be added before bottling to act as a preservative, although oils that are made for internal use should leave out the vitamin E oil.

A number of fats and oils are now used throughout the Ozarks in herbal salve making. These include oils of sweet almond, grapeseed, coconut, sunflower, etc. The specific oils themselves also have an added benefit for the skin. For example, sweet almond oil is often used in massage because of its quick absorption into the skin. Traditionally, yarb doctors and granny women exclusively used animal fats because of their availability. The most common fats were pig lard and beef tallow because these two animals were most widely used as livestock on Ozark farms. Other fats were used for their own medicinal benefit. Skunk oil, for instance, which holds some of the well-known skunk smell, was rendered and used as a salve on the chest to help relieve congestion. Rattlesnake oil, oil rendered from rattlesnake meat, was often used as a salve on sore muscles or arthritis. The thought was that trace amounts of the venom still remained in the fat and imparted an analgesic, pain-relieving quality to the salve. Other fats often used include possum grease, goose grease, owl grease, and even grease from a church bell, used to help with earaches and believed to make the deaf hear again.

SCRATCHING

Scratching the skin as a form of healing seems to have come into Ozark culture mostly by way of the Cherokee while the two cultures were still interacting in the Appalachian Mountain region, although other indigenous peoples besides the Cherokee have also employed the method. These indigenous peoples predominantly used scratching as a form of healing for arthritis and rheumatism.[30] In the Ozarks, folk healers used scratching for a variety of illnesses, not just arthritis. Power doctors also used this technique in their magical work when "bleeding" out evil spirits or curses from their client's body.

Greenbrier (*Smilax rotundifolia*) was the preferred scratcher in the Ozarks, but common blackberry (*Rubus allegheniensis*) brambles were also sometimes used. A healer would cut off a piece of the greenbrier vine or blackberry cane with plenty of thorns and then allow it to dry out for a few days. Sometimes they would twist the vine into a knot; then the two lengths left outside the knot were stripped of thorns and tied together for a handle. The healer would then run the section of vine across their client's skin multiple times until bleeding occurred. Scratching was generally performed in a downward manner so as to draw the illness or pain away from the body. Herbal poultices, washes, or powders were then rubbed into the scratches. In the case of poultices, the herbal material might be left on the scratched area for a longer amount of time.

Other materials were also used to scratch the skin. Other thorns, like those from the wild pear (*Pyrus* spp.) or honey locust (*Gleditsia triacanthos*) tree, were used. Healers also employed old plastic or wooden combs as a way of repurposing household items for a magical purpose.

Scratching is rare to see in the Ozarks today. I only met one healer who used the method, and his preferred illness was rheumatism. He showed me the tool he used, a carved scratcher made from wood. It looked like a comb, only the teeth were sharpened

---

30. Kilpatrick and Kilpatrick, "Notebook of a Cherokee Shaman."

a lot more and they were set wider apart than a regular comb. He told me that in cases of arthritis and rheumatism, scratching was the best remedy, second only to being stung on the joint by a bee, another technique widely used in the old Ozarks as a cure for similar afflictions. The idea in both cases, according to my informant, was that the sudden rush of blood to the area affected by the scratching or stinging somehow alleviated the pain caused by the arthritis, at least temporarily.

SMOKING

Smoking herbal medicines was another popular form of healing in the Ozarks, mostly because smoking tobacco was already so common. There were traditionally a couple different methods used. The first was smoking the herbal matter directly from a pipe or cigarette. This was popularly done with mullein, widely believed to loosen phlegm and relieve chest congestion. Often plants like mullein were rolled into long cigars using cornhusks and then smoked—sometimes even recreationally, along with other plants like rabbit tobacco (*Pseudognaphalium obtusifolium*), especially when stores of regular tobacco were low. Herbal material was also sometimes mixed with tobacco to aid with healing and keeping the body healthy year-round.

The other method used involved burning the plant matter in a closed room and inhaling the smoke. This same method was also widely used with steam by pouring boiling water over dry plant matter or tinctures and then inhaling the vapors. Both smoke and steam were used with highly aromatic plants like red cedar, mountain mint, lemon beebalm, or dittany (*Cunila origanoides*).

The purpose of smoke was seen as being twofold: first, it introduced the plant chemicals into the body through inhalation. Second, it physically destroyed the illness or "bad air" that was thought to be around or inside the body. This bad air was effectively purged by frequent fumigations of the house and the body itself. Common fumigants were plants with strong or pungent scents, as it was believed that strong smells would destroy or repel illness. These plants included red cedar, camphor, sulfur, and asafetida.

Smoking plants today is common as a tobacco substitute. Plants like mullein and rabbit tobacco are still used as smoking plants for both healing and magical purposes. While fumigation of the home might have been a way of destroying illness in the old Ozarks, today the majority of healers view the smoke of certain sacred plants like red cedar to be a way of dispelling evil influences, malign magic, and other bad energies. Frequent smoking—or "smudging," as many people still refer to it—is common amongst modern healers as part of both their client ritual sessions and their own daily routine.

Chapter 7

MAGICAL
HEALING
METHODS

AS WAS TALKED ABOUT IN chapter 3, the magical methods of healing illustrated in this chapter are based almost entirely upon the law of sympathy, or sympathetic magic. This form of traditional healing is then performed based on the method of "like cures like" (law of similarity) through the "rock breaks scissors" method, where one magical element might overcome another, or by creating a magical connection between doctor and client that can then be manipulated (law of contact). Many of the following methods are still in use today, and I will indicate those practices I've encountered with modern Ozark healers. Traditionally, these healing methods would have almost always been a closely guarded secret. This was first and foremost to ensure the safety of the healer, who would often be held in great suspicion by the community because of their work with magic and ritual. The power doctor who primarily used the following methods in their work would have tread a fine line between being an acceptable member of the community and being suspected of witchcraft. But, speaking of witchcraft, this was another reason for a healer's secrecy. It was believed by healers that the witch was able to use these same methods not to heal, but to magically harm others.

One example that I heard from an old story goes something like this. A certain power doctor decided to use the plugging method to cure a client. In this ritual, the doctor first went out to the woods and bored a hole in the trunk of a pawpaw tree, called a witch tree in the Ozarks. He then stuffed a few hairs, fingernail clippings, and a scrap of clothing from his client into the hole and sealed it up using a plug carved from a branch of the same tree. This created a connection between the client and the tree so that as the tree grew strong, so too would the client. The power doctor made double sure to perform this ritual away from the sight of others because it was generally known by healers that if a witch spied on the work, they could take out the plug and use the hair and fingernails in their own malign work. In this way, the work of the witch was often seen as a mirror image of that of the healer. The techniques each used might be much the same, but the outcomes and purposes were very different.

BLACK MAGIC

Black magic, or left-handed work, was traditionally believed to focus on stealing or the harming, maiming, or killing of a person. It was seen as being strictly the domain of the witch, although someone who worked with "both hands," or who worked apart from the stricter views of good and evil, might have used many of the same magical methods. In the end, it all came down to how the community as a whole viewed the person in question. If they were someone of great importance or someone very pious, they were able to get away with many of the more questionable methods of magic than someone of a much lower status. For this reason, black magic has often been associated with the magic of the poor and the minority. While many of the healers I've met today have opted to get rid of the archaic terms of "black" and "white" magic, it was still an important part of the hillfolk's worldview in the old Ozarks.

In the Ozarks, all magic—whether it was healing work or witchcraft—was believed to be based on creating a magical, or sympathetic, connection between the worker and the person being worked on, also called the target. This connection was often seen as an invisible cord between a person and their client or a witch and their victim. It was generally believed that a witch formed this powerful connection with a victim by possessing certain identifying ingredients, often from their body. Examples of these include: clothing, hair, nail clippings, spit, semen, urine, and feces. Other identifying ingredients used if these couldn't be obtained included the victim's name or even their shadow. Because these items were procured in a number of ways, some people began flushing nail clippings or hair down the toilet instead of throwing them in the trash, just in case there was a witch lurking nearby.

The methods of left-handed magic are so numerous they could fill an entire book on their own. Many of these methods were detailed alongside their right-handed counterparts in the previous chapter. In the next few sections I'd like to detail some practices and ingredients that were solely used by the witches of Ozarks past. Most of the methods offered to us today come from folklore sources written for entertainment, predominantly by nonmagical practitioners. Many of these stories portray witches as creatures from a fantasy novel, able to fly through the air, breathe underwater, or walk through walls. With this in mind, I sifted through many of the witch stories I collected on my journeys and pulled out some of the rituals and ingredients I believe might have actually stemmed from practices of real-world magical workers.

MALIGN INGREDIENTS

In Ozark folklore, witchcraft has long been associated with plant poisons, noxious chemicals, and all things to do with death and decay. Some ingredients were seen as being very specific to the work of the witch—graveyard dirt, for example, which refers to dirt that was taken from off of a grave. Graves of certain individuals were often used in particular work; dirt from the shared graves of a married couple might be used for love magic, or dirt from the grave of a murderer might be taken for darker spells. This work bears some similarity to Southern Conjure and Hoodoo and represents one of the several crossovers with this tradition, although by and large Ozark folk magic hasn't retained many of the elements some might associate with Hoodoo.

Poisonous plants like jimsonweed (*Datura stramonium*) and black nightshade (*Solanum americanum*) were often used medicinally in the Ozarks by yarb doctors, but because of their associations with death and poison, they were also associated with witchcraft. Most of the poisons employed by the witch were from the family *Solanaceae*, or the nightshades, as they are better known. Many varieties would have been known throughout Europe, like henbane (*Hyoscyamus niger*), belladonna (*Atropa belladonna*), and European black nightshade (*Solanum nigrum*). These too carry with them centuries of associations with witchcraft and the dark arts. According to Ozark folklore, witches used these poisonous plants in two similar methods: as a divinatory device for allowing them to spy on their victims, or to separate their spirit from their body in order to magically travel to where their victim resided. They were also used as a physical and magical poison in direct work against a victim.

As a divinatory compound, the nightshades were often eaten, drank, or smoked by Ozark witches in order to receive visions of their victim's whereabouts. These visions often came in the form of dreams or trances that followed consumption of the plant; they were seen as a way for the witch to keep track of any healing work they might need to reverse.

In this way, the altered state of consciousness created by the plants themselves often acted as a method of divination alongside reading tarot cards or using dowsing. In this state, witches were said to be able to invade victims' dreams or to use them as a mule to ride to their meetings in the woods.

Witches also used these poisons in direct curses against a victim. Jimsonweed seeds, for example, were ground down and mixed with graveyard dirt and then left in a person's path so that as they stepped through the material, they picked up the curse on their feet. While poisons might not have always been used in a physical way, such as depositing the material into someone's food, they were commonly used in work to magically poison someone, usually resulting in an odd sickness or wasting away with seemingly no physical connection. The witch often worked this magic using a spite doll created for their victim that they would then stuff with poisonous plants and other noxious ingredients.

Ozark folklore also includes many stories about a deadly weapon called a witch bullet. These were described as small balls of human hair, wax, poisonous plants, and sometimes graveyard dirt that were rolled up and then thrown or shot at a victim using a section of hollow river cane as a blowgun. It was widely believed that if one of these bullets hit a person, they were as deadly as an actual gunshot wound, sometimes worse because they also brought with them a terrible wasting sickness. Several storytellers have told me the only way to counter the power of a witch bullet is through reversing the work by finding and dismantling the malign object itself.

FOOTPRINTS, SHADOWS, AND NAMES

As with other identifying ingredients like hair or nail clippings, stealing footprints, shadows, and names was seen as a way for a witch to create the sympathetic connection needed to do their malign work. In some cases, a witch could carefully dig up a person's footprint out of the dirt and take it home to manipulate. Other times this act was performed in a more roundabout way by taking a nail and driving it into a footprint, then removing the nail and taking that home as a way of identifying the person who left it behind. One way for a witch master to quickly break the sympathetic connection between a witch and their victim was by burning red cedar on a witch's footprint. This was said to burn the witch's feet, thereby distracting them from their evil work. A witch master could also use the nail method on a witch themselves by driving a nail into the witch's footprint and taking the nail home with them to manipulate. Sometimes it was thought that driving the nail in the footprint alone was enough to cause the witch great pain and keep them from their work.

Stealing a person's shadow or name was another example of this work. The method used to collect a person's shadow is similar to the nail in the footprint. The idea was that a witch could sneak behind their victim and drive a nail into their shadow without them seeing it happen. Then they would pull the nail out of the ground along with their victim's shadow, or spirit. Another method involved opening a bottle in someone's shadow and then sealing it again, thereby magically trapping their shadow for use later on. It was said to be near impossible for a person to counter this rite, apart from taking back their nail or collecting the witch's shadow as a bargaining chip.

In many folk traditions around the world, names are considered a vital part of a person's essence and identity. In Ozark witchcraft, names weren't as good as hair or other personal effects, but they were still used as identifying ingredients in malign work. Capturing a person's name was as simple as writing their name down on a piece of paper, or better yet, stealing away the person's signature. There was also a belief in the Ozarks that if you heard someone call your name but you couldn't see them, you should never answer, as it could be a witch that would steal your name if you replied.

WITCH ANIMALS

In the old stories, Ozark witches were known to be powerful shape-shifters. They were often seen to take the form of the dreaded booger. The word originates from the same source as the English word "bogey," as in "bogeyman" or "boogieman." Although sometimes considered a cryptid or mountain monster alongside others like the gowrow (a giant lizard that stalks through Ozark caverns), most often the booger is seen as a witch in disguise. A booger can take the shape of any animal, forming names like booger-dog, booger-owl, or even booger-turkey. The defining characteristic of any booger is that they will always be black in color, both the body and the eyes, they will have an unnaturally long life, and they'll nearly always be able to dodge any bullet that isn't made of silver. To this day, there are stories of hunters going into the woods during the dark hours of the morning, waiting for a deer or rabbit, when all of a sudden a big black dog will appear. In tales told about "green," or inexperienced, hunters, the storyteller will add that they took a shot at the animal, but despite the quality of the hunter's aim (or the closeness of the prey), it always missed its target. Sometimes the outcome is deadlier. There are stories warning against taking a shot at any solid black animal; your gun could backfire and put out your eye.

For the witch, the main purpose of transforming into a booger was to spy on potential victims. Booger-rabbits, though, were also believed to be able to steal milk from cows and goats for use in their own home by sucking it out of their udders. After finishing, the booger-rabbit carried the milk back home, transformed into their human form, and spit the milk back into a pail. The booger was also sometimes a stronger shape for the witch. There are a number of stories where a witch attacks a hunter in the form of a giant black wolf and the hunter has to fight it off, narrowly escaping death. In most of the old tales, though, the witch prefers to take the form of a booger-owl or booger-crow in order to sit up in a tree and spy on the work of their rivals or the suffering of their victims.

Traditionally, other animals were associated with witchcraft in their natural forms. For example the owl, especially the screech owl, was a well-known "witch bird," said to fore-tell the hearer's death with its screaming. Crows were also considered spies of witches, as were black cats, rats, weasels, toads, raccoons, possums, rattlesnakes, otters, woodpeckers, redbirds, blue jays, moles, foxes, and albino animals, especially the albino deer. In this way, nearly the entire forest could be associated with witchcraft at times. This often hearkens back to the idea of the forest as the domain of the witch and other wild, untamed creatures. In most stories, the cabin represented safety supreme, while the rest of the land was almost certainly bound and determined to kill you.

Animals with specific magical qualities included the owl and crow, mentioned already, as well as the woodpecker, often called "Lord God almighty" in the old Ozarks because of its imposing size. The woodpecker was considered a magical bird and was sometimes thought to be a witch in its own respect. One tale that was told to me goes something like this:

> *Once there was an old woman living up on a mountain who kept to herself mostly. The folks down in town all called her "Red Cap" because of the little crimson hat she always wore. Some people visited her when they were sick because everyone around knew she could work the plants and heal any disease. One day some of the leaders in town turned against Red Cap, saying she was a witch who had cursed their cows to give blood instead of milk. Under the shadow of darkness, they crept up the mountain and grabbed the old woman right out of her bed. They took her down to the center of town, where they'd built up a big pile of logs and branches. They tied her to a post and set the bonfire ablaze. As folks screamed out the worst curses they could think of, much to the displeasure of the local preacher, the flames grew higher and higher around poor Red Cap. "Save yourself!" the townsfolk cackled and laughed. But the old woman just smiled, and in a flash of smoke she flew up high into the trees, escaping certain death.*

After that, no one in town talked about what they'd done, for fear or some secret
shame. From then on the friends of Red Cap always took comfort when they saw a
redheaded woodpecker light in a tree above them, and her enemies saw the presence of
the bird as a sign that harm would surely befall them soon.

Blue jays have also traditionally had a strong association with malign magic, in particular the devil. It was often said that if you saw a blue jay picking up sticks on a Friday, they were heading out to help stoke the fires of Hell. This association likely comes from the bird being a trickster. They are also often aggressive to other birds as well as humankind.

Albino animals were also looked at with great suspicion and were considered to be bad omens of death and disease. These all-white animals were considered otherworldly because of their color, and they were often seen as creatures with one foot in the world of the living and the other in the world of spirits. There's a legendary creature in the Ozarks called the snawfus, a large albino stag with blooming branches instead of antlers, who flies through the treetops creating the fog. Stories involving the snawfus, even in modern variations, present the animal as a portent that witchcraft or malign magic is at hand.

WORKING WITH BOTH HANDS

Magical workers and healers today exist in much more of a gray area, choosing to disregard or reinterpret the more conservative notions of good and evil. The magical work itself can still be looked at as a mirror image between what are traditionally referred to as "right hand" and "left hand" work. These associations have had a long history in Western esotericism and occult practices. Right-handed work encompasses work traditionally held by the healer in the community. These methods include anything that heals, protects, or helps a client be rid of sickness or evil. This work also encompasses rituals for good luck, love, and prosperity, generally considered working on the side of good. Left-handed work included the work of the witch, or what the old Ozark society labeled as a witch. These rituals sought to curse, hex, and harm the community as a whole or to use methods to improve the witch at the detriment of another, as with examples of milk-stealing rituals. Even today, left-handed work still holds many of the much older warnings, as with one healer I met who claimed that working negatively against another could come with its own set of curses upon the head of the practitioner.

METHOD	RIGHT-HAND PRACTICES	LEFT-HAND PRACTICES
Cutting	Cutting illness off of a person; cutting off a curse; cutting ties with a toxic person; separating a client from an abuser	Cutting ties in a relationship; cutting up a good marriage; cutting up someone's money or luck; cutting to harm
Notching	Cutting notches in a healthy tree so that as the tree heals, so too will the client	Cutting notches in a dead or dying tree so that as the tree grows weaker, so too will the client
Tying Off	Tying an illness to a tree; tying the worker to their client	Attaching a hex or malign ingredients to someone's house; tying the worker to their victim
Knotting	Tying prayer knots around the client; blowing and catching prayers or healing words in knots	Blowing and catching curses in knots that are then attached to a victim's body or house
Sweeping	Sweeping as a way of cleaning evil or curses; sweeping evil out of a house; sweeping illness or curses off the body of a client	Sweeping good luck out of a house; sweeping illness and evil into a place; sweeping between a happy couple to separate them
Counting Down	Reducing an illness; reducing the influence of a curse; lessening the power of a malign worker	Invading a victim's dreams; reducing a victim's life force or energy; reducing good luck
Plugging	Connecting a client's health to the growth of a living tree	Connecting a victim's degradation to a dying tree
Nailing	Nailing illness to a tree or certain spot; laying an evil spirit; nailing sickness at a crossroads; nailing good luck and protection to a house	Nailing a victim's spirit to a tree/spot; nailing evil influences into a person or place; magically harming a victim with a spite doll
Animal Parts	Naming an animal part to connect it to a corresponding body part on the client; using for symbolic value, e.g., claws for scratching out illness	Naming an animal part to connect it to a corresponding body part on the victim; using for symbolic values, e.g., claws and teeth to hurt victim
Burying	Burying healing items to be cleansed by the earth	Burying cursing items to be walked over by victim
Planting	Placing a client's name in the roots of a plant so as to connect the client's improving health to the growing process	Placing a victim's name in the roots of a dying plant so as to weaken a victim; planting a victim's name with a poisonous plant like jimsonweed

While people in the old Ozarks might have held to this more rigid separation of magical energies, the majority of informants I've encountered today prefer to look at magic as being essentially neutral in its most natural form, and it's solely up to the one gifted with the power to choose which hand to work with. Several healers I spoke with chose to refer to their own practices as "working with both hands" or being magically ambidextrous. Modern practitioners often view their work as being much freer than that of their Ozark ancestors in that they are able to choose for themselves whether working with the right or left hand is appropriate for the given situation. Amongst the majority of gifted individuals I met on my travels, there is no longer a stigma surrounding these left-handed practices, so long as they are aimed at retribution and not just harming for the sake of harming. This rule seems to be universal amongst those I met—or at least, that is what was said out in the open. Their own private practices might reflect a very different worldview.

CUTTING

Methods for magical cutting involve a knife or an axe and, as with other tools, these are almost always items already found around the house that have been repurposed for use in certain rituals. Even today, Ozark healers don't normally fashion specialized tools for their work unless they have very good reasons in mind. For example, some healers who work with the otherworld might be told by one of their spirit helpers to make a specialized tool for their work.

RIGHT-HAND PRACTICES

A healer might use these sharp tools to magically cut an illness, curse, or other harmful condition off of their client. In most cases, the knife never comes into actual contact with the physical body and is often only held up while the healer recites a certain prayer. Other times, the knife might be drawn through the client's aura a couple inches away from the physical body. As mentioned in chapter 5, the direction of the cutting is very important; cutting for a client is always done in the downward direction, which has traditional associations of removal and cleansing.

Scissors are often used to snip or cut the invisible lines connecting a healer's client to the worker who cursed them. I heard a healer one time mention a pair of silver scissors that her mentor used for this purpose. Other healers might use ordinary scissors or knives for the same purpose. The belief is that a sympathetic connection made between a person and the one who cursed them will remain intact until it severs or dissipates with time. Healers often choose to sever these cords first before any other healing rituals are performed.

Magical cutting need not be only for healing a client's physical body, though. Often these cutting rituals are employed in order to magically separate two or more people from each other. Take, for instance, the case of a toxic relationship or abusive marriage. A healer who works with other rituals besides just healing might use the cutting method here as well. In one ritual I observed, two beeswax taper candles were each carved with the name of one of the individuals in the relationship. Then the candles were lit and tied together with a string. The worker then took an ordinary kitchen knife and held it in the flame of the candle bearing her client's name, or the one who was going to come out of the relationship happier than ever, I was told. When the blade was red hot along the edge, the worker took the knife and cut it through the string connecting the two candles, magically cutting the two individuals apart.

In cases without a specific client, knives are sometimes driven into the ground to cut apart an oncoming storm. Likewise, axes are used to chop tornados and harmful winds in half so that they will disperse.

LEFT-HAND PRACTICES

Cutting as a way of cursing or hexing a person can be as simple as cutting up their name or photo while reciting a certain verse. If more personal items are available, like clothes, hair, or nail clippings, these too can be cut or chopped up with an axe as a form of cursing. One worker I met said she would write down a few names on individual pieces of paper every night, then put them in an empty coffee can she kept around for this exact purpose. The names were people who had wronged her in life, enemies of her clients, terrible people from around the world whom she saw pop up on the news, etc. They were all bad sorts, generally. Every month on the full moon, she'd take the slips of paper out to an old stump she used as a chopping block and hack them all to pieces with an axe. When she was done, she'd just let pieces of paper rot into the ground. I asked the woman if she had any words she said when she was chopping and she just laughed and replied, "I say a lot of words, but none fit for repeating in polite conversations."

As with the ritual of the two candles, a worker can use similar methods to cut apart a happy marriage, or to separate a person from their good luck and prosperity. In one rite I observed, the worker tied a lock of someone's hair into a knot at the end of a length of string and tied up a wad of dollar bills mixed with herbal matter at the opposite end. They placed the string across a stump outside of their house and then whispered some words and chopped the string in half with an axe. The half with the hair was buried under the chopping block. The worker told me it would "always weigh them down." Then the worker took the half tied around the money and hung it up above their front door inside the house. The outcome of the ritual as it was described to me was to siphon the luck and prosperity from one of the worker's local gambling rivals.

NOTCHING

Notching is a very similar method to cutting. In its most basic form, notching is connecting a client or victim to the life force of a living tree. In healing rituals, the growing, surviving tree is often invoked so that as the notches grow back together, so too will the client recover from their sickness or cursed condition. On the other hand, a person might also connect a victim to the notches made in dead wood or on a tree that is then intentionally killed so that the dying of the tree is connected to the failing health of the victim.

RIGHT-HAND PRACTICES

For those working with the right hand, a notching ritual might involve a certain set of steps that must be adhered to in perfect order. First, the healer takes their client out to a certain tree, usually a witch tree like pawpaw. They then situate their client so that their back is against the trunk of the tree. The healer takes out a knife or axe and cuts notches into the bark, usually three, right above the client's head. Then the client is pulled away without looking at the notches. The healer recites a prayer; usually something like, "As this tree heals, may my client heal." This connects the life force of the tree to the client so that as the notches heal, so too will the client heal from their illness. Finally, the client is led away from the tree and back home. An important step in the process that is often overlooked by a novice healer is turning and walking away without so much as glancing back at the tree. It's believed that by looking back—especially if it's the client who looks back—the work will be nullified. For this reason, the trees used for notching rituals are often chosen because of their isolation in the deep woods, far away from any human eyes.

In the old days, notching rituals were also commonly used for warts as well. In this ritual, a notch was made in the bark of a witch tree for each wart a person had. The belief was that as the notches healed, so too would the warts disappear. This form of notching could be performed by the afflicted themselves or by a wart charmer who specialized in the ritual.

LEFT-HAND PRACTICES

Just like the notching ritual of the healer connects their client to the growth and strength of a living tree, in a more malign magical act, a worker might induce the degradation of a person's health by connecting them to a dead or dying tree. In these rituals, the person being cursed is hardly ever present themselves. The sympathetic connection between the work and the victim is created using items connected to the person's physical body like hair, nail clippings, saliva, etc. When these items can't be obtained, a photo or just a name is sometimes used. The ritual itself is simple. It involves the worker going out to the woods and finding a certain tree to use. Instead of the tree being picked for its health or strong appearance, the tree chosen is usually one that is severely wounded, dying, or already dead. The worker will then wrap all of the items connected to their victim into a small bundle and nail it to the tree, sometimes using coffin nails to connect the work to the dead.

Coffin nails were obtained by actually digging up a coffin, or in other cases, nails might be secreted out of the coffin before burial. Today, most people get their nails from third-party individuals who claim to have taken them directly from the source, although this is rarely verifiable.

In the ritual I once observed, the worker notched a tree with a cursing number like nine or thirteen, then whispered a different curse for each notch they carved into the bark of the tree. The ritual ended with the worker saying, "As this tree dies and rots away, so too will _____ rot away!" Then we turned around and walked back home without looking back.

TYING OFF

String or rope is used in rituals where an illness might need to be magically tied, bound, or caught by the healer. Traditionally these rituals would have used whatever string could be found around the house, but today, modern healers sometimes incorporate colored strings where each color represents a different category of work; for example, white for healing, pink or red for love, green for money and prosperity, and black for working with more malign magic. A few healers I met even enjoyed spinning their own spools of magical string to be used for the purpose of healing alone.

RIGHT-HAND PRACTICES

In some cases, tying off rituals involve work similar to that of notching. A healer takes a client out to a certain auspicious tree, situates their back against the trunk, ties a string around both them and the tree, usually three times, then knots it off. The healer then says some words like, "Illness, stay behind where you are tied." The client is lowered out of the string and taken away from the spot without looking back. The string is left around the trunk of the tree along with the illness or curse that was removed.

In cases of severe magical illness or goomering, a healer might use the law of contact to help in their work. For this rite, a healer ties a string between them and their client. This creates a sympathetic connection between the two individuals. Any additional rituals from the healer are said to go straight through the magical string and to their client. This connection is severed with one cut of a knife after the healing work is done, and the cord is usually burned so that the healer's enemies won't be able to find the string and cause any trouble for their client.

LEFT-HAND PRACTICES

String can also be used in work to curse or harm other people. In these rituals, malign ingredients or amulets might be tied to someone's house in order to magically attach a curse to the inhabitants. In one case I observed, a local practitioner folded up three coffin nails into a black cloth and tied the top closed. Then we went to the house of a local man who I learned had been an ex of the worker, and a terrible one at that. Under the cover of night, we stalked into the backyard and over to a huge oak tree on the edge of the property. My companion took her bag and nailed it to the back of the tree so that it couldn't be seen from the house or most of the yard. I asked about the purpose of the coffin nails and she answered that the nails were to "keep him in place in his suffering," and that coffin nails, because they had "touched death," were considered much more powerful for cursing work than ordinary varieties.

Making a sympathetic connection between two people using string can be used for cursing work as well as healing. In this case, a worker might make a spite doll of the one they're wanting to curse, making sure to include some identifying ingredients like hair or a photo of the person. Then they tie a string around themselves, usually around the waist, and tie the other end to the spite doll. With a few magic words, the connection is made. The worker is able to send their curses directly through the string to their victim. While this technique is still used by many of the workers I've met, most prefer to create the sympathetic connection using the identifying ingredients alone and feel that the string is useful in circumstances when only a photo or name is available.

KNOTTING

String can also be used in conjunction with knotting rituals for magically catching illnesses, prayers, and curses. The basic ritual involves the worker partially tying a knot in a length of string, then blowing or whispering through the knot. Just before they run out of breath, they pull the knot closed, thereby magically catching what was sent through the knot.

RIGHT-HAND PRACTICES

In the case of prayers and verbal charms, the healer will first cut a length of string (sometimes measured out by the height of the client or how big they are around the waist). Sometimes this length is tripled to connect it to the magical nature of the triad. They then form a single knot, but before they pull it tight, they blow or whisper a prayer through the knot, making sure to catch the last word of the prayer by pulling the knot closed. In Ozark folk belief, the breath of the healer is often seen as containing certain inherent magical qualities. For this reason, many healers will simply blow through their knots, or in other rituals, they might blow across a burn or blow into the mouth of their client in order to pass along their healing energies. The knotting ritual is repeated a certain number of times, usually seven, nine, or twelve. When the healer reaches the prescribed number of knots, they wrap or tie the string around their client's wrist or waist to sympathetically connect the knots directly to the afflicted person. They will wear this string until it naturally falls off. Then it is buried, burned, or thrown into a moving body of water as a way of finally releasing what was troubling them.

LEFT-HAND PRACTICES

Workers might make themselves a more malign version of this charm by blowing curses or hexes through the knots and then hiding the entire string in their victim's house, car, or under their victim's bed. A storyteller once told me he found one of these "hex strings," as he called them, hidden away inside his bottle of shampoo. "An' I reckon that's what happened to all my hair!" he laughed, rubbing his bald head.

I once had a chance to talk to a healer about these knotting rituals; she did some left-handed work on the side. She explained that even a healer could mistakenly send a curse to their client by blowing their own anger or frustration through the knot. "What's on the brain and heart are blown through the knot," she said, warning me to keep my intentions as pure as possible during my own knotting rituals. She went on to say that she did occasionally make hex strings with curses blown and caught by the knots. She always used thirteen knots because of the number's unlucky associations. The curses she blew were mostly benign by my standards; they included hexes meant for abusive husbands, local criminals, and the occasional client who spread false rumors about her. I asked how she got her hex strings to their intended victims and she said she always hung her strings in the branches of a big elm tree in her backyard, letting the wind carry the curses away.

SWEEPING

Healing methods using brooms make a sympathetic connection between the action of sweeping or dusting the home and sweeping illnesses or hexes from a person's body. Traditionally, Ozark healers would use an ordinary broom found in their house and repurposed for healing rituals. Occasionally a specialized feather duster might be kept around for use in magical work. Brooms and dusters made with the feathers of a black chicken or rooster were considered the most powerful by hillfolk, as the color black was traditionally associated with evil and illness. For this reason, a black feather duster was believed to be able to sweep off an illness without retaining any of it in its feathers, almost like water off a duck's back.

Today, brooms and dusters come in a variety of shapes and sizes depending upon the healer. Most people keep their magical brooms separate from the ones they use to clean their house. Some even have homemade brooms consecrated for the specific purposes of cleansing and healing. Several healers I met still make use of a black feather duster in their work, considering it easier to handle when working with a client. Dusters are often used on the body, whereas a broom might be used for sweeping out or cleansing a house or other location.

Small brooms are also sometimes made from bundles of herbs, as seen in the *limpias* of Curanderismo, a folk healing based in a mixture of traditions originating from southern Europe and Latin America. These herb bundles are often picked for their fragrant quality and the specific magical associations of the plants used. In the Ozarks, these plants are mostly grown at home and include non-native plant varieties like rosemary, basil, lemon balm, and peppermint (*Mentha* × *piperita*). On rare occasions, native Ozark plants like horsemint, dittany, or mountain mint might be added to these bundles.

RIGHT-HAND PRACTICES

Just as you sweep up dust off the floor, a healer can use a broom to sweep illness off their client. In most cases, a client will stand or lie down and the healer will sweep their body from head to toe a specific number of times with a feather duster or bundle of herbs. Sometimes the healer will then sweep the illness out the front door or into a dustpan that they will then throw outside.

This kind of magical sweeping can be done for a place as well. Just like the healer might sweep their house clean of dirt, they can use a broom or duster along with certain prayers or charms to sweep a place clean of sickness or evil influences. In Ozark folklore it's believed that you should never sweep at night, magical or mundane. This time is tradition- ally associated with spirits, so sweeping dust or illness out the front door after dusk means tossing dirt right into the faces of your departed loved ones.

LEFT-HAND PRACTICES

Because left-handed magic is often seen as a mirror image of the right-handed path, rituals often involve performing acts that are opposite those for healing. In the case of sweeping, just like a healer might sweep illness or evil from a home, a left-handed worker can sweep it into the house itself. In these rituals, a worker might first put down certain left-handed ingredients like dirt taken from a graveyard, especially off a criminal's plot, mix it with the seeds or ground up foliage of poisonous plants like jimsonweed or black nightshade, and place it near the house of their enemy. Then, using a broom specifically for this more malign work, they will sweep these ingredients toward the home, ending only after the dust has touched its walls. One healer told me it's even better if you can sweep the "bad stuff" onto their front door so that they will have to walk through it and track it into their house. This bad stuff is believed to carry with it whatever curses the worker decided to add to it. Some ingredients, like graveyard dirt, come with their own set of associations based upon where it was collected. Dirt from the grave of a thief, for example, might be used to curse a home's security, or dirt from someone who died of an illness could be used to make the inhabitants of the house sick.

Sometimes this kind of sweeping is done from inside the house itself. One worker told me a story about her own experience with this kind of cursing. She was mostly a healer, and she even told me she later regretted the curse that she cast on her enemy. As the story went, she cleaned houses for a living, and one particular family was the kind of wealthy that meant they thought they could treat people however they wanted. One day as my informant was cleaning, the lady of the house tore into her about some little issue that was easily fixable. The worker had to fight back tears as the woman left in a huff. She decided this would be her last day cleaning that house. She took up her broom and swept all through the house, upstairs and down, but instead of cleaning up dirt, she said she was "sweeping up all their good luck, fortune, and prosperity." When she reached the front door, she spit on the pile of dust and swept it out of the house and into the driveway. She left shortly after and never returned to the home. When I asked what happened to the family, she just frowned and replied, "I don't have the heart to say."

COUNTING DOWN

Counting down rituals aim at magically reducing the influence of an illness or curse that is afflicting their client. Traditionally, both healers and the laity alike performed these rituals. In many cases it was believed that one just had to know the words and ritual in order to perform a successful reduction. Accompanying rituals often involve getting rid of or casting away certain objects. A popular choice is using matches, which are lit and then thrown into a glass of water as the verbal charm is recited. Other traditional items include small pebbles, bits of bread, or kernels of corn.

RIGHT-HAND PRACTICES

Traditionally, verbal charms alone are used by Ozark healers as a way of reducing a client's illness. One such charm I've heard used by several Ozark healers is:

> "Sickness you are not ten, you are nine!
> You are not nine, you are eight!
> You are not eight, you are seven!
> You are not seven, you are six!
> You are not six, you are five!
> You are not five, you are four!
> You are not four, you are three!
> You are not three, you are two!
> You are not two, you are one!
> You are not one, you are none!"

The idea is that by the time the charm is over, the illness identified by the healer will be reduced completely. Sometimes a verbal charm like this is accompanied by a simple ritual, usually involving matches or corn. In the case of corn, a healer takes a small bag filled with kernels of corn to a stream at dawn. They then recite the charm and, with each reduction, a few kernels are thrown into the stream. By the last reduction, the entire bag of corn should be completely gone. Similarly, the healer might use ten matches. With each reduction, the healer will light a match and then toss it into a stream, mug of water, or even a toilet bowl. After the last match is lit, the sickness is successfully reduced to nothing.

Similar counting down rituals were also used with warts. The number of warts were counted and then reduced with a charm like the one provided, starting with how many warts the person had. Corn was sometimes used in these rituals. A single kernel would be rubbed on a single wart, then the total number of warts was counted and reduced using a verbal charm. As each number was reduced, a kernel of corn would be thrown to a flock of chickens to eat. It was generally believed that the chickens themselves couldn't get the warts, but by eating the corn, the warts would disappear off the one who performed the ritual.

LEFT-HAND PRACTICES

There's a uniquely modern variation on the reducing method used by magical workers today to cross great distances while in their spirit form. This is generally called astral projection today, although in the old Ozarks it was sometimes just called "out wandering." This wordage was often used in witch stories, intended to say that the villain of the story was wandering in their spirit form, not in their physical body. Astral projection, or wandering, most often involves the worker falling into a trance where their spirit is able to separate itself from the body and fly to various locations across the universe. Sometimes this work is used to spy on individuals or invade their dreams while they are sleeping. In order to ease the journey, the worker might perform a ritual of reducing the miles to their target using a verbal charm like this one of my own creation:

> "(Name) you're not five miles, you're four!
> You're not four miles, you're three!
> You're not three miles, you're two!
> You're not two miles, you're one!
> You're not one mile, I'm here!"

As with charms for reducing illness, by the time the worker has successfully reduced the final number of miles, their spirit has been magically transported to their intended location.

Similarly, reduction charms and rituals can be used to reduce not only sickness, but also someone's good luck, money, love, prosperity, virility, and any other aspect of a person's life that someone might want to curse. One ritual I was taught by an Ozark healer was for reducing the power and influence of an enemy, but it can easily be applied to a multitude of situations. First, you inscribe the full name of the one you're cursing on a beeswax taper using a needle or nail. Then, you stick seven new needles into the side of the taper from top to bottom, with equal amounts of space in between each one. Every time you stick in a needle say, "Bit by bit, (name), your power is gone." At midnight on a Tuesday (connecting to the power of Mars, who rules over wrath and vengeance), light the taper and let it burn all the way down. As each needle falls out of the burning candle, the power of your target will slowly fade away.

PLUGGING

Plugging rituals were already mentioned at the beginning of this chapter, but to explain again, this is a ritual where the healer will take their client out to a tree, bore a hole in the trunk at the client's height, fill the hole with some of their client's hair, fingernails, or clothing, then close it all with a plug made from a branch of the same tree. This connects the client's healing process to the health of the tree itself.

RIGHT-HAND PRACTICES

The healer connects a client's health to the growth of a living tree. A hole is drilled into a strong tree, then items from the individual are left inside and plugged up using wax and wood from the same tree.

LEFT-HAND PRACTICES

Like the example above, a worker can connect a victim's degradation to a dying tree. The method is the same apart from choosing the tree itself; trees that are dying or dead might be used instead of a strong or living tree.

NAILING

Rituals of magically nailing involve using a nail to attach illness or curses to a certain tree or spot, the idea behind this work being that the nail, consecrated for its specific purpose, acts as a tool of binding, much like wooden plugs or string.

Nails used in these magical rituals come in many forms. Most use ordinary household nails, but there's a common belief today that they have to be new nails, from a package freshly opened just before the ritual. Others prefer to use coffin nails, believed to hold extra power because of their proximity to the spirit world. Thorns are also sometimes used in place of nails, particularly the robust thorns of the honey locust tree. From my observation, thorns and nails are used interchangeably depending solely upon the preference of the worker themselves; the one exception is in rituals where materials are physically stabbed or hung onto the thorns of a honey locust tree.

RIGHT-HAND PRACTICES

Nailing is often used for a similar purpose as methods of plugging. In these rituals, a scrap of a client's clothes might be nailed to a tree instead of plugged, thereby connecting their healing to the strength of the tree. Sometimes the healer might name a nail after their client and drive it into a tree or into the ground, which has associations with cleansing and purification.

A particularly deadly kind of nail used by right- and left-handed workers alike is the coffin nail. These are nails that were once used to hold the lid of a coffin down, and it's generally believed that in order for the nails to be effective, they must have been used for this purpose at one time. There are many old tales about Ozark healers sending out their apprentices on dark winter nights to gather up such materials that they themselves no longer wanted to risk collecting.

Coffin nails in particular were once commonly used in curing warts. Healers would prick a wart with a coffin nail until it bled, then drive the nail into a tree or into the ground. This ritual was also sometimes performed using thorns, believed to be nails provided by nature.

Certain workers with the second sight, or those who can see spirits, might use coffin nails in laying rituals. Laying refers to the calming of a spirit entity. It can also mean the trapping or binding of a spirit to a certain spot, but most of the time this form of laying is only used to keep an unruly or angry haint nailed down temporarily until they've calmed themselves. In laying rituals, the healer will take some coffin nails, usually three, and go to a place where there's a poltergeist or other angry haint. Then, using specific prayers or charms, they'll nail the spirit to a spot by physically nailing the coffin nails into the ground or floorboards of a house in the form of a triangle. The spirit is then said to be bound to that spot until at least one of the nails is removed.

LEFT-HAND PRACTICES

Nailing rituals can be used in cases of hexing and harming as well. For example, a worker might perform a ritual whereby their enemy is bound from working against them. In this case, a worker would first make a spite doll in the form of their enemy, making sure to include identifying ingredients like hair or nail clippings. Then the arms and legs of the doll are folded in on themselves and a nail is driven straight through and into the trunk of a tree. This is particularly effective when paired with the words, "(Name)! I bind you from doing harm to me until this tree rots away!" The only way for your enemy to escape is by finding and removing the nail, or they have to wait until the tree rots away.

Similar to the laying of a ghost, a left-handed worker is able to trap the spirit of a person using a nail. This is particularly important as an identifying ingredient in rituals targeting a specific individual when no hair, nail clippings, or other personal effects can be found. The ritual is simple. First the worker will take a nail—usually a new nail, but some might prefer a coffin nail—and sneak up behind the person they wish to capture without them noticing. The nail is then driven into the ground, through this person's shadow. This is usually done with the foot so as to not draw unwanted attention. The nail is then pulled up—along with a piece of the person's spirit. This nail can be used as an identifying ingredient in any ritual.

Other workers might find it useful to capture a wrathful haint or other spirit for future use. In one complicated ritual I observed, the worker had a piece of plywood about two square feet and about an inch thick. Three coffin nails had already been driven into three of the corners, leaving the fourth open.

At midnight, I followed the worker out to a barn that was widely considered by the community to be haunted. We cleared a space on the floor of the barn and the worker nailed the board into the floor using the three nails in the three corners. He called this contraption his "spirit trap" and claimed it had worked on many occasions for him.

We waited in the barn for a sign of activity. My informant took a creaking sound in the rafters to be a sign that the spirit was present. While we waited, he said a few prayers to draw the spirit toward the trap while holding a coffin nail in his left hand and a hammer in his right. As his praying intensified in volume, I suddenly heard a loud popping sound directly in the center of the board nailed into the floor of the barn. The man next to me lunged forward and smacked the fourth nail into the open corner of the board in three strikes of the hammer. Being sensitive to the spirit world myself, I could immediately feel a difference in the energy of the place. It somehow felt lighter, calmer than before.

My informant was overjoyed and set to gently prying the board out of the barn floor without moving any of the four nails stuck through the plywood square. I asked him what he could do with the board and he just smiled and told me that the ghost was now trapped in the wood, bound there by the four coffin nails, and all he had to do was take the trap elsewhere, remove a single nail, and the haint would be released. I reckoned by the tone of his voice he meant to let this spirit go in someone's home as a sort of ghostly weapon.

ANIMAL PARTS

Bones, teeth, claws, wings, and feathers of wild and domesticated animals were traditionally used by healers and other magical practitioners throughout the Ozarks. I'd reckon this category yields almost half of the physical objects used in magical work alone. It was seen as being easier to create a sympathetic connection with a client when you had similar bones to match. For example, animal teeth, particularly those from animals that were considered voracious eaters like the pig or boar, were used sympathetically to help heal toothaches. There was a specific ritual for the same purpose. A person was sent out into a field to find the jaw of a bull or cow. They then picked up the jaw with their own teeth, dropped it back on the ground, and walked home without looking back. In another variation, the person held the bone in their mouth and flung it behind them into the woods. After this, their toothache would be soothed.

Traditionally, bones and other animal parts were never picked at random, but instead were chosen because they symbolically represented a body part to be healed or some ritual work. For example, claws from various animals were used in a number of ways. A healer could use a claw to magically scratch their enemies or even to dig for a hidden secret that someone refused to divulge. The uses of these animal parts were taken primarily from observing the actions of the animals themselves; these actions were then used in a symbolic or magical way.

Today, there are still workers who use certain animal parts in their practice. Others view it as a cruel and archaic practice that has no place in modern healing work. I will say, those healers I've personally met who still use certain animal parts in their work have harvested said parts in an ethical way. Most of them have come from animals killed on the roads, animals that have died on the farm, or animals that were legally hunted. Even the old-timers, often viewed as being backward and stubborn in their traditional ways, have shared with me their beliefs on protecting the Ozark wilderness and would never dream of killing an animal needlessly. The rites and rituals of the old Ozarks that involved any animal cruelty have—as far as I can tell—been left in the past, where they belong.

RIGHT-HAND PRACTICES

There are more examples of sympathetic magic using animal parts than I can successfully list here. I will mention a few though that I've seen firsthand.

A healer wanting to cure their client's eyesight—both physical and spiritual—might name the eyes of an animal that's known for its vision for their client. They would choose animals like certain birds or a fox, put the eyes in a jar or bottle with plants that strengthen vision, and finally bury the lot in the ground. In this way, the vision of their client was said to be improved by not only the magical connection to the animal's eyes and the plants used, but also the cleansing power of the earth itself.

If a client has a bad heart, a healer might take the heart of an animal and store it with plants like bloodroot and violets, both said to be good for the blood and the heart. Sometimes these items are kept in glass or clay jars so that the work will continue for a while. (I've even seen glass beer bottles used for this purpose.) Other times the items are stored in cloth bags and then buried or hung in trees to naturally fade away.

Animal parts are often used in conjunction with other items too, like nails for instance. In one old ritual recorded in folktales, a certain goomer doctor wanted to get back at a witch that did harm to one of their clients, so they got a goat heart, named it for the witch, then said something like, "As this heart rots, let the heart of the witch rot!" The goomer doctor then pierced it with three coffin nails and left it hanging in their chimney. (In other stories, the heart is buried in the ground in a little wooden coffin.) As the story went, the witch slowly faded away as their heart was burned up in the chimney.

Chicken feet, especially those from the black chicken, are used in similar ways as they are in Southern Hoodoo or Conjure: a healer uses them to magically "scratch" an illness out of their client's body. In other cases, a claw might be worn by someone looking to scratch up a new lover. The idea is that as a chicken scratches in the yard looking for food, so too can the foot be used to magically "scratch up" other things like love and healing.

LEFT-HAND PRACTICES

Someone working with the more malign side of magic might also name certain animal parts for a person they wish to manipulate or harm. For example, they might name an animal heart for their victim and then cover it in salt so that it dries out, or they might destroy it in a fire. Another method might be naming goat testicles for the testicles of an enemy and leaving them underneath a waterfall, thereby causing the victim a great amount of pain. The most effective of these curses involve other sympathetic connections as well, like including the fingernails, hair, or clothes of the victim in the animal part being manipulated.

BURYING

Burying items or ingredients in the ground has traditionally been done for one of two reasons. First, the ground itself is seen as a place of cleansing and renewal. Patients who are severely cursed are even sometimes buried in the ground for a certain amount of time and then brought back up, leaving the curse behind. Certain items associated with healing work might be buried for a client in order to add the healing power of the earth to the ritual. Second, the ground is often used to conceal certain cursed items so that as a person walks over the area, they will pick up the curse on their feet.

RIGHT-HAND PRACTICES

Because the earth is seen as a purifying location, burying objects or people in the ground is often considered a cleansing act; for example, taking healing materials related to a client and burying them in the ground for safekeeping. This also adds the literal quality of grounding the work, or keeping the work in a practical, concrete realm.

In some cases the client themselves might be buried, either entirely or partially, for a given amount of time. If the entire body is buried, the client will usually be wrapped in a white sheet to keep them from getting dirty and to connect the work to the burial process. The head is almost always left uncovered, or at least the face, so that the client can breathe normally. This is intended to be a moment of self-reflection and meditation. The burial almost always occurs at night, and the healer will sit either beside the grave or sit nearby to keep their client calm. After the prescribed amount of time, the healer will dig up their client. The healer usually washes the client head to toe with fresh spring water. The cleansing ritual is then complete. This entire act mimics the death and burial process itself. It follows the idea of death and rebirth as a healing act. The client "dies" with their illness, is purified in the earth, then is finally reborn and washed clean. This ritual is still used in cases of strong illness or cursed conditions.

LEFT-HAND PRACTICES

Left-handed workers might also use similar methods, but their intention is to hurt their victims. Hex items, like dirt taken from a graveyard, might be buried near a person's front door so they will walk over it, thereby picking up the curse. In a ritual also involving animal parts, a worker might stuff a goat's heart with the hair of their victim (or other identifying ingredients) and then put it in a small black coffin and bury it in a graveyard, thereby cursing their victim to have an early death themselves.

PLANTING

Like burying, planting rituals involve putting magical materials into the ground for a certain purpose. The difference is that a sympathetic connection is also made to the health of a plant, usually a tree.

RIGHT-HAND PRACTICES

Healers will sometimes bury work for their clients in the roots of a potted plant or tree. This connects the work to the life force and strength of the plant. For this reason, strong trees are most often used in these rituals. It's common to see these connections in many different aspects of Ozark healing work. For example, a healer will sometimes instruct their client to drink a few sips from an herbal tea and then go out and pour the rest onto the roots of a strong tree. This creates a sympathetic connection so that as the tree grows strong, so too will the client.

Planting rituals are also commonly used for love work. In this case, a healer would plant some hair from their client and their client's lover—often the spouse in cases of healing marriages—and bury them entangled together in the roots of a flowering plant, usually a bulb like tulips or daffodils. As the flower grows and blooms, so too will the love or marriage be healed. Love work like this is usually performed in the springtime, which already has cultural associations with love, birth, and renewal.

LEFT-HAND PRACTICES

In a similar ritual, one might want to place a victim's name in the roots of a dying plant in order to weaken them. They might also entangle the victim's hair in the roots of a plant that is then intentionally killed, or one might bury their victim's hair or fingernail clippings in the roots of a poisonous plant to curse them with bad luck or magically poisoned health. Traditional plants associated with left-handed work include the poisonous jimsonweed and black nightshade.

PART
TWO

Chapter 8

HEALING PLANTS AND MAGICAL INGREDIENTS

AN INTRODUCTION

OZARK HILLFOLK HAVE HAD a wide variety of plants and non-plant supplies at their fingertips to work with for both healing and folk magic. These supplies on their own could fill an entire book, but I've chosen a few in each category that are still used today by healers and witches. These entries include both traditional herbal medicines, widely used across the Ozark Mountains in both the folklore record and today, as well as items and ingredients that aren't normally taken internally but are instead used by means of sympathetic magic or as talismans and amulets.

Chapter 9 includes a few examples of the many native and non-native medicinal botanicals found across the Ozark Mountain region. These plant entries are characterized by including both their inherent medicinal value and their use in folk magic. It should be noted that for plants, there is often a dual purpose of providing both an herbal medicine as well as a magical ingredient. Witch hazel, for example, has traditional uses as an astringent wash for sores, but hillfolk also hung witch hazel branches in their barns to protect their cattle from malign magic. Many of the plants listed are considered native to the region, but there are many others that were introduced by European colonizers. These include species like yarrow, mullein, and yard plantain.

Chapter 10 includes many of the non-plant tools and supplies that occupy the realm of Ozark folk magic. These entries include items that are traditionally used in magical amulets or in ritual acts like sweeping, cutting, nailing, tying off, etc. As with much of Ozark healing and magic, the tools and supplies used are often taken and repurposed from the home itself rather than having a specialized tool made for a single purpose.

ENTRY STRUCTURE FOR CHAPTERS 9 AND 10

OTHER NAMES: Includes any other folk names the plant or item might have in the Ozarks. This section only appears for entries in chapter 9.

CAUTIONS: Indicates any modern warnings, contraindications, or drug interactions common for a specific plant, mineral, or other ingredient. Many of the plants used in traditional Ozark medicine are not recommended in a modern setting, as many have potentially dangerous side effects or interact poorly with common medicines. These plants are still listed in this book for their historic or folk value. Likewise, many of the magical supplies listed in chapter 10 are there for their folkloric value and aren't recommended for modern use due to the unethical nature of obtaining the item.

PARTS USED: Indicates the most commonly used parts of the plant, such as bark, root, flower, leaf, etc. This section only appears for entries in chapter 9.

RECOMMENDED PREPARATION: Indicates how the plant is typically prepared as medicine today. This section includes such preparations as infusions, decoctions, tinctures, salves, etc. More detail about these preparations can be found in chapter 6. This section only appears for entries in chapter 9.

MEDICINAL USES: Details how the plant has been used medicinally, both in a historical context and today. This section only appears for entries in chapter 9.

MODERN HERBAL ACTIONS: This is a brief summary of any modern medicinal actions of the plant entries, provided for quick reference. More about herbal preparations can be found in chapter 6. This section only appears for entries in chapter 9. This section can include any of the following herbal actions:

- Abortifacient: causes an abortion
- Alterative: changes a sickly state into one of health
- Analgesic: relieves pain
- Anthelmintic: destroys intestinal parasites

- Anti-inflammatory: reduces inflammation
- Antiseptic: prevents bacterial growth
- Antispasmodic: aids or prevents muscle spasms
- Astringent: condenses tissue
- Carminative: relieves internal gas
- Cathartic: helps to produce discharges from the bowels
- Demulcent: mucilaginous principles used in solution to soothe and protect irritated mucous membranes and other tissues
- Diaphoretic: causes sweating
- Diuretic: increases secretion of urine
- Emetic: causes vomiting
- Expectorant: clears chest congestion by reducing phlegm or by suppressing a cough
- Febrifuge: reduces fevers
- Laxative: causes bowel movements
- Nervine: acts on the nerves; a sedative
- Panacea: reportedly used for many different illnesses; a "cure-all"
- Purgative: causes vomiting
- Sedative: promotes a state of calm or sleepiness
- Stomachic: aids with digestion or strengthens appetite
- Tonic: gives a sense of health or well-being; often taken during certain seasons
- Vermifuge: destroys intestinal parasites

PLANETARY SIGN(S) AND/OR ELEMENT(S): Medicinal herbs are often assigned certain planets or elements as their "ruler" based upon the qualities of the plant and their traditional uses. These give a good idea as to how the plants might affect the body or how they might be used in magical work. A list of planetary signs and their other associations can be found in chapter 5. This section only appears for entries in chapter 9.

MAGICAL ALIGNMENT: Indicates whether the item is typically used for right-handed work, left-handed work, or both.

MAGICAL USES: Details how healers and other gifted individuals have used these items for magical purposes.

TRY IT OUT: Gives specific recipes and rituals involving the listed items and plants for readers to try out at home.

HEALING PLANTS

IN THE OLD OZARKS, THE use of healing plants and herbal preparations was often the realm of the yarb doctor and granny woman. Today, many healers perform a dual role of providing medicinal remedies using healing plants as well as amulets, rituals, and other magical work. Plant healing in the Ozarks has always occupied an important part of hillfolk life. Herbal medicines were almost always taken on an empirical basis with the belief "If it works, it works," a statement I heard on my own journeys across the Ozarks.

Herbal medicines are still preferred by many Ozarkers today. As was explained to me by one herbalist, plant medicines are often seen as having fewer side effects and aren't as addictive as modern medications. This isn't always the case, though. Herbal medicines are often given a pass because they're "from the earth," as I've heard time and time again. While it's true that the earth has produced many useful medicines, she's also made a whole lot of poisons as well.

It's important that we use all available information when looking into these traditional methods of healing. A plant like bloodroot, once widely used across the Ozarks, has since been found to actually cause a lot of harm to the body. Even in my own practice, I'm constantly having to remind people that plants are made up of chemicals, whether we choose to accept that fact or not, and these chemicals have a certain effect on the body. Likewise, chemicals can interact with other chemicals, sometimes in terrible ways.

Take this story told to me by an herbalist friend. She was prescribing turmeric to a client to help with chronic inflammation of the joints. Turmeric also happens to be a blood thinner, and the herbalist made sure to tell her client several times to always tell her general practitioner she was taking turmeric in case it interacted with any other medications. Well, as it turned out, the woman didn't tell her doctor about the turmeric and nearly died during surgery a few months later.

In many ways, getting back in touch with more traditional medicines can help us better understand the power of certain plant chemical compounds. Sassafras, for example, has been a controversial plant since the FDA banned the plant in commercial products in 1960 because of safrole, discovered to be carcinogenic in animal studies.[31] To this day, there are people on both sides of the argument: those who are still pro-sassafras and those who are vehemently against it. For those still using the plant, it is reiterated that the medicine was traditionally taken as a tonic—meaning in high doses for a short amount of time, not as a year-round beverage. This was likely in part because the old-timers knew it was a healing plant that had adverse side effects if taken over a long period of time.

Despite what many might say, I think traditional medicine still has a lot left to teach us. For those interested in working with plant medicines, I have a few recommendations:

1. First, try and find a trained herbalist to work with. Check for credentials! Any herbalist worth their weight will be happy to show you where they studied or get you in touch with other students and clients. If you can't find someone in person, there are a lot of good online schools as well. The problem with a lot of the courses focusing on modern Western herbalism is that they overlook many of the native plants; this is where studying with a local in your area is key.

2. Second, keep a copy of an herbal contraindications book close by. I like to use *Herbal Contraindications and Drug Interactions* by Francis Brinker. It's a fantastic way to make sure the herbal medicines you're taking or prescribing to others aren't going to react terribly with other medications.

3. Lastly (and this is a recommendation I myself practice), don't prescribe something you yourself wouldn't take, allergies and contraindications aside, of course. Don't use your clients as guinea pigs for your experimental herbal medicines. So long as there aren't any interactions or contraindications, I recommend using the same medicines you prescribe to others for your own needs as well.

31.   Dietz and Bolton, "Botanical Dietary Supplements Gone Bad," 586–90.

APPLE
Malus spp.

OTHER NAMES: None

CAUTIONS: Seeds should never be taken internally because they contain amygdalin, which is converted to cyanide in the stomach and can be fatal in large doses.

PARTS USED: Fruit, seeds

RECOMMENDED PREPARATION: Infusion of dried apple slices

MEDICINAL USES: A common cure for stomachaches in the old Ozarks was a tea made by soaking dried apple slices in hot water. This is still used today as a digestive aid and to provide relief for internal gas.

MODERN HERBAL ACTIONS:

- Carminative: Infusion made from dried apple slices taken internally for relieving gas
- Stomachic: Infusion made from dried apple slices taken internally after a meal to aid in digestion

PLANETARY SIGNS: Venus, Saturn

MAGICAL ALIGNMENT: Both hands

MAGICAL USES: Apple seeds were once thought to be able to divine a person's true love. In this ritual, an apple seed was named for one individual, and another seed was named for the second person. After this naming, the two seeds were dropped onto a hot surface at the same time. If the sizzling seeds moved closer together, it was taken as a favorable sign that love would ensue. If they moved apart, it was generally believed that nothing would ever be able to bring them together.

Apples were also a widely used container to hold illnesses and curses. Even in certain rituals today, a healer might magically sweep or cut an ailment off their client and cast it into an apple. The apple was then destroyed, usually by burying it.

The apple can also be used in left-handed work. In a more modern ritual, a worker cores out an apple with a red-hot poker and then stuffs a rolled and sealed tube of paper containing hair, nail clippings, or other identifying objects from the one they're cursing into the center of the fruit. In order to cause the target harm, the apple is left to sizzle on hot coals or placed under running water, like at a waterfall or under a rain spout, with the belief being that the constantly falling water will cause the target joint and body pain.

TRY IT OUT—WART CHARMING: This ritual was common in the old Ozarks. See if its magic might work for you today! Take an apple and cut it in half across the middle (with the knife parallel to the top and bottom). This should reveal the shape of a star in the core. Now rub one half of the apple over all of your warts. Put the apple back together and tie up the whole thing with red string. Next, under the light of the full moon, go outside and bury the apple in the ground. It was believed that as the moon waned, your warts would slowly disappear.

ASAFETIDA
Ferula assa-foetida

OTHER NAMES: Asafedy, asafetidy, devil's dung

CAUTIONS: Due to its gastric stimulatory properties, asafetida should be avoided in cases of acute inflammation and peptic ulcers.[32] Avoid during pregnancy because of its abortifacient effect.

PARTS USED: Root

RECOMMENDED PREPARATION: Capsules of powdered root

MEDICINAL USES: In the folk herbalism of the Ozarks, the powdered root was taken internally as a decoction to help calm a sick stomach and promote digestion. It was also consumed as a panacea with the belief that its noxious odor would ward off illness from the body. Today the powdered root is taken as a stomachic, digestive aid, and laxative, although usually in pill form because of its strong taste.

MODERN HERBAL ACTIONS:
- Carminative: Resin taken in pill form helps stimulate the mucous membranes in the stomach and intestines
- Laxative: Resin taken in pill form promotes bowel movements

PLANETARY SIGNS: Mars, Saturn

MAGICAL ALIGNMENT: Right hand

MAGICAL USES: Traditionally, asafetida roots were used as magical wards against all forms of sickness, including those illnesses deriving from a magical source. Roots were carried in bags around the neck to help scare away illness with the foul smell. It was once

---

32.   Brinker, *Herbal Contraindications*, 42.

widely believed that things with pungent smells were able to keep away sickness. There are many old-timers today who swear by this cure.

Because asafetida is believed to be able to ward off evil, many people still use the roots in other ways than just wearing them in bags. Some healers will let the resin smoke and smolder in a hot skillet to clear out illness and evil spirits from inside a house. These noxious fumes are likely to clear out more than just disembodied entities. Likewise, the powdered root can be sprinkled over any object that has been "wished" or cursed as a counteracting measure.

TRY IT OUT—DEVIL'S DUNG PASTE: This is a modern version of an old ritual to make a ward against evil influences entering your home. Take some asafetida powder (easily found in any Indian grocery store, where it's called hing) and mix it with some full moon water, water left out all night under a full moon; this water is prized by Ozark healers and witches today for its power to banish evil influences. Make sure to wear gloves, as the odor of asafetida tends to stick to the skin and the yellow color can stain. Once a paste is formed, use a small paintbrush to make seven dots around the outside of any doorframe on your house that acts as both an entrance and an exit, usually the front and back door. I don't suggest using these wards inside the house, as the pungent odor is likely to offend the senses. Working clockwise around the doorframe, most people will do three dots on the left, one dot on the top of the doorframe, and three on the right side. This ward is especially useful for healers who might want to protect their work from spying eyes. The mountain magician who gave me this ward suggested repainting the dots every new moon to help maintain the protective barrier.

BLACKBERRY
Rubus villosus

OTHER NAMES: Brambles

CAUTIONS: None

PARTS USED: Root, leaf, berry, cane

RECOMMENDED PREPARATION: Infusion and tincture of foliage; decoction and tincture of root; salve of foliage

MEDICINAL USES: In addition to bearing an edible fruit rich in vitamin C, the blackberry also gives medicine from its leaves and roots. An infusion of blackberry leaves can be mixed with honey and applied to the skin as an anti-inflammatory wash. The leaves have an astringent quality, making them suitable for use externally for skin inflammation and internally to aid with diarrhea and other bowel issues.

Summer complaint was a mysterious illness in the old Ozarks that almost exclusively affected children. It was characterized by a strong fever that grew without stopping, often resulting in the child's death. It was widely believed that eating blackberries would help prevent the summer complaint.

Healers in the old Ozarks also used blackberry canes in scratching methods of healing. The cane is the part that grows out of the ground and is covered in sharp prickles. A length of cane would be cut, allowed to dry, then scraped along the client's skin until blood was drawn. Then an herbal powder, wash, or poultice was applied to the scratches and they were wrapped in gauze. Scratching was often used in cases of inflammation like arthritis and rheumatism.

MODERN HERBAL ACTIONS:

- Anti-inflammatory: Leaf infusion mixed with honey and taken internally as an aid for sore throats
- Astringent: Juice taken internally for diarrhea; root decoction or infusion of leaves taken internally for diarrhea and other bowel complaints
- Edible: Berry edible, leaf used as an herbal tea
- Expectorant: Root chewed for a wet cough

PLANETARY SIGNS: Venus, Mars

MAGICAL ALIGNMENT: Both hands

MAGICAL USES: The blackberry and raspberry have a unique quality of being able to take root in the ground at the tip of the cane as well as the base. This forms blackberry "arches" throughout the woods, which were often seen by hillfolk as portals into the otherworld. As with hag stones and hole roots, these naturally occurring doorways were considered to be a place of blessing by healers, who used them for healing by having their clients crawl under the arch a certain number of times; sometimes babies are even passed through these magical doorways to cure colic and thrush. According to Ozark folklore, witches used these magical arches to travel to their infernal meetings. A surefire way of trapping a witch in the world of spirits was by watching them disappear through one of these doorways and then uprooting one end of the cane, thereby closing the gateway.

In modern Ozark folk magic, the blackberry plant is used in a number of ways. The thorny canes are ruled by Mars and can be used in protective rituals to create barriers against evil influences. Wreaths made from blackberry canes and greenbrier can be hung up on the outside of a house near any entrance as a ward against malicious forces that might try to enter the home.

The leaves and berries of the plant are associated with Venus and can therefore be used in rituals for love, fertility, and prosperity. Carrying a small bag of blackberry leaves in your pocket is said to bring good luck, especially in matters of the heart.

TRY IT OUT—BRAMBLE FENCE: To protect your home from evil influences, try this ritual. Cut four blackberry canes, making sure to leave on any leaves and berries. Tie a sprig of red cedar to the middle of each cane. You can also pierce three juniper berries with a good-sized needle, place them on a string like they are beads, and tie this to the middle of each cane. Starting with the front of your house and working clockwise, tie or nail a single cane to each side of your house, horizontally, forming a magical fence. If you aren't able to reach all sides of your house, or if you live in an apartment building, you can fix the canes around the frame of your front door. Starting with the left side, continue clockwise to the top and right side. Hide the fourth cane under a doormat for safe keeping.

BLACK PEPPER
Piper nigrum

OTHER NAMES: Pepper

CAUTIONS: Large doses can cause stomach irritation. Black pepper can irritate mucus membranes in the nose if inhaled.

PARTS USED: Seed

RECOMMENDED PREPARATION: Infusion; seasoning

MEDICINAL USES: In addition to its use as a seasoning, black pepper had a medicinal value for many Ozark hillfolk. The crushed seed was considered warming in nature and was used in infusions to help stimulate digestion and to relieve colds and congestion. Also because of this warming effect, infusions were often taken as a diaphoretic to help a client sweat out a fever.

As an astringent, pepper infusions were traditionally used as a gargle for sore throat. Often the infusion was made with vinegar instead of water.

MODERN HERBAL ACTIONS:
- Astringent: Decoction used as a gargle for sore throat
- Digestive: Helps stimulate mucous membranes in the bowels; aids with digestion
- Febrifuge: Decoction of seed said to help lower a fever

PLANETARY SIGN: Mars

MAGICAL ALIGNMENT: Both hands

MAGICAL USES: Magically speaking, because black pepper is considered hot in nature, it can be used to energize certain rituals. For example, a worker might add some black pepper to a love satchel or amulet for a client in order to heat things up between them and their spouse or lover.

Black pepper can also be paired with other hot ingredients to aid with protection work, the idea being that black pepper will burn off any intruders. For this reason, it can also be used to drive unwanted visitors away from your home.

Because of its hot nature, black pepper has been used in left-handed work to magically burn targeted individuals, often by stuffing a spite doll with whole black peppercorns.

TRY IT OUT—A SPICY WARD: A mixture of crushed black pepper and powdered tobacco can be used as a ward against evil spirits and enemies alike. For this ritual, you can take some of this mixture and sprinkle it in the four corners of every room in your house, or you can sprinkle it under the welcome mat at your front door as a way of preventing negative influences from coming inside.

BLOODROOT
Sanguinaria canadensis

OTHER NAMES: Red pucoon, red root

CAUTIONS: The active chemical compound sanguinarine is considered an escharotic, meaning that it kills animal cells and can lead to the formation of a large scab called an eschar. Medicinal use is not recommended. For magical use, make sure to always wear gloves when handling fresh bloodroot, and wear a mask if powdering the dried roots.

PARTS USED: Root

RECOMMENDED PREPARATION: Recommended only for magical use

MEDICINAL USES: Bloodroot was traditionally used in the Ozarks for removing skin cancers, blemishes, skin tags, and warts. It's very effective at this work as the red sap of the root contains sanguinarine, a toxin that kills animal cells. After applying the juice to the skin, an eschar forms, which is a lump of dead skin cells. The eschars are then removed with a sharp object or left to fall away naturally. This sometimes leaves terrible scarring at the application site, which can become infected if not treated properly. Modern studies have found that while sanguinarine might kill the skin cells surrounding a skin cancer, it does leave behind the cancer cells in the scarred tissue. For this reason, bloodroot is no longer recommended for medicinal use.

MODERN HERBAL ACTIONS: Recommended only for magical use

PLANETARY SIGNS: Venus, Mars

MAGICAL ALIGNMENT: Right hand

MAGICAL USES: Bloodroot has had many traditional magical uses in the Ozarks, some of which are used by witches and other practitioners even today. Traditionally the dried, powdered root was sprinkled around the outside of a house for protection against illness and evil entities that might try to enter. It was also burned as a fumigation plant, the noxious odor thought to be able to drive away evil.

As a love medicine, bloodroot was used by Ozark hillfolk in a couple of ways. The dried roots were sometimes concealed in a pocket or worn inside bags hung around a person's neck; these bags were thought to be able to attract loving attention to a person. The red sap of the bloodroot was also sometimes used as a blush on the cheeks, making the wearer's appearance dazzling to all who looked at them. Because of the sanguinarine in bloodroot, application in any way to the skin is not recommended.

TRY IT OUT—A RED CHARM FOR LOVE: Love charms using bloodroot can be created in a number of ways. The simplest way is to sew a small bag or packet from red cloth and fill the inside with bloodroot and then sew closed to seal. The choicest roots in the old Ozarks were ones that were left whole, the idea being that the spirit of the plant was still intact. If a whole root is used, wrap the root in red cloth and then seal closed with red string. You can give your root a purpose by asking it to perform a task for you. "Bring me a fun date," for instance, or, "Help keep my marriage peaceful." Hillfolk believed that by carrying these charms around in their pocket, the root would perform any task they gave to it.

BUCKEYE
Aesculus glabra

OTHER NAMES: Red buckeye (*Aesculus pavia*)

CAUTIONS: All parts of the tree—including the nut—are toxic. Do not ingest.

PARTS USED: Nut

RECOMMENDED PREPARATION: Recommended only for magical use

MEDICINAL USES: Because of the toxins in the buckeye tree, it was rarely used in Ozark herbal medicine. The saponins concentrated in the nuts and roots were used to stun fish for easier catching, a technique hillfolk learned from their indigenous neighbors. The saponins work by restricting the absorption of oxygen through the gills, so the fish are essentially suffocated and can then be gathered up off the surface of the water.

MODERN HERBAL ACTIONS: Recommended only for magical use

PLANETARY SIGN: Mars

MAGICAL ALIGNMENT: Right hand

MAGICAL USES: Buckeye nuts are very popular amulets in the Ozarks. They are carried in the pocket to ward off everything from rheumatism, colds, fevers, and even venereal diseases. Vance Randolph remarked that he once heard that "no man was ever found dead with a buckeye in his pocket."[33] He, of course, doubted the truthfulness of this statement, and for good reason. But I can personally account for several of my own informants who credit carrying a buckeye for saving them not only from illness, but also catastrophic accidents as well.

The main medicinal value of the plant comes from this use as a powerful talisman. It's said a buckeye nut can only be gifted or found—those that are bought never have any power. It's also said that a buckeye needs to be kept well oiled, usually by rubbing the thing between your fingers like a worry stone.

TRY IT OUT—BUCKEYE BAG: Traditionally, most people who carry a buckeye around with them will have the nut loose in their pocket or purse, but I recommend this method for some added magical benefit. On the new moon, take your buckeye nut and put it into a small green cloth bag. You can add other herbs associated with luck and fortune, like five-finger grass (*Potentilla simplex*), red cedar (*Juniperus virginiana*), and oak bark, or you

---

33. Randolph, *Ozark Magic and Folklore*, 153.

can leave it as is. Tie the top of the bag closed with three knots, then scent with a few drops of lime essential oil. Then, while holding your bag, say: "Buckeye strong, buckeye hard, buckeye grow as the moon grows." The woman who taught me this ritual suggested anointing the bag with lime essential oil and repeating the spell every new moon to help recharge the magical energies of the buckeye.

BURDOCK
Arctium spp.

OTHER NAMES: None

CAUTIONS: Foliage can cause contact dermatitis, so handle with gloves.

PARTS USED: Root, leaf

RECOMMENDED PREPARATION: Decoction and tincture of root; root cooked and eaten

MEDICINAL USES: Burdock is native to Europe but came in with settlers as both a source of food and medicine. The root can be cooked and eaten like a carrot or parsnip. It has a bitter quality to it and is said to be good for digestion. Infusions of the leaves were traditionally taken internally as a stomach tonic to help with chronic indigestion.

A decoction of the root was thought to act as a purifier for the kidneys and urinary system. Because of the mild laxative quality of the root, it was also considered to be a blood purifier and spring tonic like sassafras. The plant's aspect is Venus, making it a good remedy against Mars illnesses like constipation and fevers.

The leaf and root both have traditionally been used in poultices and salves for boils, rashes, and other skin complaints. Caution should be taken with the foliage, as some people are sensitive to the plant and might contract contact dermatitis when using it topically.

MODERN HERBAL ACTIONS:

- Carminative: Decoction of root taken internally as a "blood purifier" or aid for digestion
- Diuretic: Decoction of root taken internally to aid the urinary system
- Skin: Root used in washes for boils and skin complaints; leaf poultice used for tumors and swellings and to reduce inflammation
- Stomachic: Leaf infusion taken internally to tone stomach and aid in digestion

PLANETARY SIGN: Venus

MAGICAL ALIGNMENT: Right hand

MAGICAL USES: Magically speaking, burdock is used predominantly as a protecting plant. Beads made from dried burdock roots were traditionally worn by adults and children to help protect from malign magic and evil spirits. Likewise, pieces of the roots and foliage can be added to protective bags that are worn or hung inside the house to ward off evil influences.

Because of its associations with Venus, all parts of the plant can be added as ingredients in any love work. One traditional method to attract a lover was to carve a burdock root into the shape of the person you wanted to attract, then to carry the figure around with you either concealed in your pocket or inside a bag hung around your neck. Similar burdock root poppets are still used today as ritual objects in work to heal and harm.

TRY IT OUT—MIGHTY ROOTS: The large taproots of the burdock can be used as a charm in their natural state. Some people dry out the taproot and nail it on the outside of their home to help protect it from illness and harming magic. These root charms were also widely used in stables to help protect livestock. Utilizing this wonderful root doesn't necessarily mean growing your own plant from scratch; most online sellers of organic herbs will carry burdock root, either whole or in pieces, for its medicinal benefits. If you want to use the whole root, I recommend drying it first to avoid molding later on. This is difficult as the root is very starchy, but you can dry it out enough in an oven set to the lowest possible temperature. (You'll need to leave it in there for six to eight hours, I've found, depending upon the size of the root.) Buying already dried root pieces is preferable. All you have to do is take some of the root pieces and add them to a small cloth bag. You can also add other protective herbs. Tie the top of the bag with three knots and hang the bags near your front and back door, outside or inside. A day when the moon is in Taurus is best for this type of work, especially during a waxing moon.

CORN
Zea mays

CAUTIONS: None

PARTS USED: Kernel, silk, husks

RECOMMENDED PREPARATION: Infusion of corn silk

MEDICINAL USES: Besides being a traditional staple food for Ozarkers, corn was also employed both medicinally and magically. To this day, infusions of corn silk are taken internally as a mild diuretic to help flush toxins from the kidneys and to assist in urinary tract inflammation.[34]

MODERN HERBAL ACTIONS:

- Diuretic: Infusions of corn silk taken internally for kidneys and urinary tract

PLANETARY SIGN: Jupiter

MAGICAL ALIGNMENT: Right hand

MAGICAL USES: Corn was often used in wart-charming rituals as a symbolic container for illness. For example, a kernel of corn could be rubbed on each of an individual's warts and then left at a crossroads, thereby transferring the warts from the afflicted to the next person to walk across the crossroads. Sometimes the warts are first pricked with a nail or thorn (or a coffin nail, for added magical benefit) and the blood is rubbed onto the kernel to create a sympathetic connection. Another method involved feeding kernels of "warty" corn to chickens, thereby magically transferring the warts to the birds, believed to be immune to having warts themselves.

There was also a common belief that burning corncobs underneath the bed of a sick client would help break their fever and aid them in recovering.

Cornhusks were often used to make spite dolls and poppets. This raw material would have been plentiful on most Ozark farms. As the cornhusk doll was made, a person might weave in strands of their client's or victim's hair, creating a sympathetic connection that could then be manipulated. These dolls would have been a way for healers to work remotely on their clients at all hours of the day. For those working with the left hand, these spite dolls could be stabbed with needles or even burned in a fire.

Corn is still grown as a staple food for many people in the Ozarks. Even those of completely European ancestry understand the importance of the plant in nourishing not only the body, but the spirit. Many farmers will plant tobacco along with their corn as an offering, and some will even leave out food and drink in their fields to receive a blessing from the Little People. I find that corn kernels or cornmeal are fantastic offerings for many land spirits and spirits of the dead. The nourishing quality of the plant helps to ground and cleanse frantic or chaotic energies. Corn represents prosperity and good luck and can be used in work for these purposes.

---

34. Easley and Horne, *Modern Herbal Dispensatory,* 218.

TRY IT OUT—A POCKET FULL OF GOLD: For luck in business and moneymaking, try out this Ozark charm. Cut out a small square of green fabric. Place twelve dried kernels of corn in the center of the square. Tie the bundle closed using green string, then knot three times. Anoint with lime essential oil and say, "Love in my heart, gold in my pockets!" Carry this in your pocket, especially while at work or when trying to find a new job. Recharge the amulet by anointing it with lime oil every new moon.

DANDELION
Taraxacum officinale

CAUTIONS: None

PARTS USED: Root, leaf, flower

RECOMMENDED PREPARATION: Decoction and tincture of root; foliage eaten cooked or raw

MEDICINAL USES: Dandelion is another food plant brought to the New World with settlers. The greens of the plant are high in vitamins and nutrients and, as a hearty green, they can last well into the winter, providing much-needed food. All parts of the plant can be consumed. The leaves and flowers can be eaten raw or cooked like other potherbs. I like to make fritters with the flowers; they're tasty with a nice dill and sour cream dipping sauce.

When roasted, dandelion root has a pleasant, coffee-like flavor—without the caffeine. Dandelion root used to be dried out, roasted, ground up, and then mixed with coffee to make it last longer, similar to chicory (*Cichorium intybus*) root.

Dandelion root is principally used in decoctions as a diuretic to help cleanse the kidneys and urinary system. The entire plant is considered bitter in taste and therefore has many benefits for the stomach and digestive system.

MODERN HERBAL ACTIONS:
- Diuretic: Decoctions of root taken internally for kidney and urinary tract
- Edible: Greens edible whether raw or cooked
- Skin: Poultice of steamed or wilted leaves applied to skin ulcers
- Stomachic: Decoction of roots taken internally for stomach pain and to aid in digestion
- Tonic: Decoction of root taken internally as a bitter tonic for indigestion

PLANETARY SIGN: Jupiter

MAGICAL ALIGNMENT: Right hand

MAGICAL USES: A traditional charm known by children is to pick a dandelion flower when its puffy, airborne seeds are present. Then they make a wish and blow. It's said that if you manage to blow off all the dandelion seeds, your wish will come true.

A lesser-known use of dandelion is with divining spirits of the dead. According to Ozark folklore, the steam created by pouring boiling water over fresh dandelion roots will show you visions of spirits that might be around you. I find it's useful to perform this ritual at a table using a wide bowl placed about a foot in front of you. On the opposite side of the bowl, place a single candle. Other than the light from the candle, the room should be completely dark for best results.

TRY IT OUT—STOMACH BITTERS: This recipe helps with gas and a rumbly stomach after eating a meal.
- 4 tbsp dandelion root, fresh or dried
- 2 tbsp fennel seed
- 2 tbsp fresh ginger root
- 2 tbsp mountain mint leaf or peppermint leaf
- Vodka

Add plant matter to a one-quart jar. Fill the jar with vodka or another 40–50 percent ABV alcohol. Let stand for two weeks, shaking every two or three days. Strain and bottle. Take ½ tsp or 1 tsp after a meal, or take up to three times daily.

DITTANY
Cunila origanoides

OTHER NAMES: Stonemint, wild oregano

CAUTIONS: None

PARTS USED: Leaf, flower

RECOMMENDED PREPARATION: Infusion and tincture of foliage

MEDICINAL USES: The dittany of the Ozarks shouldn't be confused with dittany of Crete (*Origanum dictamnus*), a much closer relative of oregano (*Origanum vulgare*). Our dittany is called "wild oregano" for a reason, though, as the crushed leaves smell almost exactly like oregano and can be used as a substitute for the herb when cooking.

Dittany and oregano can be used in similar medicinal ways as well. Both are considered warming and bitter plants, meaning infusions are often taken internally for colds, chills, head congestion, and to reduce a fever. Its bitter quality means it does well in stomach tonics and digestives.

MODERN HERBAL ACTIONS:

- Colds: Infusion taken internally for colds or head congestion
- Diaphoretic: Infusions taken internally to make the body sweat
- Febrifuge: Strong infusion taken internally to help break a fever
- Spice: Can be used in a similar way to oregano

PLANETARY SIGN: Mars

MAGICAL ALIGNMENT: Right hand

MAGICAL USES: Within Ozark folk magic, dittany was commonly used as a protecting plant, especially against boogers—fearsome, shape-shifting animals that were said to hate the smell. Ghosts with unfinished business were said to overlook houses where dittany hung outside the front door. Little bundles of dittany can be hung above the entrances and exits to your home, or you can add some of the potently aromatic leaves to protection bags and amulets.

TRY IT OUT—HERBAL BITTERS: This is a bold bitters for use with stomachaches, indigestion, and as a tonic for clearing out sinuses and fighting winter colds.

- ¼ cup dandelion root
- ¼ cup dittany leaf
- ¼ cup chopped fresh ginger root
- ¼ cup hyssop (*Hyssopus officinalis*) leaf
- 1 cinnamon stick (whole)
- 1 tbsp cloves (whole)
- Vodka

Add plant matter to a one-quart jar. Fill the jar with vodka or another 40–50 percent ABV alcohol. Let stand for two weeks, shaking every two or three days. Strain and bottle. Take ½ tsp or 1 tsp after a meal, or take up to three times daily.

DOGWOOD
Cornus florida

OTHER NAMES: Wild quinine, quinine tree

CAUTIONS: Berries and leaves of the flowering dogwood are toxic and should not be consumed.

PARTS USED: Root, bark

RECOMMENDED PREPARATION: Decoction and tincture of bark

MEDICINAL USES: Dogwood used to go by the common name "wild quinine" in the old Ozarks. While the tree doesn't actually contain the chemical compound quinine, it was used by Ozark hillfolk for many years to treat malarial fevers.

The root and bark of the tree acts as an analgesic in a similar way as willow, although it doesn't contain salicin. Decoctions of the root and bark can be taken for sore muscles and body pains, specifically for headaches. Old-timers also used to just chew the bark to gain this benefit.

Because of the tannins in the bark, decoctions of dogwood are great as washes for sores and other skin complaints.

Decoctions of the bark, often paired with other medicinal plants, have traditionally been used as spring tonics, aimed at aiding in digestion and tonifying the liver.

MODERN HERBAL ACTIONS:

- Analgesic: Root and bark chewed for headache; decoction of root and bark rubbed on skin to relieve aches and pains
- Astringent: Root and bark astringent; decoction of root and bark used externally for skin conditions
- Febrifuge: Decoction of root taken internally for fever
- Throat: Infusion of inner bark taken internally for a "lost voice" and sore throats

PLANETARY SIGN: Saturn

MAGICAL ALIGNMENT: Both hands

MAGICAL USES: There's an Ozark legend that claims the dogwood is a witch tree, like sassafras and pawpaw. It's said that the cross Jesus died on was made of dogwood and that after he died, he cursed the tree to be unfit for lumber. Dogwood flowers bear symbols of the crucifixion, namely a crown of thorns in the middle of the cluster and blood-stained petals around the outside.

Because the tree is supposedly cursed, it is useful to Ozark healers in tying off and knotting rituals. For example, a client with a fever might be taken out to a dogwood tree by a healer, tied to the trunk of the tree with a string, and lowered out, leaving the string and the fever behind. Or, as in the case of chills, a certain number of knots are tied into a string, but each time the client will blow through the hole in the knot before tightening.

Once finished, they can take the string out and tie it to a dogwood tree and their chills will go away.

Some hillfolk thought that the tree's namesake, dogwood, held some clue as to its magical uses and would carry pieces of the bark around with them to protect themselves from rabid dogs; this used to be a big problem in rural areas where there were a lot of feral dogs running around and the risk of attack was high.

Because the dogwood is considered a cursed tree, magical practitioners often use the bark and roots in left-handed rituals. For example, there's one tale that says that if a witch holds some of the bark or root in their mouth while sleeping or sitting in a trance, their spirit will be transformed into a booger-dog that they can send out to do their bidding.

There's a funny tall tale I heard once about a "root-digger" who sold an old granny woman many of her medicines, including dogwood root. One day, the root-digger delivered the granny woman her supplies as usual. He left as soon as he got his money. As he walked back down the road, he remembered he'd left behind his hat, so he returned to the old woman's shack. As soon as he got through her gate and into the yard, the root-digger saw a big black dog run out of the front door and into the woods. The man ran off immediately, fearing the dog might have been rabid.

A few days later, the root-digger was telling this story to a friend of his who was a healer. The man's friend said the granny woman was using dogwood roots to make herself into a booger-dog. He also taught the man a trick to make sure the granny woman would think twice before performing her spell in the future.

Days passed, and the granny woman contacted the root-digger for some more supplies. He remembered the healer's advice and slipped some mayapple root—the strongest laxative known to hillfolk—in with the dogwood and took the lot to the old woman's house. The man left with his money, but this time he hid in the old woman's bushes to watch the scene. A few hours passed and the man was getting tired, but just as he started to stand, the front door of the shack flew open. This time it wasn't a booger-dog leaving— it was the old woman running as fast as she could to the outhouse.

TRY IT OUT—DOGWOOD WANDS: Many magical workers today derive the benefits of astral travel by making a dogwood wand instead of putting the bark in their mouths. When the dogwood is in full bloom in the springtime, go out on a Saturday when the moon is waxing and in Capricorn (or at the very least, when the moon is waxing) and cut off a branch from a dogwood tree. With the leaves and flowers still on the branch, dry for a full moon cycle. The next time the moon is waxing, a few days after the new moon, strip off the dried leaves and flowers and save them for use later on. When using your wand to assist in astral traveling, take a pinch of the dried flowers and leaves, add them to a bowl, and pour boiling water over them to make a steam. You can also burn them on a piece of incense charcoal. Do this in a dark room with your dogwood wand in your left hand. The spirit of the dogwood will guide you on your journeys.

ELDERBERRY
Sambucus canadensis

OTHER NAMES: Elder, elderflower, elder tree

CAUTIONS: All parts of the plant are mildly toxic, especially when fresh, and can cause nausea if consumed. Fresh berries can be boiled for a few minutes before using to neutralize the toxins. Berries and flowers should be dried before using. Elderberries also cause contact dermatitis for some people when used externally.[35]

PARTS USED: Bark, leaf, flower, berry

RECOMMENDED PREPARATION: Infusion and tincture of flower; decoction and tincture of berry

MEDICINAL USES: Also referred to simply as "elder" by Ozark hillfolk, elderberry was once an important source of food and medicine for many hillfolk—if you could get to the berries before the birds did. Yarb doctors considered the elderberry to be a highly medicinal plant and traditionally used all parts of the plant in their remedies. To this day, the berries are used to treat colds and congestion, and they are favored for their use in tonics to boost the immune system. The flowers of the plant can be used in similar ways; they're even sometimes thrown into a batch of homemade hooch to add a sweet, floral taste.

Herbalists today recommend only using dried berries and flowers in remedies, as the fresh plant parts do contain toxins that can cause nausea or contact dermatitis. Traditionally, though, much of the medicinal value of the plant was in its leaves and bark. Washes were made with the leaves and astringent bark for rashes, in particular, poison ivy. It was also widely believed that carrying some of the leaves in your pocket or in

---

35. Easley and Horne, *Modern Herbal Dispensatory*, 226.

your hat would protect you from contracting poison ivy. (I don't recommend trying this one out.)

Leaves were also kept under the hat to help protect from heatstroke. There seems to be an association with elderberry and drawing off heat from the body. In this way, leaves and bark were also used in soaks for the feet to help with inflammation, another affliction associated with excess heat in the body.

MODERN HERBAL ACTIONS:
- Analgesic: Infusion of berry taken internally for rheumatism
- Colds: Berries used in infusions and decoctions against chills and colds; berries said to help support the immune system
- Edible: Ripe berries edible
- Febrifuge: Infusion of dried flowers taken internally to lower a fever

PLANETARY SIGN: Venus

MAGICAL ALIGNMENT: Right hand

MAGICAL USES: Traditionally, elderberry was used in the Ozarks in wart-charming rituals. Usually the method was by notching, where a person would cut a certain number of notches into an elderberry stick. The number of notches corresponded with many warts the person had. The stick was then buried with the belief that as the stick rotted away, so too would the warts. Some even notched directly on the live plant, the idea being that as the plant healed the cuts, so too would the warts heal.

The associations with elderberry being a healing plant are likely derived from its amazing regenerative properties. It grows in nearly every soil type, and it will even sprout up from broken branches just lying on the ground. It's amazingly resilient and prolific in its growth.

Much of the ancient European associations with the elderberry seem to have been lost on their way into the Ozarks, apart from its protective qualities. Branches and flowers brought into the house are said to protect the family from the influence of malign magic. It's also said that carrying three leaves of the plant around with you in your pocket or shoes will keep away left-handed work, particularly the evil eye.

TRY IT OUT—ELDERBERRY OXYMEL: This is great for immune support or to take care of a nasty winter cold.
- ¼ cup elderberries
- 1 cup ginger root (chopped, fresh or dry)
- Apple cider vinegar

Add your herbs and ½ cup honey to a one-quart mason jar. Fill with unstrained apple cider vinegar. Let stand for three to four weeks, shaking the jar every two days. Strain and bottle. Store in a cool, dark place or in the refrigerator for extended life. Take 1 tbsp up to three times daily.

GARLIC
Allium sativum

OTHER NAMES: None

CAUTIONS: Can cause gastric irritation in some.[36] Avoid in cases of acute stomach inflammation or acid reflux.[37]

PARTS USED: Bulb

RECOMMENDED PREPARATION: Capsules of powdered cloves; decoction of cloves

MEDICINAL USES: Garlic was—and still is—a staple ingredient in Ozark traditional food and medicine. It's a powerful plant, and I always tell people that if you're sick and have no other herbs around, garlic will do the trick.

Because of its strong smell and hot nature, garlic has associations with fighting off colds, congestion, fever, and even viral infections. There's some truth to this; garlic does contain certain antibacterial and antiviral properties and has been used in remedies for common illnesses since the Middle Ages, probably even before that.

Bulbs can be eaten raw, baked, or crushed and used in decoctions with other herbs. Personally, I like to boil garlic, onion, sassafras, and dittany together with chicken broth and drink the liquid as a fortifying medicinal beverage.

MODERN HERBAL ACTIONS:
- Colds: Decoction taken internally for colds
- Expectorant: Syrup or decoction used to clear chest congestion and aid with a cough

PLANETARY SIGNS: Mars, Jupiter

MAGICAL ALIGNMENT: Right hand

MAGICAL USES: Garlic is also a powerful protector, derived from its associations with both Mars and Jupiter. Hanging garlic bulbs outside your house will ward off evil influences

---

36. Easley and Horne, *Modern Herbal Dispensatory*, 234.

37. Brinker, *Herbal Contraindications*, 162.

and wandering witches. It's also good in work against "cold" conditions like depression, anxiety, and fear. Jupiter plants counter Saturn influences, meaning garlic is often used by Ozark doctors against spirits of the dead. Garlic planted on the grave of a restless spirit will help "lay," or calm, the ghost. These are age-old traditions going back to ancient European cultures. These same traditions gave rise to the idea that garlic is the archnemesis of the vampire.

As a Mars plant, garlic can work against the influences of Venus. This often takes the form of garlic baths when you think someone is trying to "steal your heart" by magical means.

TRY IT OUT—GARLIC OXYMEL: This is a powerful remedy to clear out sinus congestion.

- ¼ cup chopped fresh garlic
- 1 tbsp dried chili flakes
- 1 tbsp thyme leaf
- 1 tbsp rosemary leaf
- Apple cider vinegar

Add your herbs and ½ cup honey to a one-quart mason jar. Fill with unstrained apple cider vinegar. Let stand for three to four weeks, shaking the jar every two days. Strain and bottle. Store in a cool, dark place or in the refrigerator for extended life. Take 1 tbsp up to three times daily.

GINSENG
Panax quinquefolius

OTHER NAMES: Sang, sang root

CAUTIONS: Avoid using if you have high blood pressure, a fever, or acute inflammation. Can cause insomnia and nervous overstimulation.[38] Plant is listed as vulnerable and may be illegal to gather in your area outside of a certain season. Ginseng gathering is legal in Arkansas, but the plant is hard to find and has almost been completely wiped out save for a few areas. Gathering is not recommended.

PARTS USED: Root

RECOMMENDED PREPARATION: Decoction and tincture of root

---

38. Easley and Horne, *Modern Herbal Dispensatory*, 238.

MEDICINAL USES: The Ozark people have a mixed relationship with ginseng. On the one hand, it was once considered an herbal panacea, used for everything from colds to curing impotency. On the other hand, it's been overharvested in the Ozark Mountains almost to extinction. It was once a big-money item if you knew where to find it, and root-diggers sprung up everywhere in the area. Traditionally, collecting ginseng was referred to as "hunting" because the process was reenacted in many of the same ways as hunting for an animal. A group would get together, dress in camouflage, go out to the woods, and spend a day—sometimes more—wandering the hollers hunting for the roots.

Unfortunately, unlike in the Appalachian Mountains, there weren't ever any regulations put into place for harvesting, so people took as much as they wanted. It's hard to find in the Ozarks today, meaning it's no longer profitable for harvesters. There are still some people who know where to find it, but they usually go out to the Appalachians if they're looking to earn a living from the plant. This has allowed ginseng to gain a footing in the wilderness areas in recent years.

Few still abide by the old taboos surrounding ginseng, but then again, there are few who still gather it. I've met a couple of yarb doctors who still use the plant and know where to find it; that's always a closely guarded secret in the Ozarks. I've heard of families splitting apart because someone let loose about one of their secret "sang" patches.

One healer told me a story about when he was still learning healing from his mentor. They went out to gather some sang one day in a big patch his teacher knew about. Despite having been told how to approach and harvest the plant, the student made the mistake of going in on one plant and excitedly ripping its big root right out of the ground. He rushed over to his teacher, overjoyed about his find. As he walked, he lost his balance and, to steady himself, he grabbed on to a big rock set into the side of the holler. Suddenly he felt a sharp pain hit his hand and met eyes with the big timber rattlesnake that had bit him. He cried out and his teacher rushed over. The boy was sure he was going to die. The old teacher just shook his head, buried the root back in the exact spot it was taken from, and rushed the boy to the doctor in town. The healer humorously reminded me that he did in fact survive, but he still bore the scar from his lesson about respecting the natural world.

When the medicine was still widely in use, healers knew that ginseng had to be harvested when it was in season and the berries were ripe, usually in the late summer or early fall. This not only made it easier to find the plant, but the healer could also plant the seeds in the same hole they harvested from, ensuring more growth in the following years. Some healers would even plant some tobacco or corn as an offering to the spirit of the mountain and its medicine.

Medicinally, ginseng has been considered a stimulant, comparable to caffeine but not as strong. The effects of ginseng can be traced to ginsenosides contained in all the *Panax* genus of plants. The root has been used as a panacea for centuries. It's been reported to be able to help with colds, pain relief, flu, fever, chest congestion, infections, wounds, impotency, memory loss—and that's just the short list. The full medicinal benefits of ginseng are still unconfirmed; in official tests, many of the purported side effects occur as often as the placebo's side effects.

MODERN HERBAL ACTIONS:
- Analgesic: Decoction taken internally for headaches and muscle pain
- Cold: Decoction taken internally to aid with colds
- Skin: Poultice applied to wounds and bleeding cuts
- Stimulant: Decoctions and tinctures of root taken internally to improve stamina

PLANETARY SIGNS: Mars, Saturn

MAGICAL ALIGNMENT: Right hand

MAGICAL USES: In folk magic, ginseng has about as many uses as it has medicinal benefits. It's a highly protective plant—if you treat it right and don't just rip it out of the ground. Power doctors dry out old roots and keep them in bags or wrap them up in cloth as a spirit helper in certain healing rituals. Roots can also be carried or worn for protection against both physical and magical dangers as well as to draw luck, money, and opportunities to the wearer.

Healers would sometimes wear a ginseng root, particularly one that's old and wise, to bed with them to dream of remedies for their clients. This association is based on the idea of the ginseng spirit being a ruler of the mountain and therefore knowledgeable about all the healing plants that grow around it.

All of the associations I've been able to gather about ginseng say it is a fully right-handed plant. While it might be a plant that is knowledgeable about countering left-handed work, it isn't opposed to exacting its own revenge or justice against those who have wronged it. Ginseng is completely unwilling to perform these rites on demand, though.

I heard an unusual story once about a healer who had a big ginseng root that he used as a spirit helper in some of his rituals against witchcraft. One day, the healer came down with a terrible stomach sickness that he blamed on an enemy of his who was known to curse on demand. He petitioned the ginseng root to go out and kill his enemy on his behalf, but the root was silent. The next day the man was on his knees begging and pleading with the root to go out and kill his enemy so he could get better, but still there was no reply. After two more days of this, the healer took out a knife and said, "Root, if you don't help me I'll chop off your little arms and legs!" but still the root remained silent. The healer grabbed the root out of the wooden box he kept it in, took his knife, and went to cut the poor thing into pieces. But before he could, his heart was seized with pain and he fell over dead on the spot. When his family finally found the man, they wondered why he was holding the knife and what terrible sickness might have afflicted him. No one ever found the ginseng root, although many knew he used to have it. Some say a thief must have gone in after the man died and stolen the thing to sell for a fortune. Others scoffed at this theory, saying that it was a well-known fact that ginseng roots can stand up and walk if they want to, and it probably high-tailed it back to its mountain home.

TRY IT OUT—GINSENG DREAMING: Roots of the American ginseng are a little bit tricky to find sometimes because they are usually shipped off for use in energy drinks. If you can get your hands on a whole root from a reputable ginseng digger, you can do what the old Ozark healers would do: use it to dream up magical solutions for yourself or your clients.

In this ritual, the whole root is petitioned for aid before you fall asleep, then placed on the bed beside your head. I've seen some magical workers who will give their root a few drops of whiskey or milk to "drink" before falling asleep. It's said that the spirit of the root will show you what you need to know in your dreams. The next morning, the root should be carefully wrapped in a clean cloth and stored for safekeeping, usually in a box called a "spirit house" that is made specifically for such root specimens.

HORSEMINT
Monarda spp.

OTHER NAMES: Beebalm

CAUTIONS: None

PARTS USED: Leaf, flower

RECOMMENDED PREPARATION: Infusion and tincture of foliage; salve and oil of foliage

MEDICINAL USES: Horsemint is a tricky plant to identify because the name is given to many species of the *Monarda* genus, including wild bergamot (M. *fistulosa*), crimson beebalm (M. *didyma*), and lemon beebalm (M. *citriodora*). The plant most often identified with horsemint is M. *fistulosa*, or wild bergamot. All of these species are common across the Ozarks, although wild bergamot seems to occur more than the other varieties. Crimson beebalm, sometimes just called beebalm, and lemon beebalm are commonly grown in household gardens. They are popular with local pollinators, hence the name beebalm. As all the listed species are used in very similar ways, I will discuss them all together here rather than having separate entries.

Like other herbs in the mint family (*Lamiaceae*), horsemint can be used as a carminative to help with headaches and stomachaches. It's also a remedy for colds and chills. It's a cool-natured plant, so it can be used to fight fevers and inflammatory conditions. Crimson beebalm has a delicate, lemony flavor as compared to the more intense nature of wild bergamot and lemon beebalm. I use the last two in infusions for draining out the sinuses and helping clear congestion.

Externally, horsemint can be used in oils, salves, poultices, and washes for many different ailments including bug bites, stings, poison ivy, sunburn, rashes, and dermatological conditions like eczema.

MODERN HERBAL ACTIONS:
- Carminative: Infusion taken internally for gas and upset stomach
- Colds: Infusion taken internally for colds and chills
- Febrifuge: Infusion taken internally to break a fever
- Skin: Leaves used externally in oils and salves for dermatological needs

PLANETARY SIGN: Venus

MAGICAL ALIGNMENT: Right hand

MAGICAL USES: Horsemint and the other species of *Monarda* are also used as cleansing or purification plants, specifically associated with water. Baths of horsemint are still popular amongst magical workers to cleanse malign influences off the body, especially after encounters with ghosts. Healers also use bundles of fresh horsemint to sweep their clients while in a river or stream. Both dried and fresh horsemint can be added to purgative blends to help cushion the stomach and assist with easing the work; many plants from the mint family are used in this way.

TRY IT OUT—HORSEMINT BATH: Many Ozark healers use baths of horsemint leaves and Epsom salts to help detach and cleanse lingering spiritual influences. These baths were once popular after funerals and wakes to ensure the dead didn't follow their family back home. Today, horsemint baths are still used to cut any connections made with negative or unwanted spiritual influences. Several spirit mediums I know take these baths after every séance to make sure the spirits summoned don't linger.

Spiritual baths can be made in a number of ways, but the two most popular variations in the Ozarks are the soak and the standing bath. In a soak, the plant and mineral ingredients for the bath—horsemint and Epsom salt, in this case—are added to a regular tub bath. The person receiving the cleanse will soak for a given amount of time, then wash with clean water. In a standing bath, only horsemint leaves are used, and they are first steeped in a container of hot water. A popular container for these baths is a plastic one- or two-gallon pitcher, like the ones used for iced tea. After the herb has steeped for a short amount of time, the leaves are strained out and cool water is added to lower the temperature. Then, while standing outside or in a bathtub, the one being cleansed will pour the water over their heads three times, using all the liquid. They will then usually take a shower in clean water.

MULLEIN
Verbascum thapsus

OTHER NAMES: Candlewick plant, witch's taper, lamb's ear

CAUTIONS: Seeds contain the chemical compound rotenone,[39] known to be toxic. Flowers and leaves are free of this substance.

PARTS USED: Root, leaf, flower

RECOMMENDED PREPARATION: Infusion and tincture of foliage; salve and oil of foliage

MEDICINAL USES: Although native to Europe, mullein was introduced early on in America's history and is still much beloved by the Ozark people. Ozarkers have used the plant for a wide range of medicinal and magical purposes. Mullein goes by other names including candlewick plant and witch's taper, connecting it to its use as a hillfolk candle. The dried flower stalks were traditionally dipped in wax and then burned. This was particularly useful at a time when wax would have been scarce and expensive for Ozark

---

39. Easley and Horne, *Modern Herbal Dispensatory*, 270.

hillfolk. It's also said that you can use the dry, fuzzy leaves like lamp wicks, but I've never seen this in person.

Dried mullein leaves are used to help treat asthma, coughs, and congestion. This can take the form of expectorant infusions and syrups, smoking the leaves in a pipe, or smoking the leaves as long cigars rolled in cornhusks.

The leaves are also used internally and externally for their analgesic properties. Mullein can be taken internally as an infusion or tincture to help with inflammation and muscle pains. Externally, mullein leaves were traditionally wilted in vinegar and applied directly to the skin to treat a number of ailments including rashes, sprains, and arthritis.

MODERN HERBAL ACTIONS:
- Analgesic: Leaves and roots used externally in salves and washes as a pain reliever
- Anti-inflammatory: Leaves can be wilted and used in poultices for swollen glands
- Expectorant: Infusion of leaves taken internally for cough and to clear chest congestion; dried leaves smoked to clear phlegm from chest

PLANETARY SIGNS: Mercury, Saturn

MAGICAL ALIGNMENT: Both hands

MAGICAL USES: In European folklore, mullein has associations with the spirit world, especially its use as a funeral torch used to light the way for the wandering dead. In Ozark folk belief, mullein often carried similar associations as tobacco and was used in rituals for purification, unity, healing, and interaction with the spirit world. Following these associations, mountain seers often used mullein smoke to help facilitate communications with the dead as well as to filter out any harmful spirits that might try to break through. Even today, mullein is used alongside tobacco and red cedar as a smoke to clear negative or unwanted influences from the home.

Mullein has also been traditionally associated with certain divination rites, especially related to love. In one old ritual, a person could go out and bend a mullein stalk in the direction of another's home. If that person loved them, the stalk would grow upright again. If not, the stalk would die. In another ritual, dried mullein leaves were burned inside the house and then a person named their love. If the smoke blew in the direction of this person's home, it was taken as a favorable sign. Mountain healers often used this same technique to diagnose the direction a harmful curse might have come from.

Because of its associations with the spirit world, mullein has traditionally been used for left-handed magical work as well. In one ritual, a worker went out to a clearing in the woods at midnight during a new moon and lit two witch's tapers, sticking them in the ground about four feet apart from each other. The worker sat on the ground, facing the center between these two tapers, and recited a certain summoning charm. It was believed that a spirit would appear in the light between the tapers and perform whatever task the worker had in mind.

TRY IT OUT—WITCH TAPER: To make your very own witch taper, first gather up some mullein stalks. The best time to do this is over the winter because the mullein has gone to seed and the stalks are dried out. You really only want the part of the stalk where the flowers were originally, but break off the stem a few inches below this for a handle. Make sure the stalks are completely dried out.

Next, melt some beeswax. This can be done in melting pots purchased online or at any crafting store, or you can melt the wax in a double boiler made with a cooking pot and a mason jar. Do not heat the wax directly on a stove unless you are using a melting pot made specifically for that purpose.

Once the wax is melted, you can dip the mullein stalks in the wax or pour the wax over them. You'll want to build up a few layers of wax. Let the candles dry on parchment paper. Light the candles by holding the tip in a flame. Once the wax and pithy core of the mullein stalk catch, these candles will burn for several hours, depending on how much wax was used. I recommend burning them outside—they tend to smoke a lot.

ONION
Allium cepa

CAUTIONS: None

PARTS USED: Bulb

RECOMMENDED PREPARATION: Decoction of bulb; bulb cooked in broths and soups

MEDICINAL USES: It might seem strange, but one of the most powerful household cures for all kinds of illnesses was once the lowly onion. Much of our own healing starts at home with the food we eat; onions, garlic, and some strong chicken broth were often more than enough to kick any sickness right in the pants.

Herbalists have valued the onion as an effective diuretic, diaphoretic, and antiseptic. Hot onion poultices were used across the Ozarks for a variety of skin complaints and as a cure for a cough or congestion. Sometimes just having the onion was believed to be a powerful talisman for warding off illness.

Onions were also used in Ozark wart curing. It was believed that a person needed only to cut an onion in half, rub the cut side on their warts, put the two halves back together, and bury it in the ground during the full moon. It was said that as the moon waned, your warts would grow smaller and smaller until they finally disappeared altogether.

MODERN HERBAL ACTIONS:

- Colds: Decoction or syrup of chopped onions taken internally for colds
- Diuretic: Tincture of onions in gin taken internally for "gravel" or bladder/kidney stones

PLANETARY SIGN: Mars

MAGICAL ALIGNMENT: Both hands

MAGICAL USES: Because the onion is considered a plant of Mars, it can be a fierce and fiery protector. Burning onion skins can act as a fumigant against evil spirits and malign magic. Burn an onion to ash in a fire and spread the ash around the outside of your house in a big clockwise circle. It'll act as a ward against evil and illness.

Left-handed workers can also use onions for their own devices. A worker can bore a hole through the middle of an onion with a red-hot poker and then stuff the cored-out area with a sealed tube of paper. The tube holds hair or fingernail clippings from their targeted individual. This onion spite doll is then allowed to sizzle on hot coals, or the worker might hang the object in a spot where water draining off the roof will fall right on the doll, giving the victim pains and chills.

TRY IT OUT—A FIERY PROTECTOR: Need protection from another magical practitioner? Try out this traditional onion charm. First, write the first and last name of your enemy on a small square of paper horizontally, so that each name is stacked on top of each other:

FIRST LAST

FIRST LAST

FIRST LAST

If you don't know their name, just write "My Enemy" three times in the same way. If you happen to have any identifying ingredients from the person, like hair, nail clippings, a photograph, etc., add these to the paper as well, then fold it in half to hold everything inside.

Next, chop a whole onion in half. Stick the folded paper in between the two halves, then return them together. Tie the whole thing up with a good amount of red string.

Traditionally, these onion charms were hung in the branches of a witch tree like sassafras, pawpaw, dogwood, or redbud. The onion charms could also be pierced by the long thorns of a honey locust, attaching them. If none of these options are available to you, an ordinary oak tree will do. The fiery nature of the onion will ensure your enemy never tries to work against you.

PASSIONFLOWER
Passiflora incarnata

OTHER NAMES: Passion fruit, passion vine, maypop

CAUTIONS: Passionflower is a mild sedative

PARTS USED: Leaves, flower, fruit

RECOMMENDED PREPARATION: Infusion and tincture of foliage; fruit eaten when ripe

MEDICINAL USES: Many people consider passion fruit to be a tropical or exotic delicacy, but few know it grows natively throughout the Americas and has been used by Ozark hillfolk for centuries. The fruit is edible, as are the seeds inside. The fruit ripens toward the end of summer and into early fall. It's sometimes hard to tell when the fruit is ripe or has started to ferment inside. I've found many that were sweet and pleasant and then all of a sudden sucked out a mouthful of naturally made passion fruit wine.

The leaves and flowers have a sedative and nervine action, making it a perfect plant in infusions against restlessness, insomnia, stress, and even muscle spasms.

MODERN HERBAL ACTIONS:
- Antispasmodic: Infusions of foliage taken internally to calm cramps and muscle spasms
- Aphrodisiac: Infusions of foliage said to be an aphrodisiac
- Edible: Ripe fruit edible
- Sedative: Infusions of dried foliage taken internally as a mild sedative

PLANETARY SIGN: Venus

MAGICAL ALIGNMENT: Right hand

MAGICAL USES: Because of its associations with Venus, infusions of passionflower are sometimes taken by individuals wanting to attract new lovers or wanting to spice up their current relationships. Sometimes the flower or a small bundle of leaves are worn in a hat or on a shirt for the same purpose.

TRY IT OUT—DREAMING OF LOVE: Passionflower was often used to divine the identity of your future lover or spouse. First, make a passionflower leaf tea. This can be a ready-made tea that you purchase or a tea made from loose, dried passionflower leaves—just make sure it's only passionflower leaves and not a mixture with other sedative plants like valerian roots. Drink a cup of this tea before bed. To increase the power of the dream divination, some people will put a passionflower leaf under their pillow as well. It's said that the image of your love will come to you as you dream. The absolutely best time to do this work is on a Friday (Venus) when the moon is in Pisces.

PAWPAW
Asimina triloba

OTHER NAMES: None

CAUTIONS: Pawpaw fruit is a mild laxative. Tolerance to these effects comes with more exposure to the fruit.

PARTS USED: Bark, fruit, seeds

RECOMMENDED PREPARATION: Fruit can be eaten raw or added to baked breads and cakes; fruit can be made into a delicious ice cream

MEDICINAL USES: The fruit of the pawpaw is edible and a hillfolk favorite. Its taste is somewhere between a banana and a pineapple, with the texture being closer to a banana. It's a strange delicacy if you've never had it. It's also a gentle laxative, but a person can develop a tolerance to this with repeated exposure.

In addition to the fruit, trunks of the wood have traditionally been used as fence posts throughout the Ozarks. The inner bark can be woven into strong ropes. Because of the acetogenins in the leaves, an effective insecticide can be produced when boiled.

MODERN HERBAL ACTIONS:
- Edible: Fruit used for food
- Laxative: Fruit, especially unripe, used as a laxative

PLANETARY SIGNS: Moon, Jupiter

MAGICAL ALIGNMENT: Both hands

MAGICAL USES: The pawpaw is one of a few trees here in the Ozarks with very mysterious connections to the supernatural. Others of these witch trees include sassafras, dogwood, redbud, and witch hazel. These trees have traditional associations with death and witchcraft and are still used in a host of magical rites, both for healing and for more nefarious purposes.

The pawpaw and sassafras trees in particular attract the swallowtail butterfly, whose caterpillar almost exclusively feeds on the leaves of these two trees and often perches in their branches once metamorphosed. In Ozark folklore, butterflies are often seen as spirits of the dead that have returned to visit their loved ones, so seeing a tree full of these beautiful insects gives the pawpaw an eerie appearance indeed.

The seeds of the pawpaw have their own magical value in laying, or calming, spirits. The seeds can be added to protective bags and amulets or buried at the four corners of a house to magically seal the home against spirit intruders. I had a healer explain this to me once. She said the pawpaw seeds wouldn't let the spirit rise from the grave, so the ghost would be nailed or laid to the spot to think about their deeds until all the seeds completely rotted away.

The pawpaw is also a popular tree for plugging and pegging rituals, especially connected to infidelity. In that case, a person might go out to a pawpaw, bore a hole in the trunk, stuff the hole with some of their cheating partner's hair or clothing scraps, then plug the hole with a peg made from the same tree. This is supposed to cause their partner a great deal of discomfort until they confess all their wicked ways. Depending upon the temperament of the person who was cheated on, they can either go out and remove the peg or leave it in for some added discomfort.

TRY IT OUT—HANGING UP A HEX: If you ever feel like you've been cursed or hexed and want to get rid of it quick, perform this simple ritual. Cut out a small paper doll from a piece of unused white paper. Take the doll out to a pawpaw tree. It's best to do this cleansing work during the waning moon, particularly when the moon is in Cancer. Repeat this charm: "I leave my hex in a pawpaw tree! Pawpaw take this curse from me!" After you say the charm, spit on the doll. Repeat this process two more times. Then, pierce the doll on one of the pawpaw branches, right through the center of the figure. Make sure to use a tree that is hidden from sight! It's said that a worker can use your spit in cursing rites, which won't help the situation at all.

PEPPERS

Capsicum spp.

OTHER NAMES: None

CAUTIONS: Can be irritating to the stomach and intestines. Do not use in cases of stomach ulcers, acid reflux, or other gastrointestinal issues.[40] Can be irritating to skin when applied topically.

PARTS USED: Fruit

RECOMMENDED PREPARATION: Decoction and tincture of fruit; salve and oil of fruit; seasoning; can be used in cooking

MEDICINAL USES: Although it might seem counterintuitive, members of the *Capsicum* genus actually have an anti-inflammatory quality despite being associated with heat. In the Ozarks, hot peppers were traditionally used to remedy cold conditions like congestion, chills, etc.

Because of its hot nature and anti-inflammatory properties, dried and powdered red pepper has traditionally been added to salves and liniments for aching and sore muscles.

MODERN HERBAL ACTIONS:
- Anti-inflammatory: Used in salves and liniments to reduce inflammation and swelling
- Colds: Decoction taken internally for colds and to reduce congestion

PLANETARY SIGN: Mars

MAGICAL ALIGNMENT: Both hands

MAGICAL USES: Peppers are associated with Mars, both in their ability to protect as well as harm. Traditionally, little bags might be filled with hot pepper flakes and hung next to the door to magically burn away evil influences. Left-handed workers might fill a spite doll with hot pepper in order to burn their victim from the inside out.

TRY IT OUT—HOT PEPPER FENCE: To create a powerful fence around your home to protect from evil influences, try making this traditional spray. (Please note: always wear gloves when handling hot peppers and make sure never to touch your eyes or other sensitive areas of your body until you can thoroughly wash your hands.) Take around ten hot peppers of your choice and add them to a pot with two quarts of water. Boil

---

40. Easley and Horne, *Modern Herbal Dispensatory*, 202.

this for around thirty minutes. Make sure you don't inhale the steam directly, especially if you're using very hot peppers!

After you've finished boiling the peppers, let the liquid cool down. You might want to add some tobacco to steep while the liquid is cooling. Next, bottle the liquid in a spray bottle. No, you didn't just create your own pepper spray—use this spray around the outside of your house to help protect from unwanted spiritual influences, entities, and the work of other magical practitioners. As it was told to me, evil will burn its feet trying to cross the fence made by this spray.

PLANTAIN
Plantago major

OTHER NAMES: Ribwort plantain (*P. lanceolate*), white man's footprint, way bread, snake-weed

CAUTIONS: Because of its action on mucus membranes in the body, use isn't recommended with profuse or severe congestion of the respiratory system.[41]

PARTS USED: Root, leaf, flower

MEDICINAL USES: Plantain is a European plant brought to the New World with the colonizers as a winter potherb and medicinal plant. The leaves are edible but have thick veins, so picking them when they're very young is advised. Even then, they need some cooking.

The main use of the leaves today is in salves, oils, and poultices for all kinds of skin issues. The leaves of both species contain anti-inflammatory and analgesic compounds. I make a green salve with plantain and coconut oil that's great for rashes, sunburns, bug bites, and even eczema.

You can also use the leaves and roots internally as infusions for colds or breaking fevers. It also has expectorant properties, but as it is a very moist plant like sassafras, it's best used as an expectorant for dry coughs only.

MODERN HERBAL ACTIONS:

- Anti-inflammatory: Crushed fresh leaves used in poultices for inflammation
- Expectorant: Root used as a gentle expectorant for dry coughs and in helping sinus issues

---

41. Brinker, *Herbal Contraindications*, 264.

- Febrifuge: Whole plant infusions for fever
- Skin: Leaves used in poultices for bug bites, inflammation, rashes, cuts, bruises, stings, and other skin complaints

PLANETARY SIGN: Venus

MAGICAL ALIGNMENT: Right hand

MAGICAL USES: Ozark folklore says that keeping a plantain leaf in your pocket or shoe will scare snakes away from your path. I've never personally tried this folk charm, but I have met some who always keep a leaf on them and swear by its magical powers. This use of "snakeweed" can have another meaning within Ozark folk healing; healers even today will often refer to certain plants as being able to "snake" out illness or curses from a person's body. The spirit of the medicine is seen as being able to twist and turn its way like a snake through the veins and organs of a person's body, taking the complete illness or curse with it as it goes. For this reason, traditional medicines aimed at purging or releasing often include plantain.

Because of its associations with Venus, plantain can also be used in ritual work aimed at love, marriage, or strengthening relationships.

TRY IT OUT—GREEN OIL: This is an all-purpose oil for cuts, bruises, bug bites, eczema, burns, etc.

- 2 quarts oil suitable for skin use (sweet almond, grapeseed, coconut, etc.)
- ¾ cup plantain leaf
- ¼ cup comfrey leaf
- ¼ cup rosemary leaf
- ¼ cup self-heal leaf
- ¼ cup thyme leaf
- Beeswax (optional)

Heat your oil slowly in a Crock-Pot. Once warm, add all of your plant matter and set the Crock-Pot on low. You don't want to cook the herbs—if sizzling occurs, turn down the heat! Let sit in warm oil for three to four hours. If you want to make a salve that is solid at room temperature, add in ¼ to ½ cup of grated beeswax and let melt. Once the oil is cool enough to handle, strain and put in jars.

RABBIT TOBACCO

Pseudognaphalium obtusifolium

OTHER NAMES: Sweet everlasting, old field balsam

CAUTIONS: Can cause an allergic response in individuals who are sensitive to members of the *Asteraceae* family, e.g. ragweed, chamomile, yarrow, etc.

PARTS USED: Leaf, flower

MEDICINAL USES: Also called sweet everlasting, rabbit tobacco is powerful plant medicine that most people walk past without noticing. It also goes by the name old field balsam because it primarily grows in the poor soil of old hayfields. Where nothing else may be able to grow, you'll at least find rabbit tobacco.

Rabbit tobacco and mullein were both traditionally added to regular tobacco to make it last longer. Rabbit tobacco was preferred because of its smooth, maple syrup–like flavor. Both plants were also associated with opening up the lungs and clearing out mucus. These old remedies for coughs and congestion could take the form of smoking the plant or using the sweet-tasting leaves in infusions. Pillows stuffed with the flowers of rabbit tobacco were believed to help with asthma. I don't recommend this today because those who are sensitive to other members of the *Asteraceae* family will be sensitive to rabbit tobacco as well.

The plant gets its name "sweet everlasting" from the white flowers that stay on the tops of the plant even after it has died. This gives the appearance of a blooming flower even in the dead of winter. The leaves and flowers aren't harvested when green; instead, they are harvested in the fall when the tops of the leaves become silvery white and the bottoms a rich chocolate brown. The sugars in the plant caramelize, the familiar balsam or maple syrup smell becomes more pronounced, and the flavor becomes more delicate. It's said the medicine inside the plant is at its peak during this time.

MODERN HERBAL ACTIONS:

- Analgesic: Infusion used internally and externally for sores, pains, aches, wounds, etc.
- Colds: Decoction of foliage taken internally for colds and chills
- Expectorant: Dried foliage smoked and used in infusions to clear chest congestion
- Sedative: Decoction of the whole plant used as a sedative and to aid sleeping

PLANETARY SIGN AND ELEMENT: Venus, Air

MAGICAL ALIGNMENT: Right hand

MAGICAL USES: Rabbit tobacco has many uses within Ozark folk magic. Several of these uses are also associated with regular tobacco and even mullein. Rabbit tobacco smoke is said to be able to cleanse evil out of a space or off of a person. Baths made from the leaves and flowers are used for a similar purpose. Because the plant is associated with eternal life, it's said that the smoke from rabbit tobacco helps ease the dead into a better afterlife, and it can even calm angry and vengeful ghosts.

The smoke of rabbit tobacco is still used by backwoods healers in divinations for illnesses. It's thought that certain symbols and shapes will form in the smoke and lead the doctor toward a cure.

Love divinations were also traditionally performed with rabbit tobacco. For example, if you chewed up some rabbit tobacco leaves before bed and then placed the chewed up leaves under your pillow, you would dream of your true love.

TRY IT OUT—CLEANSING SMOKE: A very effective fumigation against all kinds of negative or unwanted energies and entities can be made with ordinary rabbit tobacco. In this simple ritual, hillfolk would heat up a cast iron skillet. They would then drop rabbit tobacco leaves into the center of the skillet as they walked the smoke around their cabin. Today, I prefer to drop a pinch of the leaves onto incense charcoal set in a portable burner. Then I carry the smoke around the inside of my house, starting at the front door and going clockwise through every room until I return to the front door. You can also do this on the outside of the house, but carry some rabbit tobacco with you to add to the coals, as it will burn quickly. A day when the moon is in Taurus or Cancer is best for this cleansing ritual, especially during a waning moon to lessen or banish negative influences.

REDBUD
Cercis siliquastrum

OTHER NAMES: Judas tree, bean tree

CAUTIONS: None

PARTS USED: Bark, flower, seedpod

MEDICINAL USES: This is another of the Ozark "ghost trees," along with the pawpaw. It's said that spirits hang around the trees, although few know why. It's also called the Judas tree because of a legend that Judas Iscariot hung himself on a redbud after betraying Jesus.

The redbud's bright pink flowers are edible and are a great source of vitamins in the early spring. I usually tell people to leave the flowers and let them turn into bean pods a little later on. The pods are also edible, giving the tree the name "bean tree." Harvest them while they are still under an inch and a half in length. Eat the pods raw or throw them in with other cooked vegetables. If you harvest them when they are larger than an inch and a half, they turn tough and astringent.

Decoctions of the bark were traditionally taken for coughs, particularly whooping cough, and a cold infusion of the bark and roots was taken for fevers.

MODERN HERBAL ACTIONS:
- Edible: Flowers in early spring are edible and can be used to flavor other medicinal preparations; young bean pods edible
- Expectorant: Decoction of bark taken internally for cough
- Febrifuge: Cold infusion of inner bark and roots used to treat fevers

PLANETARY SIGN: Saturn

MAGICAL ALIGNMENT: Both hands

MAGICAL USES: The main magical use of the redbud is in the making of ritual tools for calling up spirits of the dead or the land. Wands are sometimes made out of branches for this purpose, as are pendulums from the wood of the tree. The smoke of burning redbud bark is said to be pleasing to the disembodied noses of haints and ghosts. A particularly auspicious shape is a redbud root that forms a natural circle; you see these sometimes along creek banks where the water has washed away the soil that used to be around the twisting roots. I was once told that looking through a hole like this, especially a redbud circle, would allow the viewer to look into the otherworld.

TRY IT OUT—REDBUD DIVINATION: In addition to the wood of the tree, many people use the leaves as a divinatory tool. In this simple ritual, take a wide bowl and fill it with water. (Spring water is traditionally used.) Take a redbud leaf and trim off the stem. Next, float the leaf on the water. Observe the way it moves naturally at first, then wait until it is completely still. Ask the leaf to show which direction means "yes" and which means "no" based on how it turns, clockwise or counterclockwise, or if it points in a specific direction. Once you've determined this, you can begin to ask questions and interpret the redbud's answers.

RED CEDAR

Juniperus virginiana

OTHER NAMES: Cedar

CAUTIONS: Avoid if you are allergic to red cedar or juniper pollen. Topical use can cause contact dermatitis.

PARTS USED: Foliage, berry, bark

MEDICINAL USES: The red cedar tree forms a sort of holy trinity with sassafras and tobacco in Ozark traditional healing and magic. The red cedar isn't a true cedar though; there aren't any native cedars in the Ozarks from either the *Thuja* or *Cedrus* genus. Red cedar is actually in the genus *Juniperus*, or the junipers, and is often used in the same way as common juniper would be.

Infusions of the leaves and berries were traditionally used in analgesic and antiseptic washes for wounds, rashes, and other skin needs. Tinctures were also widely used for this purpose. Infusions of the foliage were also taken internally to help with arthritis, rheumatism, and colds.

Some people are sensitive to the plant, so take caution and try only a small amount at first. If you know you have seasonal allergies from the red cedar or other junipers, avoid using this tree in medicinal preparations.

MODERN HERBAL ACTIONS:
- Analgesic: Infusion of leaves used externally for an analgesic
- Colds: Decoction of twigs and leaves used for colds
- Expectorant: Smoke breathed as a remedy for chest congestion

PLANETARY SIGNS: Moon, Jupiter

MAGICAL ALIGNMENT: Right hand

MAGICAL USES: The red cedar tree has strong associations for both Europeans and the indigenous peoples of the Southeast. For the Scottish, the juniper was a powerful cleansing plant whose smoke was wafted around the house to clear out evil spirits and sickness.

Smoke from burning red cedar bark or foliage is a great fumigant for stagnant energies and lingering spirits in the home. Traditionally, bundles of dried leaves would be thrown on the coals of the fire in the morning and at night as a way for hillfolk to protect themselves and their home throughout the day. Personally, I burn red cedar in almost all of the rituals I perform.

Many healers prefer using the wood to carve magical tools. Red cedar spoons, for example, were traditionally used by yarb doctors to stir their medicinal infusions and decoctions. It was believed that the wood was able to impart its own magic to the medicine. I once met a healer who swore by cooking his broths in a clay vessel and stirring only with a red cedar spoon or stick. He told me the clay gave the yarb broth some additional healing minerals, and the red cedar spoon gave its magical sap to the mix.

Talismans and amulets are also commonly carved from red cedar. I've seen several little crosses carved from the wood, worn as a necklace to protect from evil and lightning strikes. It's also common to see these crosses, usually carved from a three-pronged branch, stuck in the ground outside a house as a "witch snare" to trip up evil magic and sickness.

For diagnosing an illness or finding out the direction of a witch, a healer will sometimes float red cedar bark or leaves in a bowl of water to act as a divination device.

TRY IT OUT—RED CEDAR PEGS: This ritual is for creating a magical fence around your house that is said to protect from malign influences, wandering spirits, and sickness alike. First, cut four red cedar sticks off a tree. The sticks can be any length. Try and find some that have three prongs at one end. If you can find a red cedar growing with its roots in running water, that is very beneficial for this work. Soak the four sticks in a mixture of spring water, asafetida powder, camphor, and tobacco. Be sure to wear gloves while you do this work! The pungent odor of asafetida is difficult to wash off.

Dry the sticks in the sun for three days. Sharpen the ends opposite to the three prongs with a knife. Take and drive each stake into the earth on the north, south, east, and west side of your house. Start with east, then proceed in a clockwise direction. It is useful to also accompany this circle with the smoking of tobacco or red cedar.

SASSAFRAS
Sassafras albidum

OTHER NAMES: None

CAUTIONS: The FDA banned sassafras in commercial products in 1960 because of the contained chemical compound safrole, which was found to be carcinogenic in animal studies. Sassafras root bark and pure essential oil are still available commercially for personal use.

PARTS USED: Root, bark, leaf

MEDICINAL USES: The second plant in the Ozark holy trinity, along with red cedar and tobacco, is sassafras, which has long been used in medicines as well as magical cures by hillfolk throughout the region. Its principle use within Ozark herbalism is as a blood thinner or blood purifier and as a spring tonic. According to the Ozark theory of medicine, the blood is seen as being intimately linked to the liver and digestive system. Plants that are said to "clean the blood," "clear the blood," or "purify the blood" all act on the liver and therefore help with digestion. Sassafras is probably the most famous of these plants.

It was said that blood's season was the springtime. Sassafras decoctions were traditionally taken in the springtime, usually at least once a day for a few weeks, to help purify the blood and cure the constipation hillfolk no doubt had after a winter eating canned and salted foods heavy in sodium and lacking in other nutrients. These mild laxatives or spring tonics were a vital part of the health of the individual. Almost all of our tonic plants have some clearing action to them, whether it's as a laxative, diuretic, or an expectorant. These all help to clear out systems of the body, thought to allow a person to get back up and running for the rest of the year.

Despite the FDA banning of safrole-containing sassafras in commercial products, hillfolk in the Ozarks still widely use the plant. There's a great amount of debate amongst modern herbalists as to the potential risks of the safrole in sassafras. Safrole has indeed been found to be carcinogenic in animal studies.[42] Herbalists who favor the plant are quick to point out, however, that this was a concentrated amount of safrole that wouldn't be consumed by the average person using the plant medicinally. These herbalists point to the traditional use of sassafras as a tonic plant. In Ozark folk medicine, tonics tend to be stronger than normal medicines, intended to be used for a short amount of time only. For example, sassafras was traditionally only drank in the springtime, and usually only in one cup a day for about a week. In the case of serious illness, the dosage might be three cups a day, but only for three days.

Preparation of the tea varies depending on who you talk to. Many I've met say to only use the "red roots" of the tree. For the longest time I was confused because all of the roots of the sassafras tree have a reddish color; then one old woman finally took pity on me and explained that it's best to use the bark of the roots that hold the reddest

---

42. Dietz and Bolton, "Botanical Dietary Supplements Gone Bad," 586–90.

color. That's favored over the white, inner core, usually reserved for a subpar version of the tea.

There's also a great debate about whether you drink the first or second boiling of the roots. In my personal work, I drink the first boiling. It's much stronger and has more of the desired "cleansing" or "releasing" effect. I'll also give the first boiling to a client if we're doing purgation work or if they're already used to drinking the tea. As with many other Ozark plants, you can develop a tolerance to the effects of sassafras through repeat exposure. Usually if I'm just making some sassafras tea for mixed company, I'll use the lighter, second boiling, which tends to be less bitter yet still retains the classic root beer flavor.

The leaves of the tree are often made into infusions for sore throats and bowel complaints. When wet, the leaves make a mucous-like substance, as with okra. The leaves then can be used to thicken soups or to help with sore throats. Sassafras leaves are also used topically in washes, poultices, and salves as analgesic and anti-inflammatory remedies.

MODERN HERBAL ACTIONS:
- Analgesic: Infusion of leaves taken internally for headaches
- Colds: Decoction of root taken internally for colds
- Laxative: Decoction of bark and root taken as a mild laxative
- Skin: Poultice of leaves and bark for dermatological needs
- Tonic: Decoctions of root usually taken in the spring as a blood tonic

PLANETARY SIGNS: Venus, Saturn

MAGICAL ALIGNMENT: Right hand

MAGICAL USES: There are many folk beliefs and taboos surrounding the sassafras tree. The most common one is that the wood should never be burned. It's said that the popping sound of burning the wood signals the devil to light on the roof of the house; according to the old tales, he'll burn the place down while you're sleeping. In other versions, he'll take all your fortune or luck back to Hell with him. I've not encountered the same belief with the leaves, which I've seen smoked with tobacco or sometimes with other plants like mullein. It still makes me uneasy, though, and I try not to even do that.

Sassafras is a cold/wet spirit, according to the four humors system. It enjoys the mountain air, soft and foggy. It lives beside streams and rivers. Its leaves have a light, lemony scent and can cool a hot temper. You can see why it might not like fire all that much. In fact, if we look at the four humors, sassafras is said to help aid the hot/dry choleric condition, linked to imbalance in the liver and poor digestion.

The magical use of sassafras is in its ability to cleanse the body of curses and other built-up negative influences. For a quick cleanse, I like to pour hot water over sassafras leaves and let it cool down to room temperature, then I use this liquid as a quick bath for washing away the stresses of everyday life. For clients who might need a deeper cleanse, I make a tea from the roots and use this along with other rituals for releasing and purification. Simply having the roots and branches around the house is also believed to help ward off evil magic and sickness. Whole roots are sometimes tied together and hung near the front door to act as a barrier for angry spirits, or they carried in pockets for protection.

TRY IT OUT—SASSAFRAS MAGIC: To pull out a curse from yourself or another, first make a small amount of sassafras tea by boiling ¼ cup root pieces in 3 cups of water for fifteen minutes. Strain out the roots and let cool.

Pour into a glass and say these words: "Water, water! As the river carries leaves away, carry this sickness away! As the river carries leaves away, carry this evil away! As the river carries leaves away, carry this darkness away! Water, water! Flow into the east. Flow back up the mountain."

Place the glass on a table near the head of the one who is cursed. Make sure the glass is near their head as they sleep. The next morning, pour the water on the roots of a strong oak tree so that as the tree grows, so too will the afflicted person recover.

SPICEBUSH
Lindera benzoin

OTHER NAMES: Benjamin bush, spicewood

CAUTIONS: None

PARTS USED: Bark, leaf, berry

MEDICINAL USES: Spicebush has been historically called Benjamin bush, derived from a corruption of the word *benzoin*, a resinous substance taken from *Styrax* trees, which bears a very similar smell to the leaves and bark of the spicebush.

Spicebush is a plant of many uses here in the Ozarks, both traditionally and in modern practice. It has a spicy cinnamon taste and therefore has been used in infusions and tinctures against colds, chills, and wet congestion. It's also been traditionally used as a fever reducer when made into a strong decoction. Internally, spicebush tea is taken as a spring tonic, sometimes mixed with sassafras, for its benefit as a blood thinner or as a laxative. Berries and bark are most effective as decoctions or tinctures. A pleasant combination is a tincture of elderberries, spicebush berries, and honey. This makes for an excellent tonic for colds, coughs, and the immune system. Leaves are best used as infusions and poultices or salves for the skin.

The berries have a strong spice flavor and were historically used by hillfolk to season game meat. They were also used as an allspice or cinnamon substitute in other recipes.

MODERN HERBAL ACTIONS:
- Analgesic: Infusion of leaves taken for headaches
- Colds: Infusion of leaves taken internally for colds
- Febrifuge: Decoction of bark and twigs taken internally for fever
- Skin: Infusion/poultice of leaves used externally for skin issues
- Spice: Red berries of the spicebush have long been used as a substitute for cinnamon or allspice

PLANETARY SIGN: Mars

MAGICAL ALIGNMENT: Right hand

MAGICAL USES: In Ozark folk magic, the twigs, roots, and berries of the spicebush are often carried to help protect against evil influences and malign magic. Like sassafras, with which spicebush is often paired as medicine, it doesn't like burning. Spicebush prefers to work in the form of baths and cleansing brews. A gentle releasing formula I like to use for beginners consists of a mixture of sassafras roots, spicebush twigs, and Solomon's seal roots, all boiled together and then drank over the course of three days alongside cleansing rituals.

TRY IT OUT—SPICEBUSH DIVINATION: One traditional method of magical diagnosis involves watching the motion of a spicebush leaf floating in a bowl of water. In this ritual, take and fill a small bowl with some water. Most healers prefer spring water because it is believed to contain its own natural source of magic. Then, take a spicebush leaf and float it on top of the water. I use a dry leaf as they seem to spin more easily than fresh, but experiment with both and see what's right for you. Ask a question and observe how the leaf moves. Traditionally, clockwise means "yes" and counterclockwise means "no." This is best done when the moon is in Pisces.

SWEETGUM TREE
Liquidambar styraciflua

OTHER NAMES: Witch ball, storax

CAUTIONS: None

PARTS USED: Bark, leaf, fruit, sap

MEDICINAL USES: The genus of the sweetgum is *Liquidambar*, so named because of its fragrant sap, often called storax or styrax, whose scent was compared to that of amber resin. For most city folk, the sweetgum is an annoyance because of the vast amount of spiny seedpods, often called witch balls, that are dropped everywhere in the fall. It always breaks my heart seeing people cutting these trees down just because they have to do some extra work to keep their lawns pristine. A good way to prevent having to do extra work in the fall is by collecting the green seedpods in the springtime before the seeds develop inside, usually when they are under half an inch in diameter. These seedpods can be crushed and soaked in alcohol to make a great tincture for colds and to help boost the immune system; they're great paired with elderberry for this purpose. You can also use this tincture as a topical astringent for many skin complaints. Salves and poultices of the leaves are used for their astringent properties.

Many folks used the sap as a backwoods chewing gum, not only for the flavor, but for the medicinal benefits. I once heard that chewing on the sap will keep your teeth and stomach strong.

MODERN HERBAL ACTIONS:
- Astringent: Gum and inner bark used in decoctions for diarrhea
- Colds: Tinctures of seedpods used for colds and chills
- Skin: Leaves used in poultices for many dermatological issues, cuts, and bruises

PLANETARY SIGNS AND ELEMENT: Mercury, Venus, Jupiter, Earth

MAGICAL ALIGNMENT: Right hand

MAGICAL USES: Smoke from burning sweetgum sap or bark is said to have many magical purposes. This smoke is used first and foremost to cleanse a space and drive away evil influences. Likewise, the sweet smell is said to attract guardian spirits to the home and can be used to communicate with the spirits of ancestors who appreciate the smoke.

I once met a power doctor who used sweetgum sap to glue together his homemade amulets, saying the sap added its own protection to the work. Along these same lines, a healer might use sweetgum sap to seal up wooden pegs in plugging rituals. The sap dries harder than wax and also has the added benefit of magically protecting and cleansing.

TRY IT OUT—WITCH BALLS: For those who work with the left hand, or those who might want to do some retribution work, the spiky seedpods of the sweetgum tree can act as a natural container for magical curses. In one ritual I observed, the worker first collected about ten of the hard, dried seedpods that were littered across the ground. He then soaked them briefly in a strong tea made from boiled hot peppers and let them dry overnight. The next day, the worker powdered the seedpods with crushed red pepper, black pepper, and sulfur powder. If you do choose to repeat this ritual, make sure you wear gloves and a mask! I didn't my first time and was sneezing and tearing up for hours. The worker then put his "witch balls," as he called them, into a paper sack and set them aside. Every time he wanted to deliver a curse to someone, he would throw his witch balls onto their property, preferably in a spot where they'd step on one.

TOBACCO

Nicotiana tabacum

OTHER NAMES: Old tobacco, wild tobacco (*N. rustica*)

CAUTIONS: Using tobacco in any form increases the risk of developing certain cancers. Avoid tobacco when pregnant or if you have certain medical conditions like high blood pressure, heart disease, diabetes, respiratory disorders, or ulcers.

PARTS USED: Leaf, flower

MEDICINAL USES: The third plant in the Ozark holy trinity alongside sassafras and red cedar is tobacco, which has had a place in Ozark and Appalachian folk healing for centuries. Historically, this controversial leaf was used in its snuff form or as loose pipe tobacco since cigarettes were too expensive for hillfolk to keep around. Tobacco was almost always grown locally to cut down on costs. My great-grandpa always had a huge patch of it on his farm that he would cure to make his own chaw and rolling tobacco. Many home remedies made use of tobacco, most often for skin complaints and bug bites where a wet plug of chaw could be taken out of the cheek of the nearest dipper and pressed to the irritated spot for relief. Tobacco smoke was even used medicinally as an analgesic for toothaches, headaches, and earaches. The plant was often seen as a panacea for many illnesses.

It's highly likely that people were using tobacco even before they came into the Ozarks from interaction with indigenous peoples in the Appalachian Mountains. Tobacco itself originates in Central and South America. Wild tobacco (*N. rustica*) flourished in South America, then physically propagated across the Caribbean Islands and into the southern part of North America. *N. tobaccum*, or what we know as tobacco today, was cultivated much later in history, predominately for sale to Europeans who didn't have a taste for the much stronger *N. rustica*.

MODERN HERBAL ACTIONS: For magical use only

PLANETARY SIGNS AND ELEMENTS: Mars, Saturn, Pluto, Fire, Air

MAGICAL ALIGNMENT: Right hand

MAGICAL USES: Many of the magical uses of tobacco reached the Ozarks through people of indigenous or mixed ancestry. Many of these uses are still around today. Some Ozark healers will blow tobacco smoke over their clients for healing and cleansing or use tobacco water as washes for the body to remove malign influences from the skin.

Tobacco smoke is also used in divination ceremonies to locate the direction the malign magic came from or to identify the one who sent the curse. According to Ozark folklore, evil spirits will always crumble in tobacco smoke, and boogers will turn back into their original forms when forced to smoke or eat the plant.

Reverence for the plant even extends to many farming beliefs. I've known several old farmers who would lay some tobacco in with their planted seeds as a blessing to help them grow better. Along similar lines, tobacco is sometimes fed to a road or river before a journey to ensure the person traveling will return unharmed. Some will even use the ground powder to make a protective barrier around their house from evil influences.

TRY IT OUT—POCKET PROTECTION: You can make a simple protective amulet using the holy trinity of Ozark healing plants. Take a pinch of tobacco, red cedar leaves, and sassafras roots and put them into a small muslin bag or onto a small square of cloth. Then tie up the pouch using some string and knot three times to close. Carry this with you in your pocket or purse to help protect from malign magic and unwanted spiritual influences.

WITCH HAZEL
Hamamelis virginiana

OTHER NAMES: Ozark witch hazel (*H. vernalis*)

CAUTIONS: Avoid using internally. The tannins contained in the plant can aggravate stomach ulcers and are also an emetic in high concentrations.

PARTS USED: Bark, leaf

MEDICINAL USES: In the Ozarks, the witch hazel bush is most often associated with face washes and dowsing. The leaves and bark are highly astringent, making it valuable for use as an external wash to help clean the skin, reduce inflammation, and dry out rashes or sores.

For this reason, the poor Ozark witch hazel, only native to the Ozark region, nearly died out. Witch hazel washes were popular enough that at one time in the early twentieth century, pharmaceutical companies would send workers out to strip leaves from all the bushes they could find to take back for processing. Luckily, with the advent of synthetic face washes and cosmetics, the Ozark witch hazel was allowed to grow and flourish once more.

MODERN HERBAL ACTIONS:

- Astringent: Infusion of leaves and decoction of bark used externally as a skin toner and wash for many skin complaints

PLANETARY SIGN: Saturn

MAGICAL ALIGNMENT: Right hand

MAGICAL USES: Branches of the witch hazel are famous for use by Ozark "witch wigglers" or dowsers, said to be able to locate water or sometimes even treasure hidden deep underground. I still know a few people who swear by the dowsing arts not only for digging wells, but also for locating illnesses in the body.

In the dowsing ritual, a Y branch of witch hazel is cut. Then the dowser will place their hands in a certain way on the two "handles" of the branch, letting the single branch in the middle point outward. As the dowser approaches what they're looking for, the middle branch will dip downward toward the ground, revealing the spot to dig. Everyone I've talked to about dowsing believes it to be a scientific phenomenon, not something magical in any way. One dowser I met scoffed when I mentioned his gift, saying, "Anyone can do it if they know how." But this doesn't seem to always be the case—most believe dowsing to be a skill that can of course be developed, but you have to start with some innate ability.

The word *witch* in witch hazel actually comes from the Middle English word *wyche*, meaning "bendable" or "pliant," referring to the branches of the shrub. Regardless, many hillfolk still connect the plant to protecting against the powers of witchcraft. Some will hang crosses of witch hazel branches in their house or barn to protect from sickness and evil.

TRY IT OUT—WITCH HAZEL WASH: You can get all-natural witch hazel extracts from most health stores as well as a handful of pharmacies. In addition to being a great topical astringent, you can add a little bit to spiritual baths to bring in the cleansing power of the witch hazel. If you have a witch hazel bush nearby, try picking some of the leaves and adding them to your bath for the same benefit.

YARROW
Achillea millefolium

OTHER NAMES: None

CAUTIONS: Do not use if you are allergic to other plants in the *Asteraceae* family. Contains thujone; avoid prolonged use and concentrated doses. Thujone is known to cause nausea, dizziness, and disorientation in high concentrations.

PARTS USED: Leaf, flower

MEDICINAL USES: Yarrow is another wonder plant from Europe that has found its way into Ozark herbalism and folk magic. It has traditionally been used as a powerful styptic and was often made into poultices to stop bleeding wounds. Likewise, infusions of the plant were used topically as an astringent to wash sores and help dry out other skin complaints.

Internally, infusions were traditionally taken to help relieve colds, stop chills, and clear congestion. Like mullein, the leaves and flowers of yarrow were often smoked for their mucus-clearing abilities. Strong infusions of the flowers could help a client sweat out a fever. It was also taken internally as an effective remedy for diarrhea.

MODERN HERBAL ACTIONS:

- Astringent: Infusion taken internally for diarrhea; infusion used as topical wash for boils, rashes, inflammation, and other skin complaints
- Bleeding: Leaves used in poultices to stop bleeding
- Colds: Infusion taken internally for colds
- Expectorant: Leaves and flowers smoked for chest congestion
- Febrifuge: Strong infusion of flowers taken internally to break a fever
- Stomach: Infusion taken internally for upset stomach

PLANETARY SIGN AND ELEMENT: Venus, Air

MAGICAL ALIGNMENT: Right hand

MAGICAL USES: Yarrow is associated with cleansing, exorcism, and protection. Bundles can be hung around the house to ward off evil and illness. Leaves and flowers are often burned with other fumigation plants like red cedar to drive angry spirits from a house or protect from the influence of witchcraft. Smelling the smoke of yarrow before you go to bed is said to make you dream of your future spouse, and drinking yarrow tea every morning is said to make you irresistible to those you are attracted to.

TRY IT OUT—CLEANSING SMOKE: Like rabbit tobacco and red cedar, yarrow can also be used as an effective smoke fumigation against all negative influences and entities. As a simple ritual, burn some yarrow leaves and flowers on incense charcoal and carry it through your house, beginning at your front door and working clockwise through every room until you get back to your starting position. Adding yarrow to other smoke mixtures for protection and cleansing will heighten the power. It's also said that smoke from a fumigation of yarrow will help you dream the identity of someone trying to curse you.

Chapter 10

ANIMALS, TOOLS, AND MAGICAL SUPPLIES

ONE OF THE MOST FASCINATING areas of Ozark folk magic for me to look at is the use of magical supplies and tools. For me, this has been a vastly under-researched area by folklorists in the past hundred years of collecting material. Historically, the approach to this form of healing and magic has been to label anything that falls outside the use of plant and mineral medicines as "superstitions"—therefore, only a part of the belief system of grannies, children, and the uneducated. Because of this association early on in the collected record, many of the researchers that came afterward feared being labeled as superstitious themselves and overlooked the opportunity to delve deeper into the more magical side of Ozark folk healing.

To this day, the focus on Ozark folkways is terribly out of balance, favoring mountain herbalism and plant remedies over the use of prayers, charms, amulets, and magical tools. Hillfolk themselves have suffered greatly from the stereotypes applied to them by the outside world and folklorists alike. Vastly important healing traditions have gone unlearned by younger generations for fear of being called a hillbilly. Like the disappearing of a rare plant from the Ozark hills, I wonder how many of our powerful mountain spells and rituals have passed into darkness as a result of this culture shaming.

What we have left from the folklore record and modern healers represents a long tradition of connecting objects found in nature and around the home with certain magical processes. Everything in the healer's world could potentially be repurposed for use with healing and folk magic; it's solely dependent upon the imagination of the practitioner themselves. I've met many modern healers who seemingly have no connection to the magical arts if you were to just walk into their homes and glance around, but when some magical work was needed, the healer would flit around grabbing what they needed—knives from the kitchen, string from a junk drawer in the dining room, candles from a supply closet upstairs, and little paper prayer cards out of an old wooden recipe box. For the Ozark healer, everything in the world is seen as being imbued with these natural magical energies, so everything in the world can potentially be used in the work of healing.

Another healer I met always took his clients out to a trail near his house. I went along on one of these "healing walks," as he called them, and observed his ritual. He and his client would walk slowly along the trail, chatting at first and then digging deeper into the heart of the issue at hand. Every once in a while, the healer would stop and pick a certain plant, which he tossed into a basket he always carried. Other times it was a rock, an oddly shaped branch, a feather, or even some bones. All the while, the healer continued to counsel his client. Once the walk was over, we returned to the healer's home and he laid out all his treasures on the dining room table. Then he brewed up a tea with the plants he picked and gave it to his client to drink. After saying some prayers and giving his client a quick cleanse using an egg and feather broom, he sent them away with a couple of the natural objects he found on the hike, and the others he added to a sort of altar he had set up in the living room. I asked about the significance of the walk and the healer replied, "The hike gives 'em energy from being out in nature. The woods talk to me and tell me what plants to pick and what rocks and such to take home. They contain power for the specific person in my mind when I found 'em."

This form of magical healing—and many more like it—are sadly in decline across the Ozarks, as fewer people are choosing to study with traditional practitioners. It's my hope that this book will spur interest in others to look into cultural traditions of their own and to help save many of these dying practices before they disappear altogether.

ANIMAL AND HUMAN PARTS

CAUTIONS: Ethical sourcing for animal bones should always be considered. Owning feathers from certain birds is considered illegal in many states, so check with your local Game and Fish Commission to be sure before attempting to purchase. The legality of owning human remains is dependent upon which state you live in, unless they are Native American remains, in which case they are illegal to own based on federal law.

MAGICAL ALIGNMENT: Both hands

MAGICAL USES: It was once common in the old Ozarks to associate various animal and human parts, such as teeth, bones, hair, fingernails, etc., with the sympathetic connection created between healer and client or witch and victim. A worker of either hand could create this connection using items like hair, fingernail clippings, spit, urine, or other identifying ingredients. This connection was often present in certain healing rituals like plugging for illnesses, whereby a few strands of hair or some nail clippings were stuffed into a hole cut in a tree trunk and then plugged with wood (and sometimes beeswax). The idea was to connect the client's health with the health of the tree so that as the tree grew strong, so too would the client.

There was also an old belief that by burying an object connected to a person (e.g. fingernails, teeth, or placenta), the ground would somehow purify the person the items came from. This is also often connected with certain planting beliefs; for example, burying a placenta at the roots of a sapling would ensure the child and mother both grow up strong as long as the tree remained alive.

Apart from humans, certain animals were associated with specific conditions or diseases according to Ozark folk cosmology. For example, owls have a long connotation with malicious magic; reptiles and amphibians with colds or flu; beavers, pigs, and squirrels with the health of teeth; etc. In these cases, the bones, teeth, or feathers of the associated animal would be used alongside related charms or songs to connect the health of the client to the health of the part used. For example, wearing a boar's tusk around your neck was once believed to help with a toothache, the idea being that the strong tooth of this animal magically made your own tooth healthier by association. Carrying a dried bat's heart in your pocket was said to make the holder quick like a bat in order to protect against a bullet wound. In this case, and others like it, certain organs have symbolic value; the heart was often seen as the seat of a person or animal's identity and spirit. In one case from the folklore record, a criminal's heart was sometimes manipulated after their death, usually by burning or driving coffin nails into the organ, in order to bring retribution and punishment to their soul.

Left-handed workers could use animal parts as stand-ins for the body parts of their victims. For example, placing an animal's testicles under a waterfall was believed to give a man a crippling pain in their groin and impair their virility. Teeth were sometimes put in mason jars filled with water and then shaken to cause pains in a victim's jaw. According to Ozark folklore, it was said that a witch could only transform into a booger animal when they wore something of that animal, like fur, bones, feathers, etc. One man once told me the more items the better. I asked if he himself ever shape-shifted, and the man just pointed over to his wall where he'd hung up a taxidermy bobcat pelt complete with teeth and claws. "If I did, I reckon I'd use somethin' like that," he answered with a grin.

BIRDS

Certain birds and their feathers often held magical significance with Ozarkers as well. Owls, for example, because of their folkloric connections to witchcraft, could be used in remedies and rituals against being hexed. For example, an owl's beak was said to bring good luck to the holder, as were the talons and gizzard when worn as an amulet. Wearing owl feathers tucked into the brim of a hat was once believed to give the wearer better night vision.

Crows were once associated with death and malign magic. Because of their association with witchcraft, crow feathers were also said to be able to protect against witchcraft when hung up in a cabin. Sometimes a crow feather fan or brush was used to magically sweep illness or evil off of a client's body.

There are several birds once used in love charms and spells. The turkey, for example, was associated with drawing in a new lover. A person needed only to carry bones or a turkey beard around with them to ensure that they were always noticed. A similar charm was made from a dried dove's tongue that was carried in a bag or sewn into a person's clothing to attract love.

Pileated woodpeckers were sometimes called "Good God Almighty," or "Good God" birds for short, perhaps because this was the common reaction to seeing one of these large birds flying by. All parts of the woodpecker were once associated with magic, and some even said the bird itself was a witch in disguise. According to the folklore, eating the meat of the bird could heal a person of any ailment; others claimed it was bad luck to ever even harm one, let alone kill it. Even today, workers who specialize in magical rituals will use feathers and claws from the woodpecker. One healer I met had a preserved woodpecker mounted on a hat he wore during some of his rituals.

Cardinals and other redbirds were traditionally considered omens of death, especially if they came tapping at your window. They also have associations with luck, money, and wishes. A simple ritual you can perform when you see a redbird is to say "Money by the end of the week" three times. If the bird flies up, your wish will be granted, and if it flies down, that's a sign it's not meant to be. Money is often replaced by anything a person might wish for.

Black chickens and roosters have a long association with illness and witchcraft in the Ozarks. An old cure for shingles was to kill a black rooster at dawn and smear its blood counterclockwise in a circle around the affected area of skin. For obvious reasons, I don't recommend this ritual today, especially since modern medicines are now very effective for shingles and there's even a vaccine available.

Feathers from black chickens have traditionally been used to make magical feather brooms for sweeping off illnesses or curses. These same feathers were sometimes burned alongside red cedar or tobacco under the bed of a client to break a fever or to expel evil influences from the room. In many cases, the body of the chicken itself was used in the old Ozarks to cure illness, as in the case of allowing a black chicken to walk over a client suffering from measles or chickenpox. In old rituals for exorcism, a black chicken was tied up in a room that was believed to be haunted or tied to a client with a string. The black chicken was watched and prayed over until it jumped as though startled or injured. At this point, it was believed that the evil spirit had entered the chicken, and it was quickly removed from the home and killed.

According to folk belief, the buzzard is a healing bird because it's able to eat carrion without getting sick. Traditionally, feathers and other parts of the buzzard's body were often employed by folk healers in amulets and tools against a range of both physical and magical illnesses. For example, buzzard feathers were sometimes worn in the brim of a hat to help ward of rheumatism and other ailments. They were also sometimes hung up around the house as a general protective measure against all manner of evil. It was often considered bad luck to kill a buzzard, so only feathers that were shed naturally were used. Other uses included making feathers into fans and brooms for cleansing rituals.

TRY IT OUT—CATERPILLAR WART CHARM: One way to cure a wart involves picking up a caterpillar and letting it crawl on your warts, then releasing it back into the wild. It's said that as the caterpillar grows into a butterfly, your warts will be healed. For this reason, the informant who gave me this charm said his grandma always kept the caterpillar in a jar, making sure to feed and take care of it until it transformed.

AXES

CAUTIONS: Always take care when working with any sharp objects.

MAGICAL ALIGNMENT: Both hands

MAGICAL USES: As with knives and other sharp tools, axes have been traditionally used in Ozark folk magic as a method of cutting both physical and magical illnesses off a person's body. In the old days, a granny woman or midwife might have placed an axe underneath the bed of a woman giving birth in order to magically cut the pain. A similar ritual was used for anyone who was bedridden with a severe illness.

Likewise, a healer might also want to cut a magical illness or curse off their clients. I've watched one of these chopping rituals before—the patient had been complaining of shooting pain through his left foot and ankle. It had persisted despite the medicines he'd gotten from the city doctor. The healer said it was no problem and took the man out to the big block where he cut his firewood. He had the man take off his boot and sock, roll up his pants, and lay his leg across the log. While I watched with great interest, I couldn't help thinking about all the horrible things that could go wrong. The healer raised the axe up and then brought it crashing down into the log, narrowly missing the man's foot by only a few inches. The man was sweating bullets. As soon as the axe struck, he tore off, swearing up a storm. The healer just laughed and asked, "How's the foot?" The man was shocked that the pain had gone away completely. I asked the old healer about his patient the next time I was through that area, and he said the man hadn't complained and was even off the medications the city doctor had given him.

Chopping and cutting rituals aren't just limited to illness and curses. A common folk belief amongst hillfolk is that an oncoming storm or tornado can be chopped apart using an axe. In this ritual, a person faces the oncoming storm, raises an axe above their head, and lets it fall right into the ground. This is said to split the storm in two, ensuring it will go around the chopper's home. There's also an old Ozark story about a witch who could fly through the air on a magic axe and used it to chop entire trees in half with one swing.

The magical ability of blades aren't limited to the folk healer; they can also be used by left-handed workers to cripple or cut their victims. In one ritual, a worker might name a chicken after one of their enemies and then chop off its head, hoping to cause some pain to the intended victim. The worker might also name a tree for a victim and then chop it down, thus causing the person serious harm.

TRY IT OUT—CUTTING UP NIGHTMARES: While I don't recommend playing with axes, here's a simple ritual you can perform in your own home to help prevent nightmares. All you have to do is place an axe underneath your bed. Make sure the blade is underneath the side of the bed that your head is resting on while you are asleep. It's believed that the axe will help magically cut up your nightmares. I've also heard that when you wake up, if the axe has turned or moved from the original position you put it in, it's a sign that there's someone intentionally trying to give you nightmares and a spiritual cleanse might be needed.

BEADS

CAUTIONS: None

MAGICAL ALIGNMENT: Right hand

MAGICAL USES: Ordinary glass or wood beads were once employed by Ozark folk healers as amulets because of their availability and relatively low cost. Prayers and blessings, often taken from simple Bible verses as indicated in the following chart, could be spoken or magically "blown" into the beads themselves and then hung around the neck of the client, thereby connecting the healing work directly to the person afflicted. Certain illnesses or conditions were traditionally connected to a color; for example, nosebleeds with the color red, or yellow for afflictions in the neck, throat, and lungs. In these cases, beads of the corresponding color were worn to magically ward off the associated illness.

BEAD MATERIAL	ILLNESS	PRAYER	NOTES
Red Glass	Nosebleed; bleeding	Ezekiel 16:6	—
Yellow Glass	Sore throat	Psalm 22:15	Gold beads have the same associations.
Amber	Goiter; thyroid; asthma	Deuteronomy 7:15	—
Blue Glass	Sore throat	Psalm 22:15	—
Bodark Wood (*Maclura pomifera*)	Summer complaint	Deuteronomy 7:15	Bodark wood is also known as "bois d'arc" or "Osage orange."
Burdock Root	Protection	Psalm 11	Burdock root is good for general magical protection from evil and illness.
Sassafras Wood	General health; magical protection	Deuteronomy 7:15	—
Persimmon Wood (*Diospyros virginiana*)	Diarrhea	Psalm 22:14	Sometimes the fruit pits are used instead of the wood.
Sycamore Wood (*Platanus occidentalis*)	Protection	Psalm 90	Also called ghost tree because of its white bark, sycamore wood provides protection from spirits.
"Corn Beads" (*Coix lacryma-jobi*)	Cough	Deuteronomy 7:15	These are also called Job's tears.

TRY IT OUT—CHARM NECKLACE: One of the many traditional folk crafts of the Ozarks is making a charm necklace or bracelet from beads and buttons that hold particular memories or associations. For example, someone might include a bead from a broken chain passed down through the family or a bead that reminds the holder of a specific memory. I've also seen charm necklaces made for magical purposes as well. One granny woman I met always wore her "special beads," as she called them, which was a length of string loaded with beads of different shapes and colors, all of which had a specific purpose: red to keep her protected from hurting herself while chopping wood, blue against the evil eye, and three silver beads, taken from a necklace her mother gave her when she was just a child, to guard against witchcraft. Making a charm necklace of your own is an easy process and only takes collecting the beads and giving them certain associations. In addition to those mentioned above, green beads are for luck, purple for good dreams, and beads made from turquoise are said to bring good health in general.

BEANS
Phaseolus spp.

CAUTIONS: None

MAGICAL ALIGNMENT: Both hands

MAGICAL USES: Beans, like other small items (pebbles, corn, etc.), have been traditionally used in many healing rites throughout the Ozarks, mostly for curing warts. In these rituals, the affliction is magically transferred to the beans by the healer and then destroyed. Sometimes this type of cure involves certain counting down rituals. In this rite, the healer—or often the client themselves—first counts out a certain number of beans. The malady is lessened as each bean is then physically cast away. This same cure is often enacted with matches instead of beans, where each match is lit and then thrown into a glass of water. Sometimes a simple charm is employed alongside the ritual.

Black-eyed peas might also be included in this section, as they were formerly part of the *Phaseolus* genus. Black-eyed peas are eaten on New Year's Day for good luck. They are also added dry to talismans and amulets, meant to draw luck and opportunity to the wearer.

Beans have a darker side as well; they are often used by left-handed workers to hold curses that are then thrown at a person or a house, or the beans are sometimes buried beneath the stoop of the front door. Dry black beans are said to be the deadliest variety.

TRY IT OUT—BEAN COUNTING: A simple ritual for removing curses, the evil eye, and other malign influences involves counting down with beans. First, take a small bowl or cup of water and ten ordinary dried beans of any variety and set them outside. Face west while holding the water and say: "Evil, I conjure you! Sickness, you are not ten, you are nine. You are not nine, you are eight. You are not eight, you are seven. You are not seven, you are six. You are not six, you are five. You are not five, you are four. You are not four, you are three. You are not three, you are two. You are not two, you are one. You are not one, you are none!" As each initial number is named, toss a bean into the cup of water. Once you're finished, throw the water and beans onto a crossroads or cast into a swiftly flowing stream. If you'd prefer, you can skip using a cup of water and throw your beans directly into a river while reciting the charm.

COINS

CAUTIONS: None

MAGICAL ALIGNMENT: Right hand

MAGICAL USES: Some have connected the use of a silver dime in folk magic to the full moon, silvery in color, which has traditionally been seen as a symbol of fullness or good health in the Ozarks. This notion might seem far-fetched to some, but healers for centuries have used the stages of the moon in their healing practice, and the full moon is almost always associated with the end of a prescription cycle, a time when the client would be fully healed.

Silver dimes are still cherished items by many Ozark healers. They're often dropped inside of bags and then hung up around the house to protect from illness and evil influences. Medically speaking, silver dimes were once a cure for nosebleeds if slipped between the teeth and upper lip. It's said the effectiveness of this charm has been lost over the years as dimes started containing less and less silver.

Healers that specialize in working against malign magic and curses sometimes employ a silver dime in their rituals and amulets. One such ritual involves placing a silver dime on the forehead of a person believed to be possessed by an evil entity as they lay out underneath a full moon. It's said that the spirit won't be able to stand the power of the silver and the moonlight and will leave the body unharmed. Silver dimes can also be thrown into haunted houses to scare away the spirits of the dead who might lurk there. One healer I met always kept a dime underneath her pillow to scare off nightmares.

TRY IT OUT—BAG OF DIMES: Most of our dimes today aren't made of silver anymore, but I've found that they work just as well as silver ones because the power derives from your intentions more than the physical composition of the item. If you'd still like to use silver dimes, they can be purchased online for relatively cheap.

You'll want to do this work at night and when the moon is completely full. Underneath the moonlight, take a small white muslin or cloth bag with a drawstring or cut yourself a small square of white cloth. Add three dimes to the bag or cloth, then repeat this charm: "Beware my silver dime! Beware my silver moon! Beware my silver bullet!" Close the bag and tie the drawstring into three tight knots. (If you used a piece of cloth, take some string and wrap it around the top so that the bag is sealed tightly, then tie your three knots.)

These bags are traditionally placed around the house out of the public view. In Ozark folklore it's generally believed that the more people who know about a work of magic, the less power it will have. Try hiding them in the attic, basement, or in the backs of bookshelves to protect your home from unwanted spiritual influences.

EGGS

CAUTIONS: Many old remedies involve consuming raw eggs, which is not recommended today.

MAGICAL ALIGNMENT: Both hands

MAGICAL USES: Because of their abundance on the Ozark farm, chicken eggs were once used for a wide variety of folk remedies. For instance, a home remedy for a boil involved placing the inner membrane of a raw egg over the afflicted area and letting it dry out. It was believed that as the membrane dried it would pull the boil "to a head," making it easier to remove. Also, a tea made from boiling crushed up eggshells was sometimes given to children with colic to settle their stomachs. There's even an old belief that owl eggs would help cure a person of alcoholism if eaten raw.

An egg also makes a useful container for magically removing and holding illnesses, both physical and spiritual. An egg placed on the throat was once said to draw out coughs and even help with heart trouble. Many healers today still use ordinary eggs in their rituals. They do this by guiding the egg along a client's body while saying certain prayers and then burying or destroying the egg, thereby destroying the illness or evil that was sucked out. Along these same lines, there's a belief that hanging eggs from a tree in your front yard will help protect you from malign witchcraft by sucking up all evil that gets near it. These "egg trees" used to be more common in the Ozarks; they are hardly ever seen anymore.

TRY IT OUT—EGG HEALING: You can use an ordinary raw egg to suck any evil or illness out of yourself or another. While facing east, pray this over the egg: "Shell and white and yolk, this evil choke, this sickness strangle and suck!" Pass the egg across your skin (or another's skin) from head to toe three times. Then go to a tree, blow three times on the egg, and throw it against the bark, leaving your troubles where the egg breaks.

HAG STONES

CAUTIONS: None

MAGICAL ALIGNMENT: Right hand

MAGICAL USES: A hag stone or hole stone is a small, flat stone that bears a naturally formed hole somewhere on its surface. In Ozark folklore, it's said that these stones are formed when snakes burrow underground and, coming across a rock blocking their path, spit out a poison that burns a hole right through the rock, allowing them to pass in peace. These stones are prized items to this day because of their protective and healing abilities. Hag stones are sometimes worn as an amulet with a string through the hole; they protect against illness and malign magic. More often, though, the stones are strung on a rope or string and then hung outside a house's front door. This is said to create a magical barrier against all evil that might want to enter.

Many healers believe that these naturally unbroken holes are actually gateways into the otherworld of spirits and the Little People. Medicinal broths and brews are sometimes even poured through the hole of a hag stone, the idea being that the medicine will pick up some blessings from the otherworld as it passes through the hole. Likewise, many healers use hag stones in their magical diagnosis process by peering through the hole as they examine their clients.

TRY IT OUT—A GARLAND OF ROCKS: If you, like me, find yourself collecting bags and bags of hag stones but don't know what to do with them, try out this simple Ozark charm. Take a thick piece of string or rope that is about four feet long (or as long as you would like). I usually use hemp cord as it's strong and withstands the elements nicely. Begin to make a knot in one end of the string, but don't close it completely. Whisper this charm through the knot: "Knot, catch my words! A stone for luck, a stone for happiness, a stone to build a wall against evil." As you say the last word, pull the knot tight.

Guide the string through the hole in your hag stone. You might need to double or triple the knot size depending on how big the hole is. Let the stone rest on the knot and then continue, spacing out the stones by a few inches, until you run out of room on the string. I like to do seven or twelve stones. Make sure to repeat the charm each time you make an initial knot in the string. Once finished, you can hang this string of hag stones anywhere you might want some magical protection.

KNIVES

CAUTIONS: Always take care when working with any sharp objects.

MAGICAL ALIGNMENT: Both hands

MAGICAL USES: As with axes and other sharp tools, knives have traditionally been used to magically cut illnesses or a curses off a person's body. There are also folk beliefs connecting knives to preventing nightmares; in this case, a knife would be placed under the pillow before a person goes to sleep. The idea is that the knife would cut through the bad dreams, acting as a sort of defense for the sleeper. Along similar lines, knives were also used in rituals to magically cut storms—tornados in particular—much like axes.

Knives can also be used in divination rites. A healer might tie a string to the handle of a knife, usually one used only for divination, and then dangle the blade over a piece of paper as a pendulum. The direction the knife turns might determine answers to certain questions. In some cases, a healer might draw symbols or words on the paper and observe which symbol or word the knife rocks toward, potentially determining what illness is present or whether malign magic is at hand.

TRY IT OUT—KNIVES FOR NIGHTMARES: As with axes, I don't recommend playing with sharp objects. Many of the old rituals involving knives are done by professionals who know exactly how to handle the knives so as to avoid accidentally cutting their patient. You can, however, use a knife in place of an axe in magically cutting up your nightmares. In a similar ritual, place an ordinary knife underneath your bed with the blade facing in the direction of your head. You are then said to be protected from nightmares and any evil influences that might try to invade your dreams.

LIGHTNING WOOD

CAUTIONS: None

MAGICAL ALIGNMENT: Right hand

MAGICAL USES: Lightning wood is wood taken from a tree that has been struck by lightning. In Ozark folk belief, this wood is traditionally seen as being imbued with power from Heaven and has been used in both healing and folk magic. The wood was often carved into toothpicks to help stop toothaches; it was also broken into small chips that were then thrown around the house to keep out insects and other vermin.

Yarb doctors have carved spoons from lightning wood to stir their healing broths and brews. Other healers might carve similar ritual implements, like wooden knives for cutting off curses or pendulums to magically diagnose illnesses. Chunks of lightning wood are also prized as protective amulets, often worn around the neck or carried in the pocket.

Because it is seen as supernatural, there is a taboo against burning lightning wood. Some believe that burning lightning wood in your fireplace will increase the likelihood that your home will be struck by lightning.

TRY IT OUT—LIGHTNING FENCE: If you're lucky enough to find yourself some wood from a lightning tree, you can use it to craft a magical fence of protection around your home. First, collect or carve four stakes of the wood, about a foot long and half an inch around. Then, using a hammer, drive each of the stakes into the dirt on each of the four sides of your home, starting on the east side and continuing clockwise. Each time you secure a stake, say these words: "Lightning, strike not this home for as long as this stake shall stand. Lightning, strike not me, but the one who would wish me harm."

You can also do this inside if you live in an apartment or don't have access to all sides of your house; choose the main room of your house, usually where the front door is located. Hang the stakes on the wall starting in the east and working clockwise so that there is one stake hanging on the wall for each of the four directions. Make sure you say the charm while hanging each stake.

NAILS

CAUTIONS: Be careful when handling nails, especially rusty nails.

MAGICAL ALIGNMENT: Both hands

MAGICAL USES: Nails have traditionally been a part of the Ozark healers' toolkit because they are easy to find and usually plentiful around the house. In certain rituals, a sickness itself can be taken off a client by magically nailing it to a tree. In this way, the sickness is left behind when the client leaves. Trees often used for this ritual include those associated with strength or health, like oaks.

New nails were once included in many rituals and amulets for protecting against evil influences. In one common rite, three new nails were hammered into the frame of the front and back doors of a house in the shape of a triangle, point facing up. This was believed to protect the home from evil by magically nailing the intruder to the spot before they could enter. It was also once believed that if someone with evil intentions entered the home, the nails would pop out of the doorframe (although sometimes not all the way).

Coffin and gallows nails were traditionally seen as having added magical powers because of their proximity to death. Coffin nails specifically were once commonly carried by hillfolk as an amulet to ward off certain venereal diseases. In left-handed work, coffin nails could be driven into the footprints of their victims or into wax dolls filled with a person's hair or fingernail clippings. Such magical nailing can also be done using thorns from certain trees like the honey locust.

TRY IT OUT—A BAG OF NAILS: This is one of many examples of an Ozark house charm. Take three new nails or three large thorns and place them in a cloth bag. Tie the bag closed using three knots, then hang the bag near the front or back door of your home. It's said that the nails or thorns will trip up intruders who might try and enter.

STRING

CAUTIONS: None

MAGICAL ALIGNMENT: Right hand

MAGICAL USES: String is a repurposed household item still used to today in tying-off rituals. In this case, a string might be tied around a person's body and then taken off along with the illness. A client might be walked through a hoop made from string for the same purposes. There is also a remedy where the healer blows prayers through knots made in a string, and after a certain number of prayers and knots, the whole thing would be tied around the client's waist or wrist, thereby symbolically attaching the blessings to them.

Sometimes a string can be used as a physical stand-in for a client. First, a healer measures the height of their client with a string. They then snip the string to match the client's exact height. The healer can then take that string out and bury it or tie it to a tree in order to remove the illness completely.

TRY IT OUT—STRING ON A TREE: This is a traditional Ozark ritual for removing curses, the evil eye, and other malign influences. Take a spool of regular white string. Cut a section a few feet long. Make a knot toward one end, but before you close it completely, say, "Curse, I tie you up! What I tie here, I leave here." Blow through the circle made from the unformed knot. While you're blowing, close the knot up tight. Repeat this all the way down the string, ending when you reach a total of nine knots. Take the entire string out to an oak tree and wrap it around a branch three times. Turn and walk back to your house, leaving your curse behind you.

WATER

CAUTIONS: Water from certain sources like springs, caverns, wells, etc., while once used in folk medicine, should be avoided today. Many natural springs these days are contaminated not only with parasites, but with runoff from industrial farming or livestock ranching. Contaminated water can be dangerous when consumed.

MAGICAL ALIGNMENT: Both hands

MAGICAL USES: A simple bowl of water can be a powerful tool for the mountain healer. Rivers and creeks are valued for their use in washing rituals to remove anything from a cold to a curse. In many cases, water from specific locations like natural springs, caves, waterfalls, etc. have traditionally been favored over what comes from the tap at home. Spring water is traditionally used in the brewing of medicines as well as in healing rituals because it's thought to be closest to the natural world. The most auspicious water source, I've been told, is a spring inside a cave that's never seen the light of the sun or moon. When collected, this water is almost always covered in a towel or sheet to keep the light from spoiling it.

There are other types of specialized water used, usually involving ordinary spring water that has gone through an additional ritual. Moon water, for example, is water left out under a certain moon phase in order to be infused with magic. Water from a full moon is said to be the most powerful for healing rituals and herbal medicines, while new moon water is often used as an ingredient in left-handed work because of its associations with darkness.

War water is another specialized water, made for the purpose of causing strife, anger, or conflict. This water is made in a number of ways, but it always involves soaking certain other items like rusty nails, thorns, blades, and sometimes even bullets in water. The water is strained off and bottled after a certain amount of time. One left-handed worker I met showed me a jar of their own homemade war water that they used on various occasions by simply pouring a little in a spot they knew their victim would walk.

There's also a folk belief that just the presence of water will have a cooling effect upon the body. Following this notion, a bowl of water was sometimes put under the bed of a person with a fever to help cool them. Likewise, it was commonly believed that if one suffered from night sweats, they needed only to put a bowl of water underneath their bed and they'd have relief.

Water can also be employed in certain rites of divination. A healer might diagnose an illness by suspending a dry leaf, especially from the spicebush, on top of a bowl of water and examining how it moves. As with a pendulum, the healer designates the directional meanings—for example, clockwise meaning "yes" and counterclockwise meaning "no"—asks a question, and observes which direction the leaf turns.

Water is also used in a variety of love divinations. In one such ritual, three bowls were brought into a room. One was filled with clean water, one with dirty water, and the third was left empty. A person was then blindfolded and brought up to the bowls. If they picked the one with clean water, it was said they would soon be happily married. The one with dirty water indicated that they would be married but would lose their spouse to death or divorce. The empty bowl indicated they would forever be alone.

TRY IT OUT—A CLEANSING BATH: For a cleanse after a stressful week at work, or for when you're feeling a little under the weather, follow this simple recipe. First, fill a pitcher or large bowl with water. This can be from the tap or spring water. Once filled, you can bless the water in a number of ways. Traditionally, Ozark healers will cross the water three times with the blade of a knife: up-down, then left-right. Others will think about their intentions and then blow across the water three times, a physical method for transferring their thoughts and feelings into the work.

After the water is blessed, you can use it as is or add other cleansing herbs and minerals. Some healers add salt and a little lemon juice; others have a more complicated recipe of plants. My favorite Ozark native plants to use are any of the *Monarda* genus (or horsemint, as they are called), rabbit tobacco, sassafras leaves, and red cedar. Let the plants you use soak in the water for at least an hour; some leave them overnight. Strain and discard the plants.

Before the bath, put a small cup or bowl at your feet and whatever water is collected there as you pour the bath you will take outside and pour onto the roots of a strong tree. When you're ready, you will stand in your shower (or outside) while facing east, then pour the water over your head three times. With the third pour, the pitcher or bowl should be completely empty.

MODERNIZING FOLK MAGIC

AFTER LOOKING AT MANY OF the old traditions of the Ozarks, it's important to also examine the position of folk magic and healing today. What practices are still alive? How has the cultural landscape changed? Questions like these are important to ask when looking at any traditions carried into the present. The situation for most of the old Ozark folkways today is grim, I'm sad to say. There are remnants still around in reenactment circles, museums, and folk centers, but for the most part, the living traditions that folklorists like Vance Randolph and Mary Parler collected have disappeared altogether. It's a difficult fact for me to admit. As a cultural representative, I like to imagine that there's still the same magic left in the hills and hollers of my homeland. That's not the reality of the situation, though, nor should it be! Folk practices change, evolve, and grow as they come into contact with new traditions, cultures, and technological advancements. While I'm sad to see that certain practices have died out, I'm happy to see how far we've come in the modern Ozarks and what new traditions are being born here.

In northwest Arkansas, where I live, almost everyone has access to clean water, electricity, a local doctor, and Wi-Fi—that's including even the most rural areas. The region today looks very different from when I was growing up; the amount of urbanization that's happened in such a small amount of time is staggering. People who once lived in very rural areas have now been thrust into heavily populated communities as cookie-cutter houses have sprung up around them. The values of the culture have also changed. While it's still generally a conservative area, we're far more diverse now than ever before, and not just racially. Ozarkers are diverse in religions, languages, and other cultural traditions. For me, all of this is still Ozark culture. We were never a unified people, not even in our traditions. The organization of those first settlers was based around the family and clan system. Each individual family came with their own beliefs, values, and traditions, and later these mixed and merged into something bigger.

For me, Ozark culture now is better than it ever has been, but we're still not without our problems, especially when it comes to recognizing our own bloodstained past. Few know that the pre-1900 Ozarks used to be home to at least ten large, thriving communities of freed slaves. These were towns in their own respect, bigger than many on the map even today. But tensions finally broke around the turn of the twentieth century when the Ozarks saw years of lynching and expulsions of these communities out of the area.[43] This sickening and terrible piece of our historical tapestry can't be covered up, and it shouldn't be. By recognizing the racial tensions of our past and present, we're given the much-needed opportunity to heal and look toward a very different future.

MY OWN WORK

I'm a storyteller by nature, so I can't help but talk with the words of the old-timers I've met. Telling yarns is in my blood. I'm also a practicing healer, someone with the gift. My personal practice is based on a combination of my own family traditions, things I've learned from others, things I've picked up along the way, and things that were given to me by spirits, guides, the Little People, and other magical sources. Healers today are much more eclectic than they were in the past, like the granny woman I know who runs an herbal school in Eureka Springs that combines healing methods from across the world to create a holistic system. Or the yarb doctor I know who measures all his medicines using the traditional Chinese medicine weight system and talks about Ozark native plants in terms of liver, qi, yin, and yang. Or the conjure woman who is trying to reclaim the practices of her ancestors who were driven from their home by the lynching of the Ozarks. Or the number of modern Ozark witches I know who happily bear the name that would have meant so much trouble for them in the past.

My own practice is hardly what you would call "traditional," whatever that might mean. I've always viewed my path as respecting the voice of my ancestors while trying to live in the modern world. This has meant changing beliefs that many of the old-timers have really

------

43. Harper, *White Man's Heaven*.

tried to hold on to. In an effort to encourage others to look into their own ancestral folk healing traditions, I've come up with a list of suggestions for beginners. Let this be a guide, but not a guide so stiff that it breaks in the wind like the oak tree. Be instead like the reed that bends and dances in the storm.

MOVING WITH THE TIMES

Helping to preserve cultural practices is noble work. It can also be a constant uphill battle, especially if you are trying to work with a dying culture. With the Ozarks, for instance, there are so many gaps in information. One informant might say one thing, another something completely different.

We have to remember that these traditions were born in isolated communities, so often traditions might be similar, but with regional or clan differences. Take the use of the horseshoe, for example. Across the Ozarks the horseshoe is a symbol of good luck and prosperity. It's usually nailed above a house's front door or up in a barn to protect livestock. But which way should it hang? Should the prongs be pointing upward? Or should they point downward? Some say upward because you want the shape to fill up with luck and you don't want it to pour out. Others say the horseshoe should always point downward because you want the power of the object to pour out onto the household. But who is correct? Well, it's not an answer many like, but they both are.

This is one of the issues with trying to modernize folk practices; there are different variations from nearly every informant. Who can you trust, then? The way I usually work is to collect everything and sort through it all later. Everything is interesting to me, from the simplest wart charm to the most mystical or esoteric ritual. It's all good stuff because it all gives us important glimpses into culture and folkways. After collecting all my anecdotes, I try to look and see where there might be common connections with other Ozark traditions.

Let's go back to the horseshoe. Perhaps one of my informants says a horseshoe should always hang with the prongs pointing upward. I can then add it to a category with all the other anecdotes that say the same thing. I can repeat this process with people who say the prongs should point downward. Then I see that this group has far fewer people with this belief. I might even have an informant who denies all of these notions and says a horseshoe should only hang sideways, with prongs pointing to the right. Well, he's the only one in that category, so he might be correct, but it's more likely he got that tradition from someplace very different than the others.

Going into this work, I had to accept the fact that there will always be holes in my information. Even when it comes to traditional herbalism, there is room for varying opinions, especially with folk names for plants. I had one informant tell me, "We used to stop high blood pressure with the heart plant."

"What plant is that?" I asked.

"I don't know. We always used to call it the heart plant."

"Can you describe what it looks like?"

"Oh you know, it grows on the ground in the woods, sometimes in old fields. It's shaped like a heart."

"Are the leaves shaped like a heart? Or is it the flowers?"

"Yes. It's all shaped like a heart."

"So leaves or flowers?"

"Yes."

"Gotcha."

You might laugh, but this conversation is so common in the Ozarks, especially with the old-timers who still use the folk names for plants. It seems like every farmer has a different name for every yarb out there, and sometimes the same name is used across plant species. For example, the heart plant could refer to the redbud tree, several species of violet, or the sorrels—wood sorrel (*Oxalis acetosella*) or yellow sorrel (*O. articulate*). Even using the name "sorrel" is itself an example of what I'm talking about, as true sorrels are not in the *Oxalis* genus. Our "sorrel" was so named because it tastes sour, which Europeans would have been used to with the true sorrels, *Rumex acetosa*. None of these heart-shaped plants have any effect on blood pressure, though. They could still be the heart-shaped plant in question because plants were often used according to the law of similarity, meaning a plant was often seen as good for a certain organ in the body simply because it was shaped like that organ.

These gaps in information might never be filled. Sometimes I can trace a ritual, remedy, or belief back to its European or indigenous roots, but some traditions are isolated to only one community or even one family. In this case, I try and collect what I can, but I always keep in mind that we're living in a very different world today. Traditions change, they evolve—and yes, sometimes they die. Most of the time, the traditions I've collected aren't worth bringing into a modern setting; this includes both folk magic elements and plants or compounds that are definitely not recommended for medicinal use today. For example, kerosene was at one time taken internally for sore throats. Poisonous plants like jimsonweed were smoked for asthma, but this is a very powerful poisonous plant if eaten or swallowed, especially if people consumed the seeds. Pokeweed was once used in baths for skin complaints like boils, rashes, eczema, etc., but it works by giving you a painful chemical burn all over your body. Bloodroot was very effective at removing skin cancers and warts, but it could also cause severe scarring. With all of that being said, many plant remedies do still work, and they have little other interactions with modern medicines or contraindications for certain conditions. These plants can be worked into our own home medical routine, and there are many trained herbalists and professionals in the Ozarks working tirelessly to further study these old remedies.

Sometimes you have to be very discerning about what folk traditions you choose to modernize and which ones are better left in the books. This is especially true if you are walking down any sort of healing or folk magic practice. There are many rituals that might be very interesting to look at but that aren't worth using in a modern setting. Take, for instance, those rituals that involve the harming or killing of an animal, like the infamous black cat rite. I can't stress enough that many traditions of the past need to be left in the past.

CONFRONTING BELIEFS

It's not just the folk traditions themselves we have to examine, but also the entire worldview that gave rise to these beliefs. While there might be those today who'd love to go back to the "good ol' days" of yesteryear, the fact remains that the good ol' days weren't so good for the majority of people living in the Ozarks. Women were still being oppressed within rigid systems of patriarchy and conservative ideals that valued servitude at home over education and personal fulfillment. For those with debilitating health issues, little hope for recovery could be had apart from the few who were able to travel great distances for medical care or had the money to pay for stays in institutions. Mental health care was nonexistent apart from some counseling with the local preacher. To this day, too few people in the rural areas seek readily available help for fear of being ostracized by their families. For those with gender or sexual identities that didn't fit within the strict boundaries of the community, there was only a life of hidden shame and suppression of one's true nature. The good ol' days were then only good for a very small number of people, and those old-timers I've talked to who glorify this past seem to have forgotten how terrible it was for them too. As humans, we often hold on to just the good memories and leave behind any moments of pain and sadness.

By and large, the Ozarks today are very different. There are still pockets of more traditional culture out there. Unfortunately, with this traditional culture comes many of the same problems faced in the old Ozarks. Even this is changing, though, as more and more Ozarkers are moving from the cities back out into the forested hills and hollers. Many of the healers I met on my travels were from this group of people. These days, you can't simply judge a rural community by its location; there are many out there that no longer fit the stereotypes of backward, gun-toting, conservative Christians. Many of my informants who proudly identify as witches and pagans alike are living in these small communities where they are supported just like anyone else. One feeling I encountered amongst the healers, witches, and other magical workers was that of safety. With the exception of a few, most experienced a level of community love and support for their gift that the healers of the past would never have had.

In my own experience, many of these small towns have been aching to run headlong into the twenty-first century but have been held back by stubborn old-timers holding on to their "good ol' days" of oppression, racism, and bigotry. As one informant told me, commenting on the state of his little community in recent years, "Once Pastor Daniel died, things got better! The old folks left the church, but our numbers doubled with young people and we started helping people out." The help he mentioned was a community food pantry that was actually condemned by Pastor Daniel, one of the "pull yourself up by your bootstraps" kind of old-timers who often preached that being poor was God's punishment upon people without faith. As it turned out, only a handful of people in town actually sided with the man, but because he had so much pull in the community, no one dared speak out until he was dead and buried. This same situation is common across the rural Ozarks.

The radical merging of cultures has been happening since the '70s when the area received a sudden rush of back-to-the-landers from around the country looking to the hills and hollers of the Ozarks for homestead and farming sites. Many of these "hippies," as the locals called them, formed communes, many of which were centered practices of free love, Paganism, and modern witchcraft, notions that would have been very foreign to hillfolk. As many of these communities and even individual farms became more and more integrated in the wider Ozark landscape, they added many of their own traditions and beliefs to the greater culture around them. As a result of this "opening" of the region, areas in Arkansas like Fayetteville and Eureka Springs (as well as Springfield in the Missouri Ozarks) have become centers for more liberal beliefs as well as modern Ozark magic.

More and more people today are looking to cultural representatives to be able to add Ozark traditional practices to their own work as healers or witches. As a person with one foot in the old Ozarks and the other in the modern world, I absolutely love seeing practitioners and lay people alike who are interested in Ozark folkways. It's because of this interest that I first began teaching workshops and giving talks on Ozark healing and magic, and I will continue for the rest of my days, I reckon. I take as my guiding light the work of countless people over the years who made it their mission to drag Ozark magical and healing practices into the modern world despite what the old-timers might say.

TRADITIONS REINTERPRETED

Confronting the beliefs and traditions of the past doesn't mean just throwing everything away and starting fresh. There's already such a powerful foundation here in the Ozarks to work from; let's not ignore it. This foundation is based upon the intimate connection between the individual and the natural world. It's this connection that originally gave rise to the stereotypes of hillfolk, or "hillbillies," as a wild, primitive, and shoeless people. Local communities often looked at hillfolk with great suspicion because of their "backward" ways and "superstitious" beliefs. Despite this, many knew that the hillfolk meant big business if you were willing to hike up into the hills and find them. Pharmacists and country doctors frequently hired root-diggers to bring them pounds and pounds of valuable medicinal plants like ginseng, goldenseal, and bloodroot. Even though they did all of the backbreaking labor, most hillfolk were paid less than a quarter of what the pharmacists would earn from the same roots.

Ozark folktales often idealize hillfolk, depicting them as possessing an inborn knowledge of the land and magic. In some tales, hillfolk were even said to be able to speak the language of the birds and to transform themselves into animal forms. These tales, while hinting at the powerful connection that hillfolk had to the land, completely ignored the real value of this traditional knowledge. In fact, much about life for those living in the isolated hills and hollers was ignored by the wider world, and still is. The rampant poverty, lack of education, and proper medical care—not to mention the widespread abuses suffered by women and children—were once labeled as just "hillfolk problems," not to be the concern of townsfolk. This is still the case in many places around the Ozarks.

Looking beyond the folktales, a different picture emerges. At one time, because life in the hills was so difficult, the people who lived there had to have a very different relationship with the natural world. Everything took on a life of its own, from the plants and animals to the weather, fire, and other elemental forces. The world became full of spirits, and not just ghosts of the departed, but spirits of the land like the Little People. During a thunderstorm, the lightning itself was petitioned to strike elsewhere. The rain was petitioned in times of drought, and the sun in times of flooding. The entire world became animated, and those with the gift were seen as being valuable links between the world of humans and that otherworld of spiritual forces.

This heart of Ozark folk belief is what we can bring with us into the modern world. This mountain animism in its simplest form views the natural world as full of living entities with spirits, personalities, and opinions of their own, not as unintelligent and dead matter. This worldview once influenced all aspects of life for hillfolk and there are many powerful ways we can incorporate these beliefs into our own lives today. Loving and respecting nature often means protecting certain areas from development and destruction or working together as communities to plant gardens of native plants, supporting those species that are most at risk. An example of this in recent years can be seen with the Ozark chinquapin (*Castanea ozarkensis*) trees. This is a species of *Castanea* that is only found in the Ozarks, particularly the Arkansas Ozarks. It was very nearly wiped out by the chestnut blight that swept across the nation in the early part of the twentieth century. In recent years, botanists and lay naturalists have been working with local communities to plant these trees in large numbers, and now the Ozark chinquapin is having a second chance at life.

The Ozark Mountains are full of other plants just as at risk as the Ozark chinquapin. At one time, Ozark witch hazel (*Hamamelis vernalis*) almost suffered the same fate when in the early twentieth century, pharmaceutical companies hired hillfolk to overharvest the bushes every spring for use in cosmetics and face washes. Only when much cheaper synthetic alternatives were developed did the Ozark witch hazel begin to gain a footing in the Ozarks again.

Although I currently live in town, planting my yard full of Ozark native plants—especially those that are edible and medicinal—is a good way for me to stay grounded in my connection to the land and my heritage. So much of Ozark folk healing and magic is based on the relationship between the practitioner and the natural world that just being outside in the hills is a revitalizing experience for me. I keep this relationship in mind in all aspects of my work, from harvesting plants, to their use, to working with the spirits of the land itself. I always make sure that my footprint on the land is the smallest it can possibly be.

In many ways, this connection to nature is all that we have from the healers and magical workers of our past. So much has been lost through the years, but this connection has remained true. No matter if the worker is male, female, or anywhere in between, no matter if they are Christian, Pagan, or any other religious identity, this deep connection to nature remains as the heart of the tradition. I can't say it any better than one healer I met: "If you need answers, sit outside. The land will teach you." Because we have so little left by way of actual teaching and guidance with these traditions, we often have to work in a very dynamic way, changing what we need to change, evolving practices with the world around us, and taking time to listen to the land itself.

WORKING CREATIVELY AND DYNAMICALLY

Healing and magic are often called "arts" because they have been traditionally seen as creative acts. As magical practitioners, we work with forces we can't always see. We work with intention, visualizations, and rituals made up of aesthetic, symbolic, and practical aspects. We have to be able to understand our clients and to figure out not only their physical ailments, but what mental or spiritual factors might be affecting the situation as well. We have to work in a creative way, especially when we work within traditions that have provided very little by way of concrete instruction.

When I'm working with a client, I try and do everything within the boundaries of what I've learned from the Ozark tradition. But that's not always doable. We have new illnesses, new problems in the twenty-first century. For example, how do I help a person who is concerned about balancing their screen time and time with their kids? What Ozark ritual is there out there for someone who is a staunch atheist but feels like an ancestral spirit is contacting them through dreams? Or what should I do for a person struggling with their gender identity?

There are hundreds more of these situations that I've encountered. What they all point to for me is this need to work creatively and dynamically. Working dynamically means being able to shift and change at a second's notice. You might have been talking with a client about one issue, but what they bring to you the day of the work is completely different. As workers, we can't be so caught up in our own heads and in our own cultural traditions that we are too quick to refuse work that is asked of us. I encourage workers not to just say, "I don't know," but instead to say, "Let's see how we can rephrase the question," or maybe even, "Let's explore what factors are affecting your situation now."

I've encountered many issues that have made me throw my hands up and say, "I don't know!" Some of these I've been able to revisit at a later time with more information, but others have gone unsolved. There's no shame in not knowing what to do. But if you just stop and take the time to think through the situation creatively, most of the time a solution will come to you. Do another divination reading—do five more if you need to! Maybe it takes some time, so give it a few days. Maybe monitor your dreams and see if anything comes through that way. Don't give up immediately.

Let's look at a situation like gender identity, which is a concern I've encountered more and more lately, as well as one that I've struggled with in my own life. The first client I had with this question came at me as a shock. My own issues of being nonbinary rose up to the surface immediately. I thought I might not be able to help them, and I didn't really know what I could do within the Ozark context, which traditionally worked within the male-female binary. I had to stop myself and go sit in the woods for a while. The voice of the trees called to me and I immediately realized that gender identity isn't a new concept, it's been around since the beginning of time, even in the old Ozarks. Back then, I could imagine it was something people kept hidden behind labels like "tomboy," and it was something few ever thought to approach a healer about. "Change is good," I heard myself saying as I sat there in the woods, embraced in the branches of an ancient oak tree.

When I got back home, I made a plan of action. I talked with my client for hours, working out everything in their life that might be affecting their situation. Then I gave it a couple days while I sat with my own guiding spirits and ancestors. The message I received from them was to do the work that I would want to do for myself. What had helped me get through my own identity crisis? So we came up with a creative way to work out this issue. We started with transformative cleanses in a nearby river over the course of a certain number of days. I paired these baths with herbal decoctions that the client drank every day. This was to cleanse their body inside and out in preparation for the next step. Finally, we did a cleanse paired with a light emetic, smoking ceremony, and a ritual burning of the clothes my client identified as holding them prisoner in one identity. I ended the work by having them put on their new clothes and a new name. It was simple but profound work. You always know your work is spot-on when you and your client both get something out of it.

CHANGE IS HARD

For many people I've met, moving with the times has meant getting rid of everything they might hold near and dear. The process of change is a hard one for many people, especially those who might see change as losing a part of themselves or their history. I can't say that my opinions about Ozark culture and folkways are popular across the board. I've been met with a lot of hostility from people who are stuck within their own rigid views of culture and traditions: people who still hold to the idea that Ozark folk healing is always based in Christianity; people who still believe in the firm separation of genders in healing work and passing along magical knowledge; people who still see the witch as an evil character who uses their power to ruin lives. When I first started sharing my stories with the public, I'd get up in arms when confronted by people like this. I'd go out of my way to try and prove to them that their opinions weren't the whole truth of the matter. While I was wasting my time fighting, the work I needed to do was left undone.

As the years have gone by, I've mellowed out significantly. A friend and fellow healer put it to me in the best way possible, saying, "Don't worry about the haters. They're wrong, and people will see it." *Don't worry?* I thought to myself. *But I'm always worrying!* For the longest time, I was afraid these people would somehow convince everyone that I was a fraud and Ozark culture would take ten steps back again. I figured out that wasn't the case at all. While I was busy arguing with one crazy member of the audience, there were thirty others who sided with me and thought the person was crazy too, but I was too engaged to notice them. I had to stop and ask myself where I wanted to put my time and energy—with the haters or with the people who are actually interested?

Change is hard, there's no denying it. I even find myself coming to terms with a changing culture on almost a daily basis. Being a healer doesn't make it any easier. In the past year alone, I've had seven of my informants die. Their stories and power went with them into that other place. I've had to face the fact that I too will one day die, taking what I know with me. Keeping a strong connection to nature and the cycles of birth, life, and death has helped me loosen my fear of leaving this world. I also know that as one tradition dies, another is always born to replace it, often bearing a likeness to its parent but perhaps in a much more important form.

THE IMPORTANCE OF SECRECY

One of the most important lessons I've had to learn is to keep my work only between my clients and myself. It's hard when we're living in a world dominated by social media. We often feel a compulsion to show others our rituals and practices. Of course, there's nothing wrong with wanting to share; after all, that's how ideas spread and grow. At the same time, it's important to be mindful of what you're sharing. Is the photo you're posting to Facebook or Instagram of a ritual? If so, would the person you were working for approve of you posting it? I see a lot of people in the magical community who are of the opinion that photos are just photos and there's no way anyone could do anything by just having an image of the ritual. The tradition I work within says this is absolutely false. Even seeing a photo of a ritual means someone might be able to reverse that work. Secrecy is very important in the Ozarks, and I understand others might have different opinions, but even on a basic, fundamental level most of us can agree that we at least don't want inexperienced workers trying to replicate our rituals.

There's a certain amount of irresponsibility in posting photos and detailed descriptions of complicated rituals online. I think it encourages beginners to copycat the work without understanding what they're doing. It's as dangerous as someone posting herbal misinformation online. One example I've come across was a reputable herbal information site that posted an article about jimsonweed as a great remedy for asthma without any understanding of how the plant was used traditionally. They also failed to mention that the plant is highly poisonous when ingested, especially the seeds, which are often fatal. You might be saying, "Well, who would just take a remedy without asking more questions?" The answer is, a lot of people. There's often a certain amount of inherent trust put in anything that is published, whether in print or online. I see this a lot when I give workshops on herbal preparations. I always get shocked faces when I say, "Did you know essential oils can poison you?" People use them all the time, mostly because there are quack websites and companies telling people that essential oils will cure all their problems, without explaining what they are, where they come from, or how they should be used.

I once met a man after one of my herbal preparation workshops who asked if he could share one of his home remedies with me. I said of course; I'm always curious about people's stories. He told me for a stuffy head and allergies, he takes a bottle of oregano essential oil, sticks the open end to his nose, and inhales the vapors sharply three times on each side. I asked how this worked and he replied that his sinuses drained instantly, but that he was dizzy for about a minute afterward. I then asked him how often he did this and his response was, "A few times a day, more when I really need it." I didn't know what to say. I asked if he was concerned about the fact that he was getting dizzy after snorting the fumes off concentrated plant chemical compounds and he just shrugged and said, "Hasn't killed me yet!" I then explained to him why I wouldn't recommend his remedy, and we left the conversation with both of us disagreeing with the other.

These dangers aren't limited to herbal medicines, though. Rituals can sometimes be just as dangerous. There's always a risk when dealing with spiritual forces, and there's always a temptation for beginners to get in over their heads too quickly. An example to illustrate this: I once met an amateur "conjurer," as he called himself, who was making a "tongue charm" to silence one of his enemies. This ritual isn't really seen in the Ozarks, but it comes from cross-connections with Hoodoo or Southern Conjure. Basically, the ritual involves a raw cow's tongue that is split open and filled with a target's name and certain noxious ingredients, then sewn up with string. This work is supposed to make the target "tongue-tied" and unable to speak ill of the one who cast the spell.

On this occasion, the target of the work was my informant's neighbor, who was a witch and also another informant of mine. She was a witch in the new sense of the word, the reclaimed version. In fact, she did far less malign work than her so-called "healer" neighbor, who was currently splitting open a cow's tongue as a curse. The conjuror and the witch had gotten into some argument, and unfortunately the nature of apartment buildings is that you can't really escape from arguments. The conjuror was convinced this tongue charm of his would shut the witch up for good. Unfortunately for him, I sided with the witch in this particular quarrel.

My relationship with the conjuror started when he emailed me and introduced himself as a fellow healer interested in Hoodoo. He was mostly self-taught, as many are these days. There's nothing wrong with that, but not learning from someone experienced meant the conjuror was constantly running his mouth about the work he was doing. He even had an Instagram account devoted to his ritual work. Since I sided with the witch, who was much more reasonable in general, I made sure I watched the conjuror closely as he made his tongue charm.

After we finished, I left his apartment and went over the witch's place. She was home and excited to see me. As she was a budding folk magician herself, I asked if she wanted to learn about how to reverse work done by others. She happily answered yes and we got to work. Reestablishing the natural order of the world generally takes precedence over other healer taboos. So, whereas normally I would keep information private, I felt like this cursing was flippant and childish and would cause only harm, not healing. I sided with the target of the spell. If the work had been justified, I wouldn't have intervened.

The rest of the evening was spent recreating the tongue charm as closely as we could to the conjuror's version, down to the number of nails and hot peppers he used. Once we had a recreated version, we then worked on ritually disassembling the charm, piece by piece, starting with what we made last. With each element I'd have the witch say something like "I pull these nails from this tongue, so that these nails might be pulled from my body," or "I cut this string, so that my tongue may no longer be bound." The last element was a paper with her name written on it. We took this and burned it with cleansing red cedar twigs.

Once everything was disassembled, we wrapped all the separate pieces up in a trash bag and threw it in the dumpster outside. After that night, the witch took a cleansing bath once a day for three days, and nothing ever manifested from the conjuror's ritual.

Workers, try and keep your information secret, especially work for clients and the really powerful stuff. Leave it between you and the powers you serve. You won't regret it. And for those just beginning with all of this, find good resources for beginner's work—there are lots out there—or try and study with someone who knows what they're doing. If you're working within a certain cultural tradition, there are usually old-timers out there who are just itching to pass on their knowledge and gifts. All it takes is some time and a willingness to be humble and listen.

COLLECTING STORIES

There's so much information I wish I could have collected from my family members before they passed on. It sometimes haunts me what I could have learned from them. Like my great-uncle Bill, the wart charmer. I only ever heard stories about him, but not actually from him, even though he was around when I was a kid. I just wasn't interested in those sorts of stories. For one thing, like many other Ozarkers, I desperately wanted to separate myself from the "hillbilly" stereotype. One way hillfolk have found to do that is by forgetting. We forget our accents, we forget the stories, we forget the land itself. I'm just glad I got to an age where forgetting was no longer an option. Unfortunately, it was too late to collect a lot of traditions from my own family.

It's the same story across the Ozark Mountains. Old-timers get older, and if there's no one there listening, their stories just die with them. Sometimes we take those stories for granted. We hear them so many times growing up that they become commonplace. We don't think to record them from the source until it's too late. Then we struggle to get the details right, knowing it'll never be the same.

Learn from cultural representatives today, in the present. There's only so much information we can glean from books and collections. Sometimes we have to go out and hear the stories ourselves. It's not such an overwhelming task. Start with your family first; they'll be the easiest to collect from since they know you. Keep the conversations simple and lighthearted if you can. Make your interviews a fun activity, not a chore. This will help encourage others in your family to maybe do their own research and will bring out more and more stories from your elders. And probably one of the greatest pieces of advice I can offer is to stick with it. Don't be discouraged by some of the racist and bigoted gobshite that might fall out of people's mouths; I've experienced plenty of this when talking to informants. These might be opportunities for you to help update your grandparents, or maybe even parents, on the way they talk and what they think about the world. But don't let the differing viewpoints keep you from learning more about your ancestors and their stories.

Bibliography

Andrus, Carley Ann. *The Wizard of Oto: The Mystery Doctor Who Became the "Wizard Healer."* Self-published, 1985.

Banks, William H. *Plants of the Cherokee: Medicinal, Edible, and Useful Plants of the Eastern Cherokee Indians.* Gatlinburg, TN: Great Smoky Mountains Association, 2004.

Bilardi, C. R. *The Red Church or the Art of Pennsylvania German Braucherei.* Sunland, CA: Pendraig Publishing, 2009.

Blevins, Brooks. *Arkansas/Arkansaw: How Bear Hunters, Hillbillies, and Good Ol' Boys Defined a State.* Fayetteville, AR: University of Arkansas Press, 2011.

———. *A History of the Ozarks, Volume 1: The Old Ozarks.* Urbana, IL: University of Illinois Press, 2018.

Brinker, Francis. *Herbal Contraindications and Drug Interactions: Plus Herbal Adjuncts with Medicines.* 4th ed. Sandy, OR: Eclectic Medical Publications, 2010.

Campbell, John Gregorson. *Witchcraft and Second Sight in the Highlands and Islands of Scotland: Tales and Traditions Collected Entirely from Oral Sources.* Whitefish, MT: Kessinger Publishing, 2004.

Carter, Kay, and Bonnie J. Krause. *Home Remedies of the Illinois Ozarks.* Ullin, IL: Shawnee Hills Craft Program for Illinois Ozarks Craft Guild, 1974.

Davis, Hubert J. *American Witch Stories.* Middle Village, NY: Jonathan David Publishers, 1990.

Dietz, Birgit, and Judy L. Bolton. "Botanical Dietary Supplements Gone Bad." *Chemical Research in Toxicology* 20, no. 4 (2007): 586–90. https://doi.org/10.1021/tx7000527.

Easley, Thomas, and Steven Horne. *The Modern Herbal Dispensatory: A Medicine-Making Guide.* Berkeley, CA: North Atlantic Books, 2016.

Frazer, James George. *The Golden Bough: A Study in Magic and Religion.* London: MacMillan, 1923.

Gregory, Lady. *Visions and Beliefs in the West of Ireland.* New York: Knickerbocker Press, 1920.

Grieve, M. *A Modern Herbal: The Medicinal, Culinary, Cosmetic, and Economic Properties, Cultivation and Folklore of Herbs, Grasses, Fungi, Shrubs, and Trees with All Their Modern Scientific Uses.* London: Tiger Books International, 1998.

Harper, Kimberly. *White Man's Heaven: The Lynching and Expulsion of Blacks in the Southern Ozarks, 1894–1909.* Fayetteville, AR: University of Arkansas Press, 2012.

Irwin, Lee. "Cherokee Healing: Myths, Dreams, and Medicine." *American Indian Quarterly* 16, no. 2 (1992): 237–57. https://doi.org/10.2307/1185431.

Kilpatrick, Alan Edwin. "'Going to the Water': A Structural Analysis of Cherokee Purification Rituals." *American Indian Culture and Research Journal* 15, no. 4 (1991): 49–58. https://doi.org/10.17953/aicr.15.4.h7r56274k32r1t11.

Kilpatrick, Jack Frederick, and Anna Gritts Kilpatrick. "Notebook of a Cherokee Shaman." *Smithsonian Contributions to Anthropology* 2, no. 6 (1970): 1–83. https://doi.org/10.5479/si.00810223.2.6.

Levey, Martin. *Chemistry and Chemical Technology in Ancient Mesopotamia.* Amsterdam: Elsevier Publishing Company, 1959.

Milnes, Gerald C. *Signs, Cures, and Witchery: German Appalachian Folklore.* Knoxville, TN: University of Tennessee Press, 2007.

Moerman, Daniel E. *Native American Ethnobotany.* Portland, OR: Timber Press, 2010.

Mooney, James. *James Mooney's History, Myths, and Sacred Formulas of the Cherokees.* Fairview, NC: Bright Mountain Books, 1992.

———. *The Swimmer Manuscript: Cherokee Sacred Formulas and Medicinal Prescriptions.* Edited by Frans M. Olbrechts. Washington, DC: Government Printing Office, 1932.

Parler, Mary Celestia. Papers. Special Collections Department, University of Arkansas Libraries.

———. *Folk Beliefs from Arkansas.* Self-published, 1962.

Pompey, Sherman Lee. *Granny Gore's Ozark Folk Medicine*. Self-published, 1961.

Randolph, Vance. *The Devil's Pretty Daughter and Other Ozark Folk Tales*. New York: Columbia University Press, 1955.

———. *Ozark Magic and Folklore*. New York: Dover Publications, 2003.

———. *Sticks in the Knapsack and Other Ozark Folk Tales*. New York: Columbia University Press, 1958.

———. *The Talking Turtle and Other Ozark Folk Tales*. New York: Columbia University Press. 1957.

———. *Who Blowed Up the Church House? And Other Ozark Folk Tales*. New York: Columbia University Press, 1953.

Rayburn, Otto Ernest. Papers. Special Collections Department, University of Arkansas Libraries.

———. "Bloodstoppers in the Ozarks." *Midwest Folklore* 4, no. 4 (1954): 213–15. https://www.jstor.org/stable/4317482.

———. "The 'Granny-Woman' in the Ozarks." *Midwest Folklore* 9, no. 3 (1959): 145–48. https://www.jstor.org/stable/4317804.

———. *Ozark Country*. New York: Duell, Sloan & Pearce, 1960.

Wilson, Charles Morrow. *Backwoods America*. St. Clair Shores, MI: Scholarly Press, 1979.

TO WRITE TO THE AUTHOR

If you wish to contact the author or would like more information about this book, please write to the author in care of Llewellyn Worldwide Ltd. and we will forward your request. Both the author and publisher appreciate hearing from you and learning of your enjoyment of this book and how it has helped you. Llewellyn Worldwide Ltd. cannot guarantee that every letter written to the author can be answered, but all will be forwarded. Please write to:

Brandon Weston
℅ Llewellyn Worldwide
2143 Wooddale Drive
Woodbury, MN 55125-2989
Please enclose a self-addressed stamped envelope for reply,
or $1.00 to cover costs. If outside the U.S.A., enclose
an international postal reply coupon.

Many of Llewellyn's authors have websites with additional information and resources. For more information, please visit our website at http://www.llewellyn.com.